BALAAM'S

How Israel
Lost Its Way,
And How It Can
Find It Again

CURSE

by
Moshe
Leshem

Simon and Schuster
New York   London   Toronto   Sydney   Tokyo

SIMON AND SCHUSTER
Simon & Schuster Building
Rockefeller Center
1230 Avenue of the Americas
New York, New York 10020

Copyright © 1989 by Moshe Leshem
All rights reserved
including the right of reproduction
in whole or in part in any form.

SIMON AND SCHUSTER and colophon are registered trademarks of Simon
& Schuster Inc.

Designed by Nina D'Amario/Levavi & Levavi
Manufactured in the United States of America

10   9   8   7   6   5   4   3   2   1

Library of Congress Cataloging-in-Publication Data
Leshem, Moshe.
     Balaam's curse : how Israel lost its way, and how it can find it
again / by Moshe Leshem.
    p.   cm.
  Bibliography: p.
  Includes index.
  1. Zionism—History. 2. Israel—Politics and government.
3. Jews—Politics and government—1948- I. Title.
DS149.L342   1989   89-11365
320.5'4'095694—dc20   CIP

ISBN 0-671-67918-X

Contents

"And Balaam said . . . from the top of the rocks
I see him, and from the hills I behold him: lo,
the people shall dwell alone, and shall not be
reckoned among the nations."

—Numbers 23:19

Prologue

This is the story of an exodus. Not the Exodus from Egypt related in the Second Book of Moses, but the second Exodus of the Jews—the Exodus from the ghettos of Europe.

The Biblical Exodus was a divinely inspired move from slavery to certain freedom. The Israelites knew they were going to the Promised Land, even if they first had to roam the desert for forty years. They had God's word for it, and God's active help: "And the Lord went before them by day in a pillar of cloud, to lead them the way; and by night in a pillar of fire..." (Exodus, 13:21). They had a leader, Moses, through whom God's word was transmitted to them, and they had a common national goal—nationhood, which they believed they would achieve by an act of allegiance to God's rule.

Three thousand years later, in the late eighteenth century, when the second Exodus began, things were not nearly so certain. The Jews leaving the ghettos of Europe were leaderless. They had no pillars of cloud or fire to guide them in their wanderings. They were going out into the unknown: the world of

9

the gentiles. Instead of the certainty their faith had provided through the long centuries of the Exile, they now found themselves in a maze they did not understand, butting up against walls not of their making. Not surprisingly, they tried to tear these walls down, often angering the gentiles in the process.

The second Exodus was a fateful turning pointing in Jewish history, for the Jew outside the ghetto was not the same as the one who had lived within its walls. What changed him wasn't the breaching of any physical walls, but rather the collapse of the spiritual walls that had been erected by Rabbinical Judaism to prevent the Jew from being contaminated by the outside world and straying from his divinely ordained mission: to be the chosen instrument of mankind's collective redemption. (The Jews would admit of no other destiny, however far in the future its fulfillment might lie.)

The Enlightenment and emancipation, the twin secular godheads that drew the Jews out of the ghetto, forced the Children of Israel to seek an answer to a difficult question: How could they maintain a Jewish identity while assimilating European culture and values that were not merely alien to Rabbinical Judaism but often irreconcilable with its teachings? Many Jews wrestle with the problem to this very day as individuals; so does Israel in its vocation as the Jewish state.

Before emancipation, there had been no such conflict. The Jews were truly one nation. Although dispersed geographically, they lived apart from the rest of the world. Rabbinical Judaism permeated Jewish life, Jewish culture, Jewish thinking, Jewish philosophy. There could be nothing of value outside it.

Emancipation shattered this unity, exposing the peculiar Jewish body politic to the world, to novel influences through which the Jews (except for those who remained wrapped up in Orthodoxy) refracted their heritage. Rabbinical Judaism no longer had the strength to rally the now doubly dispersed members of the nation: to the physical dispersion was added a spiritual atomization.

By itself, physical dispersion had proven to be no danger to Judaism. On the contrary, the Exile had fostered a canonic creativity that actually strengthened Judaism by adding layers upon layers of interpretations, glosses, glosses on interpretations, and interpretations of glosses on the ever rising wall of the Law. Spiritual dispersion, on the other hand, represented a very real threat, not least because the egalitarian and humanitarian ideals of the Enlightenment, which inspired the emancipation, were doomed to fail. (And fail they did, even though the emanations of those ideals still waft through our world, inhabiting, like a benign dybbuk, well-meaning people who all too often unwittingly wind up playing the role of useful fools for cynical politicians.)

The Enlightenment certainly failed the Jews. Consider its legacy. The Enlightenment begat emancipation; emancipation begat anti-Semitism; anti-Semitism begat Zionism—and the Holocaust.

Had political Zionism succeeded in creating a Jewish state at the beginning of the twentieth century, as Theodor Herzl dreamed and thought possible, it might well have spared Jewry the loss and trauma caused by the Holocaust. But it would not have healed the crisis of Judaism brought on by emancipation and assimilation, a crisis that is still with us. (On the contrary, judging by the State of Israel's impact on Judaism, it probably would have exacerbated the crisis.) The aim of political Zionism, after all, was to transform the Jewish people into a conventional nation. It never meant to solve the crisis that beset Judaism from the day the ghetto walls fell to the trumpet blast of the Enlightenment. What Zionism wanted to cure was the sickness known as the "Jewish problem"—the rising tide of anti-Semitism that flowed over Europe after the Age of Light burned itself out.

As long as the Jew sat in the ghetto, he was not responsible for the fate of the Jewish people. That was in God's hands. All he had to do was to observe the 613 commandments as best he could. A noble task, indeed, but one that naturally blunted the political sense of the Jewish people.

The absence of a well-developed political sense among the

11

Jewish people seriously hindered the growth of political Zionism. Though individual Jews demonstrated impressive political aptitude in the service and affairs of other nations, no one was able to mobilize the Jewish people in the pursuit of their own national interests. As a result, most Jews remained indifferent, and many hostile, to political Zionism. Even those who embraced it lacked, in the main, the courage of their convictions. To a degree, this was because they did not believe that a return to their ancient homeland was a realistic possibility. This disbelief, fed by the diaspora's chronically inert and generally optimistic belief in its own viability, became a self-fulfilling prophecy. It was easy to disclaim responsibility: Zionism was an idea whose time had not yet come.

The emergence of an independent Jewish state in 1948 changed the rules of the game. An important segment of the Jewish people now constituted a sovereign nation. Jews had, at long last, taken their fate into their own hands. As far as most newly enfranchised Israelis were concerned, it was Zionism— and not the Holocaust—that had begotten the State of Israel. To the young nation, the Holocaust represented a nadir of Jewish powerlessness and passivity in which a people had allowed itself to be "like sheep driven to slaughter." It was the final cataclysm in which the "old" diaspora Jew had perished. The "new" Jew, epitomized by the Israeli, would never allow such a catastrophe to happen again.

That attitude was soon to change. With the capture, trial, and subsequent execution of Adolf Eichmann in 1961, a deliberate effort to make the memory of the Holocaust part of the Israeli ethos shifted into high gear. It has not been arrested since. The original impulse may well have sprung from a simple desire to bring the man in administrative charge of the "Final Solution" to justice when no one else could or would. But the trial's most significant result may have been to force Israel to face up to the legacy of the Holocaust—and in the process accept its own very real link to diaspora Jewry.

Previously, Israelis had tended to dismiss, even disparage, the diaspora. In their eyes, diaspora Jewry had too much of the old Jewish mentality in its make-up. Besides, if Zionism was correct, as it seemed to have been in predicting the establishment of the Jewish state, the diaspora had forfeited its right to existence. It was barren. It was undignified. It was doomed. The only way open to diaspora Jews was to join their brethren in Israel.

The Ashkenazi diaspora, however, showed no such inclinations. (The Jewish communities of Arab countries may have reacted similarly had Arab hostility not virtually robbed them of a choice. Indeed, Algerian Jewry, which did have a choice, did not flock to Israel; instead, some 130,000 Algerian Jews chose to resettle in France.) As a result, it slowly dawned on Israelis that the diaspora would continue to be a permanent feature in the life of the Jewish people. Israel thus had no alternative but to become a partner of the diaspora.

The implications of all this were troubling, to say the least. If Zionism was wrong in its assessment of the diaspora, then perhaps the State of Israel was not the state Zionism had envisaged. (It certainly was not the kind of state Herzl had in mind.) To be sure, Israel is in many respects a conventional nation-state, and that was one of Zionism's principal aims: normalization. On the other hand, one cannot overlook the fact that Israel is also unique—it is, in a sense, the Jew among nations.

To a Zionist, this continuing "specialness" might be a sign that the task of Zionism is still unfinished. However, that is not the direction in which Israel has found itself pushed by the newfound emphasis on the religious significance and eschatological role of the state. The new emphasis grew out of the 1967 war, which brought all of the Land of Israel under Israeli control. The immediate result was a sense of imperious power paradoxically accompanied by a religious revival and a growth of influence of the religious sector, which viewed the state in a new light: as an instrument of redemption. Zionism had thus returned to what Maurice Samuel called its "historic, religious, moral and cultural identity with eternal Judaism"—precisely

13

where many Jewish thinkers had always felt it belonged.

In the millennial view of Judaism, the nation-state must ultimately cede to the rule of God. Or to put it another way, eternal Judaism—and, with it, messianism—necessarily supersedes Zionism and the nation-state. (Marx transformed this Judaic tenet into the theory that the proletarian state will wither away with the achievement of true Communism.) The conflict this presents is clear. As a nation-state, Israel cannot become an instrument of messianic redemption. To do so, after all, would be to place its disappearance at the center of its policy.

The fact is, the State of Israel did not come into being as a link in an eschatological chain, but rather in recognition of the need for the Jews to have a country of their own, like most other nations. This is the natural order of things, and it is likely to remain so for the foreseeable future in spite of all the talk about the interdependence of the global village created by the magic of electronics and cybernetics.

Israel can no more conduct its affairs according to the tenets of Judaic ethics than the princes of Renaissance Italy could govern in conformity with those of Christianity, as the much maligned Machiavelli has tried to make clear. Nonetheless, the religious right argues that even though it violates the tenets of Judaism, the State of Israel is still an instrument of redemption. And as such, it must be nudged into becoming a Torah state, a state walled in by the Law, a state where Jewry can find spiritual as well as physical security.

Orthodoxy, in short, wants the Jewish people and their state to "dwell alone" and "not be reckoned among the nations," as Balaam prophesied in the Book of Numbers. The Orthodox do not ask themselves whether such a state could survive in the modern world or whether the majority of its population would wish to live in such a state. In their desire to re-establish the conditions that had in the past given the Jews a certainty of faith, they embrace a circular view of history. In a sense, they wish to turn the clock back to the era of the ghetto—with the critical difference that there is now a new starting point on the road to redemption: the Jewish state established in the whole of the Land of Israel.

It is a doctrine fraught with dangers for the state's existence. The most terrifying danger is the one presented by Israel's control over a large hostile Arab population in the occupied territories. Yet the religious nationalists persist. To them, the "wholeness" of the Land of Israel created by the victory of 1967 was a portent that redemption had begun. In their view, if that control were to be relinquished, as seems inevitable, the state would then be guilty of having retreated on the road to redemption. It would become the equivalent of a false messiah and share the fate of a false messiah.

I

Within the Walls

Before the Enlightenment, and the second Exodus it ultimately inspired, the Jews of Europe had no concept of liberty, equality, or the pursuit of happiness. That's not to say they were hopelessly downtrodden. Their forebears may have been slaves in Egypt, forced to do hard manual labor, but the ghetto Jews were nobody's slaves. True, they could not settle wherever they wanted or live in any house they could afford. And they were invariably subject to the will and whim of rulers who often found their presence obnoxious. Nonetheless, they enjoyed the one freedom they needed to survive, the one freedom they could understand: the freedom to worship their God.

Of course, while the Jews had the freedom, they often lacked the security—physical as well as economic—to follow the difficult road their faith prescribed. They were set upon, spat upon, mauled, and massacred. And all they could do about it was pray to be spared. On Passover night, they called upon God to "Pour out Thine indignation upon them, and let the fierceness of Thine anger overtake them. Pursue them in anger, and

17

destroy them under the heavens of the Lord." There was no need to specify the identity of "them." As the Haggadah pointed out, "in every generation there have risen against us those who would destroy us."

Still, when the Jews prayed to be "next year in Jerusalem," it was not a prayer for liberation from their ghetto condition. Rather, it was a prayer for the coming of the Messiah, for redemption, for the salvation not only of the Jewish people but of all humanity. (After all, what good would it do the Jews to be the only redeemed people in an unredeemed world?)

Until the Messiah came, the mission of the Jewish people was to work toward becoming "a nation of priests and a holy people." And while ghetto life may have had its drawbacks, it was the perfect environment for the fulfillment of this mission.

After all, what held the Jews together was not simply the Law, custom, and fear. At bottom, what held them together was the conviction that theirs was the only true religion, that they alone among the nations had a Covenant with God and a divinely inspired mission. In their eyes, the Jews were a very different and superior kind of people.

To preserve that sense of spiritual uniqueness, isolation from the outside world was essential. Jews therefore limited their contacts with gentiles to the strictly necessary. They might do business with the goyim, but they would not break bread with them.

In short, it was the Jews themselves who insisted that their communities be spiritually self-contained and self-sufficient. The gentiles may have built physical walls around the ghettos, but the real barrier was the Jews' own "Fence of the Law." Indeed, the rabbis saw to it that layer upon layer of intricate interpretation made that fence ever higher and spikier. In the nineteenth century, Benjamin Disraeli wrote of two nations "between whom there is no intercourse and no sympathy; who are as ignorant of each other's habits, thoughts and feelings, as if they were dwellers in different zones or inhabitants of different planets." He was referring to the rich and the poor in Victorian England, but he could just as well have been describing ghetto Jews and their gentile contemporaries.

To be sure, the gentiles were quite happy to see the Jews return to their ghettos each evening before the curfew hour struck. The Jews were obviously useful in filling the economic niches (such as moneylending) that good Christians were unwilling or unable to occupy. But at best they were a necessary evil.

Christians, after all, took their religion just as seriously as the Jews did theirs. They did not want to be constantly reminded that there was a "certain people," as Haman called the Jews in the Book of Esther, who denied Christ and who regarded gentile ways as blasphemous, erroneous, and foolish. What was especially irritating was that the Jews couldn't be accused of doing so out of ignorance; they weren't pagans who didn't know any better.

The refusal of the Jews to recognize Jesus as the Savior was both irksome and incomprehensible to the gentiles, at least before rationalism trimmed religion's reach. The refusal must have also gnawed at the certitude of the Christians' faith. It is not surprising, therefore, that the Jews were considered to be deserving victims of whatever exploitation might serve gentile interests. Not only were they heavily taxed, but collective fines were imposed on Jewish communities for imaginary transgressions. In Prague, for example, the Jews were obliged to erect a giant cross on the Charles Bridge topped by an arch proclaiming in large, golden Hebrew letters *Kadosh, Kadosh, Kadosh* ("Holy, Holy, Holy"). Similarly, if even more onerously, Jew-baiting was encouraged—to the point where it became the favorite sport of the age. This not only distracted the populace from its own misery, it also made people feel righteous. After all, they could claim they were merely taking revenge on the descendants of the people responsible for the death of Christ. (The Jews' collective responsibility for the crucifixion remained Catholic doctrine until 1962, when the Second Vatican Council officially exonerated the Jews.)

19

Not surprisingly, there was hardly a Jew in pre-Enlighten-
ment Europe who considered the particular country in which
his ghetto was located to be his fatherland. After all, how could
he possibly regard as his fatherland a country that would not
give him the right of permanent residence, a right conceded
even to the serfs? In any case, he already had a fatherland
(though it was spiritual rather than tangible)—the Land of
Israel.

In free association, the noun "ghetto" often evokes the adjective "squalid." And in most Jewish ghettos sanitary conditions
certainly left a lot to be desired. For one thing, a great number
of people were crammed into very limited acreage. Even the
rich could not build themselves townhouses. There simply was
no space. (A few privileged financiers were allowed to build
mansions, often outside the ghetto, but they were exceptions.)
Nor was there much sunlight; the streets were narrow, and the
houses were warrens of small rooms and chambers.

But while living conditions within the ghettos may have
been poor, the people generally weren't. On the contrary, there
was more wealth per square foot inside the ghetto than out.
Indeed, in some cities, such as Frankfurt, the gentile authorities
would not let poor Jews into the local ghetto for fear that they
would dilute the tax base. And even poor ghetto residents were
better off than their gentile counterparts. While the gentiles
could refer their poor to their posthumous rewards, the Jews
were commanded by the Prophets to provide justice in the here
and now. They were obliged to practice *tsedaka* ("philan-
thropy")—a Hebrew word that has its root in *tsedek* ("justice").

Semantics, of course, do not necessarily create realities. In
practice, the ghettos were ruled by the rabbis and the wealthy.
Learning, however, was available to anyone with enough brains.
And education provided an avenue out of poverty, for the
wealthy were always eager to find learned husbands for their
richly endowed daughters. Still, the simple folk were not universally happy. Hasidism, for example, was not only a flight

forward into mysticism. It was also a social protest against the coalition of rabbis and wealthy merchants that controlled ghetto life.

The Torah and the Oral Tradition were the law of the ghetto. The Jews believed in the inerrancy of the Bible—as well as in the inerrancy of their rabbis. Over the centuries, the rabbis produced mind-boggling masses of responsa, most of which remain uncatalogued and unresearched to this day. And although there were variations in rabbinical opinions, ghetto life was everywhere regulated by the same set of strict rules.

In the seventeenth century, uniformity was further strengthened by the wide dissemination of the *Shulhan Arukh*—the Prepared Table. It had been written a century earlier by Rabbi Joseph Caro as a kind of home-companion Talmud. As a result of the *Shulhan Arukh*, a literate man—and literacy rates among the male inhabitants of the ghetto were high—did not have to be a Talmudic scholar to look deeper into the sources and understand why he was living the way he was. Of course, the *Shulhan Arukh* first had to be adapted to Ashkenazi conditions and tastes. (Caro was a Sephardi whose writings the Ashkenazi rabbis believed appropriate for the Sephardi public only.) This was done by the glosses of Rabbi Moses Isserles of Cracow. The work covered every facet of life from the sublime to the trivial, from the legalistic to the ritualistic, from communal activities to the most intimate relations between man and wife.

There was no way a Jew could slip out from under the yoke of the commandments and remain in the ghetto. The constraints were too rigid and the social pressures too high. The rabbis had no taste for deviations or dissent. Of course, dissent did exist, but it had to be carefully concealed from the rabbis, much as the Marranos concealed their crypto-Judaism from the Inquisition. The only way out of the European ghetto was into Christianity.

That was a route few chose to take. After all, for a Jew to embrace another faith meant cutting himself off from his people and his nation, their culture and way of life. It was far more than a change of religion. A Christian such as Martin Luther was no less a German after he rejected the Catholic Church. If anything, he became more German by casting off the authority of the Pope in Rome. But a baptized Jew could no longer be a Jew.

What distinguished, say, a German from a Frenchman was of a different order than what distinguished the Jews from all the other peoples of the world. And the reason for it was metaphysical, not simply the historic circumstance of the loss of their country. The Jews wanted to have nothing to do with history. They did not know what it was.

Endless tracts, commentaries, glosses, responsa, and treatises were written during the era of Exilic Judaism. Not one dealt with history or the philosophy of history. The Jews were a strictly self-contained collectivity, and as Oswald Spengler wrote in *The Decline of the West:* "For the self-contained type of consciousness there is certainly no world history, no world-as-history." The passage does not specifically relate to Jews, but it describes the ghetto consciousness to a T.

Spengler defined history as "that from which man's imagination seeks comprehension of the living existence of the world in relation to his own life." To the ghetto Jew, that would have been totally meaningless. What mattered to him was the living existence of God in relation to his own life. The quest for God might prove as elusive as the quest for history, but at least the Jews had definite, binding guidelines: the Torah and the towering edifice of interpretation built on it.

The Enlightenment, however, asked the Jews to give up all this "obscurantist rabbinical humbug." A new era had dawned. A new secular dispensation was available for the asking. The Jews ought to see the light, leave the darkness of the ghetto, and become citizens of the emerging new Europe, the Europe of nation-states.

At first, the Jews did not know what to make of the proposition. Certainly, the conservative ghetto establishment didn't like it. New ideas—especially secular ones—could not be "good for the Jews." The ghetto may have had its drawbacks for certain individual Jews, but it was the right environment for Rabbinical Judaism. Indeed, until the Enlightenment, it was the only conceivable environment.

Still, the ghetto walls were not impervious to secular thinking. In Amsterdam, for example, intellectuals enjoyed wide access to secular works—most prominently Spinoza, who based his philosophical system on other than traditional Jewish sources. In 1656, the rabbis of Amsterdam still had enough authority to expel Spinoza from the community. A century later, however, the rabbis no longer had that power. No ban was proclaimed against Salomon Maimon, the Kantian philosopher who eventually left both traditional Judaism and his native Lithuania.

II

Liberté, Egalité, Judeité

At eight o'clock in the evening of March 23, 1912, the curtain
in Copenhagen's Royal Theater rose on a new play. Called
Within the Walls, the play was a comedy on a serious topic: the
love between a girl from a traditional Jewish home and the gentile son of a Danish state counselor. Its author (as well as director) was Henri Nathansen, a Jewish lawyer who preferred
literature to legal briefs and was more at home in the court
theater than the courtroom.

The play was highly successful, and has remained so. (In 1988
it was revived as a musical.) Its message was that of enlightened
optimism: differences in race, religion, and social standing
should not be allowed to stand in the way of human happiness.
As Old Levin, the father of the bride, says to his wife in the last
line of the play: "Somewhere I read, Sarah, that if the human
race could agree on life's blessing, there would be enough for all
of us. Let us hope that time will come." The joke, alas, was on
the Jew.

Nathansen's dramatic optimism was shared by a leading the-

ater critic of the time, Arié Henriques, a descendant of the Sephardi Jews whom King Christian IV had invited to Denmark in
the early seventeenth century in the hope that their presence
would replenish the financial resources he had squandered in
pursuit of glory on the battlefield and grandeur in building. In
his review of Nathansen's play, Henriques remarked: "It is extremely likely that twenty-five years from now it will be...
difficult to find a home in Denmark that can be called typically
Jewish."

Henriques was certainly right with regard to the Sephardi
Jews who had come to Denmark in the seventeenth century.
Very few of their descendants are still Jewish today. Intermar-
riage, which Nathansen's play reluctantly celebrated in the
name of humanitarian ideals (the happy ending was added at
the insistence of the Royal Theater), has reduced the Sephardi
presence in Denmark to little more than fondly cherished
echoes reverberating in the Spanish-sounding family names of
many good Lutherans. It also persists as mute memories chis-
eled into the tombstones in the Jewish cemeteries of towns like
Fredericia, where one will not find a single living Jew.

Nathansen's life exemplifies the tragedy of the many Jews
who believed in the humanitarian vision of the brotherhood of
man that the prophets of the Age of Reason and the Enlightenment had promised with such arrogant self-assurance. He committed suicide in 1944. The rare example of brotherhood in
action provided by the Danish anti-Nazi Resistance, whose
courageous members ferried virtually all of Danish Jewry (including Nathansen) across the øresund to the safety of neutral
Sweden was not enough to defuse his despair.

Although Nathansen called his play *Within the Walls*, a better title might have been *The Walls Within*. After all, the outer
walls shielding Judaism against alien influence had been
breached—from the outside—well over a hundred years before
he wrote the play. By the beginning of the twentieth century, all
that remained were the not-so-solid inner walls maintained by
the Jews themselves in order to preserve their Jewish identity.

The play's protagonist, Old Levin, well reflects the dilemma into which emancipation and the Enlightenment had cast European Jewry. Should he accept the gift of liberty and equality offered to his daughter through marriage with a Danish Christian at the price of her Jewishness? As the change in the ending of the play indicates, the author was of two minds.

In fact, by the time Nathansen wrote his play, the dilemma had been largely resolved for the Jews—not by them, it should be noted, and not in their favor. The Enlightenment was a thing of the past. For the Jews of France, Germany, and the Austro-Hungarian Empire, the dream of emancipation had turned into the nightmare of the "Jewish problem." (The Jews of Russia had never had much to dream about to begin with. Only England's Jewish population fared well, though England was hardly free of anti-Semitism.)

Nathansen was by no means the only Jewish writer attracted by the ideals of the Enlightenment at a time when they were no longer a living force. So, too, were the Jewish writers of Eastern Europe who can be considered the fathers of modern Hebrew literature, as well as the prominent Yiddish writers of the time. "Entirely different winds were blowing in the reality of Europe when the Jewish writers discovered Enlightenment," noted Baruch Kurzweil, perhaps the most eminent Israeli literary critic of his day. "Schiller and Lessing, Kant and Montesquieu, Shakespeare and Milton filled them with enthusiasm at a time that was already the era of Flaubert and Dostoyevsky, of Darwin and Marx, of Nietzsche and the poets of the fin de siècle. They were still dreaming of the ideals of emancipation and reform at a juncture of history in which the masses that had come to power negated the postulates made in the name of divine reason and surrendered to the new myths of race, blood, and class."

The gradual breaching and destruction of the ghetto walls had begun toward the end of the eighteenth century. The process proved to be a fateful turning point in the life of the Jewish people, marking their re-entry into the mainstream (or, some might say, maelstrom) of history, which they had deliberately left after the destruction of the Second Temple. It was a profound cultural revolution.

The strict separation in which the Jews had lived until the Enlightenment had guaranteed that their spiritual nourishment came from sacred scriptures and from nowhere else. This secured the cultural unity of the Jewish people as well as providing them with a certitude of faith. Inevitably, the opening up of ever widening avenues to the increasingly secularized world outside the ghetto shattered that unity and undermined the certitude of faith, perhaps irretrievably.

France's President Raymond Poincaré once said: "Those who thirst before all for certitude do not really love truth." To which the eminent Israeli historian Jacob Y. L. Talmon added: "Neither do they love freedom." Truth and freedom were the all-pervading themes of the Age of Reason and the Age of Light, as the French poetically call the Enlightenment. The Jews would have to learn to worship them, too.

To most philosophers, this was a good thing. Moses Mendelssohn, the first Jewish philosopher of the Enlightenment, was happy to note "the fortunate coincidence that the betterment of the situation of the Jews [was] identical with the progress of mankind." (Until then the progress of mankind had been of no interest to the Jews at all.) And Hegel saw in Jewish emancipation an important criterion by which to judge the modern state.

As the enlightened intelligentsia saw it, all men had the right to be free, free to engage in the pursuit of happiness as individuals. These were the ideas the Founding Fathers of the American Republic incorporated in their Declaration of Independence. If these ideas were alien to the ghetto Jew—and they were—he would simply have to learn to appreciate them. After all, to claim that the philosophical tenets of the Enlightenment did not apply to Jews would have been as absurd as maintaining that some bodies were not subject to Newton's laws of gravity.

The rationalists of the Enlightenment believed in one *humanitas*, one humankind, each member of which was moved by the same aspirations and the same moral impulses, irrespective of race, creed, or nationality. For the thinkers of the Enlightenment, the True, the Good, the Beautiful came only in one variety. The rationalists wished to establish one principle that would govern human relations, just as modern physicists search for a grand unified theory that will explain the workings of the universe. (The physicists haven't yet found it, either.)

Not everybody was in favor of Jewish emancipation. Some thinkers claimed that the Jews neither deserved nor desired to be emancipated. Prominent among them was the Protestant theologican Bruno Bauer. In a pamphlet published in 1843, he made the point that the Jews "have resisted the movements and changes of history" and always "wanted to stay forever what they are." Bauer may have been an anti-Semite, but he correctly read the spirit of Rabbinical Judaism.

Rabbinical Judaism, however, was less rock solid than Bauer thought. It had been profoundly shaken by the appearance, in the middle of the seventeenth century, of Shabbetai Zvi, a Turkish Jew who proclaimed himself the Messiah and soon gathered a wide following. Not only did he promise that redemption was coming within a matter of months at most (contrary to what the rabbis preached) but his religious practices were more hedonistic and were believed to include sexual licentiousness (also contrary to what the rabbis preached).

Unfortunately, Shabbetai Zvi did not deliver. Captured by the Turks, who viewed with alarm the possibility of a mass Jewish migration into "their" Palestine, he converted to Islam to save his life. It was a hard blow to his many followers, some of whom refused to give up hope in spite of all.

Rabbinical Judaism was successful in containing the damage caused by Shabbetai Zvi. But it could do no more than that. It could not quite heal the deep wounds the collapse of the messianic hopes had left in the Jewish soul. The danger remained that disappointment would breed despair, and despair beget apostasy. Indeed, Gershom Sholem, the leading authority of his time on Jewish mysticism, sees a clear dialectic development leading from the faith in Shabbetai Zvi to the disintegration of the religious basis on which it rested, and from there to the Enlightenment. Be that as it may, the Enlightenment succeeded in unraveling the cocoon in which Rabbinical Judaism had so tightly encased the ghetto Jew. It persuaded the Jews that they, too, could become butterflies and fly into the world, if they only dared.

Whether it was the fault of Christian society or not, the enlightened intelligentsia believed that the ghetto Jews lived in a deplorable state of cultural decrepitude. Before long, the Jews came to believe it themselves. Hitherto, Jews had looked at themselves from inside the ghetto. They liked what they saw, even if they keenly felt the physical insecurity of their existence. Now, however, they began to look at themselves in the mirrors provided by non-Jews. And they no longer liked their self-image. In the new mirror, they appeared as wretched victims of sociopolitical conditions and of outdated traditions, persons of warped body and mind—or, as Theodor Herzl later put it, of "diminished human substance."

Enlightened intellectuals, including the Jews who joined the movement in the early phases of emancipation, considered Rabbinical Judaism as ritualistic and retrogade; they saw the ghetto community as senselessly imprisoned in a strait jacket of rigid rules and festering fanaticism. The Jews were thus held to be morally, socially, and culturally inadequate to merit full civil rights. But the champions of emancipation were convinced that it was within the grasp of the Jews to improve themselves sufficiently to attain the required standards.

The eighteenth century was an age of remarkable intellectual ferment. At no other time in modern history has an intellectual elite enjoyed a greater influence on the shaping of society. And in no other era have the autocratic powers that be allowed so much freedom of expression to those who honed the tools for their ultimate demise. In fact, many a ruler found enlightened ideas to his liking—as long as they were applied gradually and in moderation.

One of the first autocratic rulers to embrace the Enlightenment was the Austrian Emperor Joseph II (1741–1790). His conservative court was wary, and the Catholic clergy liked it even less. But the Emperor wanted to improve the conditions of the peasantry and abolish torture and other cruel forms of punishment. He did not forget his Jews, either.

In spite of opposition, the Emperor issued, in 1781, the *Toleranzpatent*. Among other things, it ordered that all Jewish children in his realm receive a secular education. The Jewish educational enclave that had existed undisturbed for centuries, almost hermetically closed to outside influences, was suddenly broken up by a stroke of the imperial pen, much to the chagrin of the ordained defenders of the faith. If the Jews were to be the equals of all of the Emperor's other subjects, they would have to be taught like all the others, and taught in German.

Similar ordinances passed in other countries quite openly spelled out the intention of weakening the hold the rabbis had on the Jewish community. They abolished the jurisdiction rabbinical authorities had hitherto legally exercised inside the community. Rabbis and religious teachers were now obliged to acknowledge and teach the supremacy of the law of the land, including the duty of the Jews to serve in the army (since military service had become an important criterion of good citizenship). The Jews were no longer allowed to be a community living apart from the rest, a kind of nation within the host nation, ruled by laws other than those that applied to everyone else.

Emancipation was "not intended to benefit the welfare of the [Jewish] community as such," as the German historian Helmut Schmidt remarked in a 1956 essay, "but rather to create conditions which would in time bring about the social liquidation of that community within a wider society bounded and molded by the state." If individual Jews were to be full citizens of the emerging nation-states, there would be no room for a separate Jewish national or cultural identity.

Count Stanislas de Clermont-Tonnerre, one of the few French aristocrats who threw in his lot with the Revolution, expressed the new enlightened attitude toward the Jews in a formula that had all the attractiveness—and all the pitfalls—of a slogan. Speaking in the French National Assembly on September 28, 1789, he proclaimed: "The Jews should be denied everything as a nation, but granted everything as individuals."

If a Jew desired to practice his religion, he was, of course, entitled to do so by the same right that enabled Christians to practice theirs. An enlightened Jew was, however, expected to disengage himself from the rigidity and medieval obscurantism of ghetto Judaism. Reason had to be the guiding light of Judaism. After all, the Enlightenment demanded no less of Christianity.

True to their unitary view of mankind, the intellectuals of the Enlightenment regarded Judaism as a religion no different from Catholicism or Protestantism. Reform Judaism tried hard to conform to that view. But the rest of Jewry did not see it in the same light. To them, Judaism was more than a theology; it was also an assertion of a particular national and cultural identity, something that went beyond religious practice. The Enlightenment couldn't accept this. What it saw was not a people attached to their past and their deep roots, but a group of individuals held in thrall to archaic rituals prescribed by reactionary rabbis. The White Knights of the Enlightenment urged, and wished to help, the Jews to get out of the darkness of the ghetto and walk toward the brightness of the Age of Light.

And walk they did. This exodus was quite unlike the one that led the Children of Israel out of Egypt. Not all of the Jews left the ghetto at the same time. They had no Moses to lead them and no sign of God's guidance. On the contrary, the authoritative interpreters of God's commandments, the rabbis, were deeply alarmed at the sight of Jews breaking away from centuries-old traditions. Aside from everything else, this meant a loss of authority for the rabbis, and being human, they resented it. But they could not stop the outgoing tide.

Not all Jewish communities were affected by emancipation in the same measure. Those in Islamic countries felt nothing of the changes that were so acutely transforming the way of life of many of their European brothers. In Eastern Europe, the Enlightenment, like everything else, moved at a slow pace. It was the Jewry of Western and Central Europe that was touched most profoundly. And it was also in the West that the failure of the Enlightenment eventually grew its most poisonous fruits.

By the beginning of the nineteenth century, emancipation seemed irresistible to masses of Jews. Some jumped in headlong, others waded in carefully, trying to keep their Jewish heads above what were to them the unknown, strange, and treacherous waters of the gentile world. Any Jew who wanted to enter this un-Jewishly cold world in one way or another had to undergo a profound personal change in outward appearance, manners, habits, speech, and, ultimately, way of thinking. He had to conform to norms determined by non-Jews—a stunning change from the days when the only norms he recognized were his own, which he held to be superior to the contemptible ways of the goyim.

It was a painful process. John Murray Cuddihy, the American sociologist who wrote a book about Jewish emancipation and assimilation (a process he believes is still going on today), called it—and his book—*The Ordeal of Civility*. The *Oxford English Dictionary* defines civility as "conformity to the principles of social order, behaviour befitting a citizen, good citizenship, senses connected with civilization and culture and, now obsolete, secularity." In the ghettos, none of these concepts meant anything to the Jews. Once they were out, however, they had to contend with all of them, not least the now obsolete one: secularity. They were overwhelmed by "culture shock," to use Cuddihy's expression. And while they often overcame it with varying degrees of success, the effort was never without pain.

A great number of Jews were so overcome with the desire to be like "them" that they converted to Christianity. Max Nordau, who in his day was one of Europe's best-known writers and intellectual celebrities (and who later became Herzl's most eloquent and loyal lieutenant), estimated that by the middle of the nineteenth century two-thirds of all the prominent personalities of Jewish origin no longer identified with Judaism in any form.

It is difficult to believe that these converts suddenly became convinced of the divinity of Christ. More likely, they never felt any obligation to accept the tenets of their new religion. They simply went from being non-practicing Jews to being non-practicing Christians. After all, enlightened intellectuals who carried no burden of Jewish origin manifested much the same attitude toward religion.

Though opportunism often seemed to lie at the bottom of conversion, it was not always a crass opportunism geared toward material gain. Rather, it was often an honest desire to buy a "ticket to European culture," as the poet Heinrich Heine (himself a convert) put it. (He later regretted his conversion.) It was, in other words, a desire to be fully united with their national and cultural surroundings—surroundings, in which they began to feel quite at home.

The act of conversion, however, implied the unintended acknowledgment that Christianity was a superior religion, a higher stage in the spiritual development of mankind, a religion that had superseded Judaism—a religion in which Judaism found its fulfillment, as Joseph Cardinal Ratzinger, the head of the Vatican's Congregation for the Doctrine of the Faith, stated in an interview in October 1986 (thus reaffirming that, theologically, the Roman Catholic Church still finds it difficult, perhaps impossible, to acknowledge the validity of Judaism).

The Jews did not like that. (They like it even less today.) As a small people, the Jews have always been painfully affected by any loss of "co-religionists."

On the other end of the spectrum were those who took the ghetto walls with them and internalized them. Perhaps better than other sectors of Jewry, they understood that ideas alien to Judaism had shaken Jewry's faith in the sanctity of its sources, and almost voided it of the sacred. They noted with abhorrence that the Bible had become an object of historic and historiogra-

phic research. They saw the wealth of rabbinical exegesis rejected as totally irrelevant to modern Judaism and the affirmation of the Jewish past transformed into a romantic myth.
Perhaps worst of all in their eyes, they watched chosenness become something that had to be explained away by the new enlightened Jewish clergy (an innovation in itself) that suddenly
appeared on the religious scene.

The majority of Western and Central European Jewry placed
itself at different points of the spectrum defined by the two
extremes: Orthodoxy and conversion. Jews had to cope with a
paradox. While Europeans were now defining their identity in
terms of nationality, the Jews were still obliged to identify in
terms of religion. The paradox boded ill for their future.

It is only recently that a social climate has emerged in the
West, particularly in the United States, that allows Jews to disidentify, to belong to no congregation, no Jewish association or
organization, not even a Jewish country club—to be nothing
more (or less) than ordinary people who simply want to enjoy
the basic human rights to a home, a family, a livelihood, and
full citizenship. That choice was not open to the Jews coming
out of the ghettos after centuries of isolation and segregation.
Those Jews had to either convert to Christianity or become
known as Germans, Frenchmen, Englishmen, Italians, and so
on of Jewish, Mosaic, or Israelitic confession, as the Jewish religion was then variously designated and officially recognized. In
Berlin, Herr Kohn might think of himself as a German; in Paris,
Monsieur Cohen as a Frenchman; and in Rome as an Italian,
possibly going by the name of Sacerdote—but they were all,
inescapably if fatuously, linked to the ancient priestly caste of
Israel.

To the emancipated Jew, this was not supposed to mean anything. His God was more of a cosmic superego than the living
and notoriously jealous God of Israel. He was a God that modern Jews, especially Reform Jews, could worship without undue
fear of contamination by rabbinical obscurantism.

Although modern Judaism could not make Jewish citizens

altogether indistinguishable from their gentile neighbors, it could help phase out Jewish peculiarities that were considered jarring, in bad taste, and apt to generate anti-Semitism. Reform Judaism in particular did not accept the notion that anti-Semitism was as eternal as the Jewish people. Reform Judaism believed in the perfectibility of man.

To help the process along, Reform Judaism introduced a religious service that tried to emulate that of the Protestants. Judaism had become attentive to aesthetics; indeed, it is no coincidence that Moses Mendelssohn's first philosophical work dealt with aesthetics. (Judaism has a problem with aesthetics to this very day, and so have the Jews.) The new preoccupation with style found expression in the form of worship, the attire of the rabbis, and the architecture of the synagogues (or temples, as Reform Jews preferred to call their houses of worship).

Whatever they were called, they were not shuls. That word evoked unappetizing visions of none-too-hygienic bearded Jews swaying back and forth, shouting and gesticulating their prayers at services that never started on time.

The Reformed services were sanitized, civilized, and shortened. The black-robed rabbis were academically trained professionals. They resembled their Protestant colleagues more than their antecedents of the ghettos. Unlike the latter, their task was not to teach Torah, but to preach modernity—to preach not only a novel form of Judaism but also the assimilation of bourgeois virtues and values, appropriately underpinned by quotations from acceptable Jewish sources.

The farther one traveled in an easterly direction, the fainter became the signs of the gentrification of Judaism. But even in Russia, the winds of modernism stirred Jewish intellectuals and brought forth a bountiful crop of *Maskilim* (literally, "enlightened ones"). The *Maskilim* were secularized Jewish intellectuals who hoped to hitch Jewish particularity to the wagon of humanist universalism by using Hebrew or Yiddish as the national language of the Jewish people. They could expect little help from Russian intellectuals and none from the authorities.

35

The Tsarist regime had no intention of bestowing any rights on the Jews or letting them out of the Pale of Settlement to which they were confined. The *Maskilim* had, therefore, a more difficult task in getting their fellow Jews to abandon the old ways.

They did try, though. As early as 1841, a group of them, advocating Russification, petitioned the governors of the Pale demanding the elimination from Jewish education of the "harmful influence of the Talmud." In the same petition, they expressed the view that "inasmuch as Jewish dress has no relation to religious law, the Jews ought to be ordered to change their dress for clothing commonly worn throughout the country in accordance with the social class to which they belong."

In some jurisdictions such ordinances were actually passed. Like many other regulations, these were often disregarded or their edge blunted through bribery. Even so, the number of Jews who worried about the proper ritual composition of their clothing material diminished, while the number of those interested in contemporary fashion grew steadily. In Russia, too, the hold the rabbis exercised weakened, though more slowly than in Western and Central Europe, where dress assimilation had long ago become the rule. (The Jewish bourgeoisie there tended to be both overweight and overdressed.)

In spite of signs of outward assimilation, the majority of Jews continued to cling to the religious symbols of the past. They celebrated holy days, they held traditional weddings, they attended religious services on the Sabbath. But though they fasted on Yom Kippur, they ate on other traditional fast days. They also lit up cigarettes on holy days, and they began to be lax in matters of kashrut (compliance with dietary laws), especially outside the home. Still, they rarely married shiksas. And virtually all Jewish males were circumcised, a sure (albeit mostly discreetly hidden) sign that their parents wished them to retain a Jewish identity. Circumcision, however, was not necessarily taken as an act by which the Jewish male entered into the Covenant of Abraham in a way that would oblige him to keep all the commandments. It was merely a time-honored custom. Besides, the custom could be rationalized; doctors proclaimed it healthy and hygienic.

Despite all the visible signs that distinguished the modern Jew from his ghetto ancestors, he had not become completely assimilated. Perhaps he did not want to become completely assimilated. The suspicion was not easily allayed that the Jews, in whatever form their Jewishness expressed itself, knew in the depths of their hearts that they were a distinct, separate people. Public protestations to the contrary, the sincerity of which was often in direct proportion to the degree of assimilation of the protestor, did not help much.

It is not surprising that the gentiles were not easily convinced that a people who had for centuries dwelt apart would renounce all that kept them apart, particularly their claim to chosenness. Besides, the gentiles often did not want to be convinced. It took close to two hundred years and two world wars before some societies were ready to accept Jewish apartness. The issue was even more complicated with regard to Jewish chosenness. The matter still raises theological eyebrows and keeps American rabbis (though not the Orthodox among them) busy explaining it away for the benefit of their rightly suspicious Christian colleagues.

In the nineteenth century, there was one very prominent gentile who was uneasy about Jewish apartness: Napoleon Bonaparte. Napoleon wanted assurances from French Jewry that it no longer considered itself a separate entity, forbidden to intermarry, with one set of rules dictating relations with fellow Jews and another governing commerce with non-Jews. Napoleon was especially worried about "usury"—in other words, the money-lending activities of the Jews. Moreover, Napoleon suspected that somewhere in a remote corner of their hearts the Jews longed for a *patrie* other than France.

Napoleon wanted to have all these matters authoritatively cleared up. In 1806, he convened an Assembly of Jewish Notables and presented them with twelve questions that, if answered to his satisfaction, would make definite the entry of

French Jews into the French nation. The following year he con-
voked a Sanhedrin that was to give doctrinaire sanction to the
answers provided by the Assembly. The Assembly and the sev-
enty-one members of the Sanhedrin, two-thirds of whom were
rabbis and one-third prominent laymen, did not have an easy
task. They had to convince Napoleon that the Jews were perfectly loyal Frenchmen and that they did not now, nor would
they in the future, have any other fatherland but France. "Yes,"
the notables proclaimed resoundingly, "France is our country;
all Frenchmen are our brothers." In deference to their Emperor's anglophobia, they added, in an act of gratuitous groveling, that a French Jew would feel as foreign among English Jews
as any Frenchman would feel among Englishmen.

At the same time, however, the Sanhedrin had to reassure
French Jewry that their subordination to the secular law of the
state did not mean that they should disregard Jewish Law and
custom. Max Nordau retrospectively denounced the Sanhedrin
as "lacking in courage, dignity, and honesty." In fact, the Sanhedrin was merely being diplomatic. To gain *Liberté* and *Ega-
lité* for French Jewry, it compromised on *Judeité.*

In essence, the Sanhedrin assured Napoleon that the heart of
a French Jew beat for France, and for France alone, though it
remained a Jewish heart. The Sanhedrin had no choice but to be
ambiguous. How different—different also in the quality of its
ambiguity—the situation of French Jewry is today can be
gauged from a remark attributed to former President Georges
Pompidou. Pompidou, who had been for many years the director of the Banque Rothschild, reportedly said of his former boss,
Guy de Rothschild: "His heart beats for Israel, but it is a French
heart." The Baron must have loved the formula.

The entry of Jewry into the maelstrom of modern Europe was
not an easy one. In leaving the spiritual and psychological security of the ghetto, Jews were subject to what Cuddihy described as "stresses, maladjustments, feelings of backwardness
and other ambivalences." Though all this was similar to the
experiences of other peoples forced into a clash with a "higher"

foreign civilization, the predicament of European Jewry was more acute. Unlike Japan, for example, which opened its ports to the Black Ships of the West and thus to alien influences at about the same time, European Jewry did not present a solid social structure. There no longer was a coherent, unified Jewish community. There was no recognized leadership (such as the Japanese shoguns and their successors) to guide them through the process of emancipation and assimilation. Even had there been such leadership, its task would have been impossible: emancipation addressed the Jew as an individual, not as a collective.

Europe never promised the Jews a comfortable journey into its civilization. In the heady days of the Enlightenment, all it promised was liberty and equality. As it turned out, with the possible exception of England, Europe never kept the promise. On the contrary, it reneged on it, with a vicious vengeance— above all, in the case of Germany.

III

The Maze

What emerged from the revolutionary ferment of the eighteenth and nineteenth centuries was not a brotherhood of man that made no distinction between Frenchman and German, Jew and gentile, but rather a selfish national bourgeoisie that placed its own country and its own class interests *über alles.* As long as the idea of equality served as a weapon against the privileges of the aristocracy, the bourgeoisie had embraced it with enthusiasm. But once the bourgeoisie gained political power, the humanitarian ideals of the Enlightenment lost much, if not all, of their attraction.

The revolutionary ideas of the era were rooted in abstract conceptions of the nature of man and society that (as seems to be the rule in history) did not survive their translation into the realities of power. It did not take long before the philosophical underpinnings of the striving for liberty, equality, and brotherhood collapsed. The new philosophies of Schopenhauer, Nietzsche, and romanticism (which Nietzsche called a "malignant fairy") no longer looked to rationality to provide the answer to the enigma of man, no longer had faith in man as a rational being.

Not surprisingly, the newly powerful national bourgeoisie had little tolerance for the phenomenon of a persistent Jewish identity, the less so as it was ill-defined and often annoyingly ambiguous, seeming to cling even to those who wished to be rid of it. By the middle of the nineteenth century, the Jews of Western and Central Europe had formally attained full citizenship of the countries in which they lived. Yet the Jews became part of the bourgeoisie of their host countries without being completely absorbed into them. The Jews insisted that they were, indeed, Germans, Frenchmen, Englishmen, and so on of the Jewish or Mosaic or Israelitic faith, or whatever designation local custom dictated. Some were very vociferous in their insistence, and even those Jews who knew better thought it impolitic to say otherwise. But the gentiles largely considered the Jews as a separate entity and viewed their acquired nationality as a qualifier of their Jewishness rather than the other way around.

Historically, there was, of course, a difference between, say, a French Catholic and a French Jew, however strongly French both felt. It may be largely a myth for a Frenchman to see himself as a descendant of the ancient Gauls, but it is a plausible myth. Not so for a French Jew. His ancestors had come to France from some other country. Tombstones in old Jewish cemeteries could attest to that, as did records kept by the authorities.

Then there was the matter of the interest Jews showed in the fate of Jewish communities in other countries, an interest that transcended national boundaries, and therefore was a sin against the ethos of nationalism. That interest, however vague, was persistent, and it often, as in the case of the infamous Damascus blood libel of 1840, served to revitalize the sense of worldwide Jewish solidarity, a phenomenon wildly exaggerated by the gentiles, particularly those hostile to the Jews.

French Jewry went so far as to institutionalize Jewish solidarity by founding, in 1860, the Alliance Israélite Universelle. Its philosophy was based on the precept that "All Israel are friends and vouch for each other." The precept was not always honored, but it did help to strengthen the perception of the supranational—and thus alien—nature of the Jewish people. Still, it did not prevent Jews from fighting and dying for the greater glory of their respective fatherlands, even though that meant they had to face the possibility of fighting and killing other Jews. Jews were, or had to be, no less patriotic than the Social Democrats of different countries had proved to be, their adherence to the Second International notwithstanding.

But however much patriotism Jews displayed—and even young Martin Buber greeted the outbreak of World War I enthusiastically and regretted his physical inability to be a soldier—the suspicion persisted that the Jews constituted a people and a nation apart, distinct from the host nation, more than just a non-Christian religious community. Moses Hess, a nineteenth-century philosopher who emerged from the chimerical maze of radical socialism to become a born-again nationalist Jew, severely criticized Reform Judaism for disregarding the question of national identity. A large part of his principal work, *Rome and Jerusalem*, was devoted to demonstrating the futility of religious emancipation at a time when the rising tide of nationalism had all but drowned the sociopolitical significance of religion.

The friends of the Jews were perhaps ready to accept the thesis that the Jews were different only in their religion. But their enemies—and their numbers grew ominously in the second half of the nineteenth century—were out to prove that, despite the evident signs of their acculturation, the Jews were a separate nation, not simply a separate creed, and as such were not assimilable. Since the Jews could neither be disenfranchised and pushed back into the ghetto, nor be seamlessly integrated into society, they found themselves as a collectivity in a sociopolitical limbo. In other words, they became a pariah nation, a diagnosis first made by the French Jewish writer Bernard Lazare, an early adherent of (and deserter from) the cause of Herzlian nationalism. The essential futility of assimilation wedded to its practical necessity had given birth to the Jewish problem.

The ambiguity of the Jewish situation did not prevent individual Jews from occupying places of prominence in the life of "their" countries, or from attaining a considerable degree of wealth. In 1843, Bruno Bauer tried to bolster his argument against the emancipation of the Jews by asking rhetorically: "Who worked for eighteen hundred years to educate Europe? Who fought the battles in which a hierarchy that wanted to rule beyond its time was defeated? Who created Christian and modern art and filled the cities of Europe with enduring monuments? Who developed the sciences? Who developed theory of state constitution?" And Bauer answered his own question: "There is not one Jewish name. Spinoza was no longer a Jew when he created his system." (The very Christian Bauer had no use for the civilization of Moslem Spain, in which Jews had played a significant role.)

Not long after Bauer's outcry appeared in print, Jews were to be found in all the fields enumerated by Bauer, except Christian art. Jews even sat in the legislative bodies of European countries, though not as representatives of Jewry. The defense of Jewish interests as such was anathema. With the formal entry of the Jews into civil society, they could by definition have no particular interests and concerns as a collectivity except in religious matters. Even in the Parliament of the Austro-Hungarian monarchy, in which ethnic groups were recognized as such, Jewish deputies were not permitted to form a Jewish parliamentary group or an official caucus, a privilege granted to Czechs, Poles, and Ukrainians. (Hungary had a parliament of its own.)

In an era of nationalism, the Jews alone were required to relinquish the national component of their identity and to be content with a religious differentiation. Even so, they were still distinguishable from their gentile neighbors, the more so as there were always gentiles who made the point that the Jew was unlike them, an alien who must remain an object of suspicion at best, of persecution at worst.

The ultimate logic of assimilation would have been mass

conversion. Unrealistic as it was, the idea had its advocates among both Jews and non-Jews. The proponents of the idea must have been unaware of or chosen to disregard the predictable reaction of most Jews to a method that proposed to make the Jew acceptable by eliminating him. (The example of Queen Isabella of Spain's Jewish policy should have made it clear that even coercive methods failed to convert all Jews.) It is a sign of how acute the Jewish problem was at the time that such ideas were even considered. (Herzl, who once proposed mass conversion as a solution, must have been aware of its flaws, for he rejected conversion for himself.)

In short, the Jews of Western and Central Europe found themselves on the horns of a dilemma whose points pressed painfully into their conscience. Legally, they were full-fledged citizens of the countries in which they resided, often going back for many generations. But in what sense were their countries truly theirs? This was a painful question to which there were many possible answers, but no real one. The voices that shouted, with growing intensity, that the Jews belonged elsewhere (but where?) could not be ignored. They provided threatening evidence that large numbers of their fellow citizens did not consider the Jews as "belonging."

There was also the troubling question of Jewish identity. How was that identity to be defined now that the cultural-religious unity of the Jewish people that had prevailed in the ghetto was a thing of the past? There was no longer only one Judaism. Now there were many forms of Judaism, even a secular Judaism. The desire to be part of the host nation while still retaining a Jewish identity that extended beyond mere formalized participation in religious rites and customs presented the Jews of Western and Central Europe with a gnawing moral dilemma.

Had the Enlightenment actually given birth to a world in which reason was the measure of all men and all things, in which both free nations and the free citizens within them lived in perfect harmony with one another, the Jews would have been spared the dilemma. Unfortunately, that was not the case.

The Orthodox, of course, had no dilemma. For them, the route to take was clearly marked: they would continue as commanded by God and their rabbis. They would deal with the gentiles only to the extent necessary for their material existence, while disregarding (even holding in contempt) gentile culture, ideas, nationalism, politics, and other foibles and vanities. In short, they would continue to live as though the ghetto walls had never been breached.

The emancipated Jew, however, could not do that. He had become too much a part of his host nation's life, even if he was not fully accepted by large sectors of its society.

Russian Jewry did not have to face the dilemmas that bothered their Western brethren, either. Except for a small number of individuals, Russian Jews did not have to ponder the question whether or to what degree they were Russians. They knew exactly where they stood, however distressing that was. The Enlightenment had left but a faint impression on the absolutist government of the Tsars, although Catherine the Great corresponded with Voltaire and read Montesquieu. The thin shafts of light that penetrated into the Pale of Jewish Settlement during the reign of Alexander II (1855–1881) were snuffed out when he was assassinated by radicals on the very day he put his signature to a new, liberal constitution. Ironically, Alexander's assassins (a Jewish woman among them) acted because they considered his reforms to be insufficient.

His successor, Alexander III (1881–1894), not only abrogated the constitution but sharply reversed the liberal trend initiated by his predecessor. The spiritual father of Alexander III's regime was Konstantin Petrovich Pobedonostsev, a fanatically religious man who rejected all Western ideas. Not surprisingly, the Jews particularly felt the oppressive weight of his reactionary policies. Again, the Jews could be harassed, persecuted, and, on occasion, even murdered with impunity. Anti-Semitism was government policy.

What East and West had in common was that, in both parts of Europe, governments, politicians, theologians, writers, journalists, and sociologists raised the question: "What are we to do with our Jews?" No one seemed to be able to propose a practical solution. Instead, the energies of those seeking to solve the problem were devoted, with growing viciousness, to anti-Semitic propaganda. Frustration over the apparent intractability of the problem was only part of the explanation. Often, anti-Semitism appeared merely to have shifted its basis from rejection on theological grounds to excision by reason of the "depravity and inferiority of the Jewish race." It was the old game in new garb.

The notion that there were only two ways of getting rid of Jews—either by sending them back to Palestine or by killing them—has a long pedigree. The nineteenth-century French social theorist Pierre Joseph Proudhon (1809–1865), who accused the Jews of having infected Europe's bourgeoisie with their heinous brand of capitalism, suggested the extermination of that "infernal race," though he did leave open the possibility of their expulsion to "Asia."

The Tsarist Minister of the Interior, Vyacheslav Pleve, a notorious anti-Semite and organizer of numerous pogroms, envisaged a three-part solution to the Jewish problem. When Herzl, much to the dismay of Russian Zionists, met with him in 1903 in order to enlist Russia's help in persuading the Turkish Sultan to allow Jewish settlement in Palestine, Pleve, who liked the project, estimated that the Palestine Charter, if granted, would result in the emigration of one-third of Russia's Jews. Another third, he figured, would become fully integrated and assimilated into Russian society. The rest, Pleve thought, would perish in one way or another.

Still, in spite of the French slogan *Mort aux Juifs,* and the old Russian cry to "Kill the kikes—redeem Russia," no one at the time envisaged anything like the Final Solution invented by Hitler. Even pogroms were primarily meant to persuade the Jews to move somewhere else. (Initially, that was also the thrust of Nazi policy; unfortunately, the Jews had nowhere to go.)

Even as notorious an anti-Semite as Hilaire Belloc rejected the notion of physically destroying the Jews as "abominable in morals." Belloc's solution, which he outlined in a book published in 1922, was "amicable segregation." He proposed a modern ghetto without walls but with functional restrictions, such as barring Jews from high finance and what he called "monopolies." One can well imagine that the idea appealed (and may still appeal) to those who wanted to see the Jews excluded from their particular profession.

Toward the end of the eighteenth century, yet another revolution, Jewish nationalism, began to question the quality of the civic fundaments on which the Jews of Western and Central Europe relied for their well-being and the preservation of their identity. Once again, restricting walls were very much the issue—walls erected by gentile society in order to keep the Jews "in their place." What that place was was never clearly defined. Legally, no such place existed, since the Jews had supposedly attained full equality. But it was understood that certain positions, if not hermetically closed, should be difficult for Jews to attain. The same was true of being accepted in "society."

Marcel Proust's *Remembrance of Things Past* offers a deep insight into the dilemma the emancipated Jew encountered in the second half of the nineteenth century. Although his mother, née Jeanne Weil, came from an old Alsatian Jewish family, Proust himself was not a Jew. He was baptized at birth. His Jewishness came mainly from his "Jewish sensitivity."

Proust was ambiguous about his Jewishness in the same way that he was ambiguous about his homosexuality. Indeed, the two often became inextricably intertwined in his creative mind. To Proust, there was something that linked both "accursed races." Accursed through no fault of their own, both faced the thorny problem of acceptance. (A curious echo of this affinity could be heard during the hijacking of TWA flight 847 by Shiite terrorists in June 1985. When asked to state his religion, Richard P. Herzberg, an American Jew, answered "agnostic," which, luckily for him, left the hijackers nonplussed. Two other passengers, Jack McCarthy and Victor Amburgu, were similarly intent on concealing their homosexuality, for fear that the fundamentalist Moslem terrorists would kill them for their "sin." The commonality of reaction by Jew and homosexual would have struck a sympathetic chord in Proust: in the face of danger, both retreat into the closet.)

In the section of *Remembrance* entitled "Cities of the Plain," Proust discourses at some length about the plight of homosexuals in society, likening it to that of the Jews. In fact, what Proust says about "his" inverts applies just as much (if not more) to Jews seeking to be admitted to society than to homosexuals, toward whom French society of his time had, as a rule, been more forgiving provided, of course, that they kept their sexual preferences discreet. Indeed, one may well wonder if Proust really had homosexuals in mind when he described their practice of "shunning one another, seeking out those who are most directly their opposite, who do not want their company, forgiving their rebuffs, enraptured by their condescensions; but also brought into the company of their own kind by the ostracism to which they are subjected, the opprobrium into which they have fallen...having finally been invested, by a persecution similar to that of Israel, with the physical and moral characteristics of a race."

In another passage, the precedence Proust gives to the problem caused by his Jewishness over that of his homosexuality is even more transparent. "These descendants of the Sodomites," Proust wrote, "have established themselves throughout the entire world; they have had access to every profession and are so readily admitted into the most exclusive clubs that, whenever a Sodomite fails to secure selection, the black balls are for the most part cast by other Sodomites, who make a point of condemning Sodomy, having inherited the mendacity that enabled their ancestors to escape from the accursed city. It is possible that they may return there one day. Certainly they form in every land an oriental colony, cultured, musical, malicious, which has charming qualities and intolerable defects."

Surely the passage makes better sense if "Sodomite" is replaced by "Jew." Homosexuals nowhere formed an "oriental colony." This was a label attached to the Jews, mainly by those who did not wish them well. The attributes of "cultured," "musical," "malicious," "charming qualities," "intolerable defects," though they may fit homosexuals as well, were more often brought up when the "Jewish problem" was discussed, whether in serious or frivolous terms. In fact, there never was a homosexual problem. At least no one ever suggested that they all return to Sodom, as it was suggested that the Jews return to Palestine.

And what is one to make of Proust's "provisional warning against the lamentable error of proposing (just as people have encouraged a Zionist movement) to create a Sodomist movement and to rebuild Sodom"? The parenthetical parallel makes it clear: Proust is talking about the Jews and a possible solution to the Jewish problem, a solution he rejects. His ambiguous feelings about his Jewishness, aggravated by his neurosis, do not permit him to be open about it.

Nevertheless, he qualified his warning as "provisional." Was Proust endowed with a premonition of things to come, such as is often attributed to Kafka? Did he envisage the establishment of a Jewish state? He couldn't possibly have envisaged a "Sodomite" colony such as the one established in the Castro district of San Francisco in the 1970s. But a Jewish state was another matter altogether.

Proust's sensitivity to his Jewishness and the humiliation involved in the barriers gentile society placed between itself and the Jews was poignantly expressed in the scene in which the narrator of *Remembrance of Things Past* (that is, Proust himself) is placed in a section of a café reserved for "foreigners," instead of in the prestigious section where he was to meet his aristocratic friend Saint Loup. Though the two sections are separated only by a railing decorated with greenery, the partition is an insuperable obstacle that the narrator cannot negotiate without the help of his "pure French" friend.

The denizens of the "foreign"—in other words, Jewish—section are oblivious to the existence of the partition. Proust views them with both repulsion and admiration. He describes them as "intellectuals, budding geniuses of all sorts, resigned to the laughter excited by their pretentious capes, their 1830 ties and still more by the clumsiness of their movements, going so far as to provoke that laughter in order to show that they paid no heed to it, who were yet men of real intellectual and moral worth. They repelled—the Jews among them principally... those who could not endure any oddity or eccentricity of appearance.... Generally speaking, one realized afterwards that, if it could be held against them that their hair was too long, the noses and eyes were too big, their gestures abrupt and theatrical, it was puerile to judge them by this, that they had plenty of wit and good-heartedness, and were men to whom, in the long run, one could become closely attached. Among the Jews especially there were few whose parents and kinsfolk had not a warmth of heart, a breadth of mind, a sincerity, in comparison with which Saint Loup's mother and the Duc de Guermantes cut the poorest moral figure."

Proust the French aesthete had a problem with the insufficiently assimilated Jew. Yet Proust's "inalienable spiritual sensibility," to use a definition of Jewishness coined by Gustav Landauer, through the prism of which he rationalized any rejection he encountered, admired the Jew who struggled to retain his authenticity in one way or another.

Though he was not really part of European Jewry, Proust, too, wandered in the diabolical maze into which the Enlightenment and emancipation had unintentionally led the Jews. It was a maze within a house of horrors, where at any unlucky turn frightening anti-Semitic apparitions jumped out at the wanderer. There seemed to be exits: conversion, cosmopolitanism, socialism, withdrawal into oneself, escape to the New World. But most of them proved to be illusory, some tragically so. In the end, some six million of Europe's Jews were forced to exit not only from the maze but from the world, by way of Hitler's death camps.

Half a century before the catastrophe occurred, an attempt was made to demonstrate a way out of the maze: through Jewish nationalism. But the majority of the Jewish people refused to heed its call.

IV

The Lure of Nationalism

By the middle of the nineteenth century, the Jews of Central and Western Europe had gained membership (on paper, at least) in the patriotic association called the nation-state. As new members with a suspect past, they were required to renounce the idea of a separate Jewish national identity. That idea, after all, was incompatible with the prevalent notion that nation and state were inseparably fused into one.

The neo-Kantian Jewish philosopher Hermann Cohen (1842–1918) probably spoke for the majority of westernized Jews when he said that it was "our religion that solely and exclusively constitutes the difference between us and our State, and, therefore, our nation." By "our nation," he meant the German nation. By "our religion," he meant a Judaism of reason. How strongly this view was rooted among an important section of German Jewry can be gauged by the fact that even in the Nazi era many German Jews held on to it with exasperating tenacity; indeed, many may have gone to their deaths thinking of themselves as truer Germans than their murderers.

This outlook was hardly unique to German Jews. The nineteenth century saw the emergence of culturally distinct French, English, German, Italian, Austrian, and Hungarian Jews (to name just a few)—distinct, that is, from each other. To be sure, Jews could not ignore the fact that something both distinguished the Jews from their gentile compatriots and also drew the Jews together in a way that transcended political boundaries. But most Jews felt it wasn't nationhood. Rather, it was religion. If that was not the whole truth, it was at least a useful convention that enabled the Jews of Western and Central Europe to participate in ever growing numbers and prominence in the economic, cultural, and public life of the countries in which they lived.

There were, of course, Jews who were not willing to renounce their sense of national separateness in return for emancipation, Jews who did not think anyone had the right to exact such a price. They were a disturbing phenomenon. Their insistence that the Jews *were* more than just a religious community amounted to a Jewish confirmation of the thesis that Jews were an alien national element in the midst of a supposedly homogenous national body politic. This was a view expressed mostly, though not exclusively, by anti-Semites who saw Jewry as a sinister, dangerous cabal bent on undermining state and nation from within. The affirmation by Jews that they were in fact a national minority thus seemed to play right into the hands of their worst enemies.

Johann Gottlieb Fichte, the eighteenth-century philosopher whose political theories had a profound influence on European nationalism (including its Jewish version, Zionism), had nothing good to say about the Jews. To his mind, they were an alien state within the state. In 1793, in his famous work "Contribution to the Correction of the Public's Judgment Regarding the French Revolution," Fichte wrote: "...through almost all countries of Europe there is spreading a powerful, hostile state, which is perpetually at war with all other States, and which in some of them oppresses the citizens with the utmost severity:

it is Jewry." (Though Hitler probably never read Fichte, he launched his war against the Jews on the same premise.)

It was Fichte who first sounded many of the themes that later became the staple fare of the modern anti-Semite: Jewish exclusiveness, their belief in their inherent superiority, their predilection for trade, their disdain of gentiles. He wanted the Jews to go to Palestine not so much for their own good as simply to get rid of them. "Again," he wrote, "I see no other means of protecting ourselves against them than conquering their promised land for them and sending them all there."

Fichte was later to change his mind about the Jews (though not necessarily for the "right" reasons). He changed after coming under the influence of the German literary salons presided over by such enlightened, assimilated Jewish ladies of great charm and keen intellect as Rachel Varnhagen and Henriette Herz, and also as a result of his friendship with the daughter of Moses Mendelssohn. But the damage was done: the Jews had been identified by an eminent nationalist philosopher as an alien nation that ought to live in its own land.

By contrast, when Fichte's contemporary, the great eighteenth-century thinker Johann Herder, insisted that the Jews were a nation, and not simply adherents of a particular religious creed, there was no trace of hostility in his pronouncement. On the contrary, Herder had great admiration for the cultural heritage of the Jews. Indeed, as Isaiah Berlin tells us, "it was despite his passionate addiction to their antiquities [that Herder blamed] the Jews for not preserving a sufficient sense of collective honor and making no effort to return to their home in Palestine, which is the sole place where they can blossom into a *Nation.*"

That the Jews ought to live in their own land was by no means a novel idea, and certainly not one invented by anti-Semites. As early as the sixteenth century, no less an authority than Rabbi Juda Liwa ben Bezalel proclaimed that God had granted every nation a land of its own, and that the Jews had been given the Land of Israel, which was therefore the natural place for the Jewish people to be. The Maharal, as he is known to the cognoscenti, considered Jewish existence in Exile to be anomalous and contrary to the natural order of things. At the same time, however, he warned against "hastening the end." The Jews, he insisted, would be returned to their land only when they were found worthy of redemption. Their exile was a punishment for not having fulfilled their mission to be a Holy People in the Holy Land when they had the opportunity. As soon as this sin was expiated, Rabbi Liwa asserted, the Jews would be restored to Israel.

Somewhere in the back of his prolific mind, the Maharal may have envisaged a man-made (and, hence, incomplete) redemption. Byron Sherwin, a modern biographer of Rabbi Liwa, points to the latter's preoccupation with the "anomalous" nature of the redemption narrated in the Book of Esther. "In the biblical text," writes Sherwin, "no divinely engineered miracles are mentioned; indeed, God's name never even appears in the Book of Esther. The redemption seems to be the result of human effort and not of divine providence. The people are saved from annihilation by God elusively operative within history."

But while the Maharal may have believed in the possibility of redemption by human effort, the idea that the Jews might be restored to their ancestral land before the coming of the Messiah evoked few, if any, echoes among rabbinical authorities. It wasn't until the second half of the nineteenth century that some rabbis began to envisage the possibility of Jewish settlement in Palestine as a desirable preparatory step on the road to redemption. They undoubtedly did so under the influence of the surge of nationalism in Europe, not out of any new theological understandings. They were simply convinced that the Jews would be better off waiting for the Messiah in their own country. Christian writers, too, thought of the restoration of a Jewish commonwealth in Palestine. Some were inspired by the belief that the return of the Jews to their land was a precondition for the Second Coming of Christ. Others, like Herder, were truly concerned with the spiritual health of the Jewish people.

The great nineteenth-century Polish romantic poet Adam
Mickiewicz wanted the Jews to enjoy freedom in their own land
as much as he desired liberty for his own people. He went so far
as to try to found a Jewish Legion in Constantinople (in addition to a Polish Legion) to undertake the reconquest of the ancient homeland. It was a very romantic notion, worthy of a
poet. Mickiewicz died in Constantinople before he could carry
it out.

Jean Henri Dunant, the founder of the International Red
Cross, approached the problem from the point of view of international politics. In a memorandum published in 1874 under
the title "The Question of the Diplomatic Neutralisation of
Palestine," he advocated Jewish settlement in Syria and Palestine. As a Swiss, Dunant saw a neutral Jewish commonwealth
in Palestine as providing both a good solution for the Jews and a
service to international peace. (Though the dream of Swiss-
style neutrality continued to haunt many Zionists even after
the establishment of the State of Israel, political realities de-
creed otherwise. In any case, it is an irony that the organization
Dunant founded still refuses to accept the Red Star of David as
an internationally recognized symbol equivalent to the Red
Cross and the Red Crescent.)

The anti-Semites, who began to proliferate dangerously in the
second half of the nineteenth century, did not care where the
Jews went as long as it was somewhere else. But even they
preferred to send them to Palestine. Though expulsion to another country would only shift the "problem," not solve it, they
had few compunctions about throwing it into the lap of the
Turkish Sultan, whose empire teemed with many different and
dubious nationalities already. None of the anti-Semites were
prepared to wait for the Messiah to solve the problem once and
for all.

That was also the view of the new breed of nationalist Jews.
"Our nationalism came in," wrote essayist Jacob Klatzkin (best
remembered as the founder of the Encyclopaedia Judaica),
"when and to the extent that the national reality of religious

Judaism fell apart.... In fact, Jewish nationalism grows as the Jewish 'rabbinical' reality fades away."

Klatzkin was not concerned with the Reform Judaism of the assimilated Jew. After all, there could be no Jewish "national reality" for Jews who rejected the notion of a Jewish nation as being incompatible with the universal mission they believed Judaism was supposed to fulfill. In Reform theology, messianism was no longer an absolute faith in an inevitable redemption toward which a Jew had to attune his whole heart and being. Rather, it was a sublime concept placed at a spiritual asymptotic limit—in other words, a humanitarian ideal that is forever approachable yet can never be realized.

For the many Jews who placed themselves between the two camps of Orthodoxy and Reform, secular Jewish nationalism appeared to have potential. In the past, the Jews had been warned to keep their distance from the gentiles, to shun their customs, foods, and languages in order to preserve their unique essence. Inspired by the deceptive sun of the Enlightenment and the march-of-progress tunes struck by the French Revolution, they strove to emulate the gentiles and follow them into the thickets of secular history. They had done so individually, and with problematic results, going through the painful wringer of emancipation on conditions stipulated by the emancipators —conditions that seemed at every turn to be revocable. As a result a need began to be felt for a cathartic self-emancipation on terms proposed by the Jews themselves. This self-emancipation could be achieved only by a supreme collective effort, through a born-again national will, a goal that looked well nigh unattainable.

Henceforth, Jewish history was to be secular, not sacred. And the return to Palestine would be an event placed in the context of a secular historic development, not "a mystical doctrine about an elect people led by God to its sacred land to the beat of the Messiah's drums." Baruch Spinoza, identified by the Israeli historian Yirmiahu Yovel as "The First Secular Jew," had said that much as early as the seventeenth century.

That did not mean that Jews would have to give up the sense of mission that had always been part of their mythos. Being a national Jew could be just as much of a sublime duty as keeping religious commandments. Besides, one did not necessarily exclude the other.

If Fichte could preach that being a German was as much of a mission as being a disciple of Christ, and that nationalism had now taken upon itself the tasks that once belonged to religion, why shouldn't the Jews apply the same principles to their newborn sense of history? Since religion did not hold out the prospect of a return to their ancestral land any time soon, Jews increasingly felt they had to pay heed to the words of the nineteenth-century Italian patriot Giuseppe Mazzini: "Without a country, you have no name, no vote, no right, no baptism of brotherhood between the peoples. You are humanity's bastards, soldiers without a flag. Israelites among the nations, you will win neither trust nor protection: none will be your sureties."

If that was the situation faced by the Italians, who actually lived in the land of their ancestors (though not in a unified Italian state), it applied with even greater poignancy to the Jews, who had yet to return to theirs. The Italians had to change political reality in order to become a full-fledged nation; the Jews had first to create it. But to create it had become a necessity if they were to become a historic nation. There is no history without a state, Hegel taught. The Jews began to accept the idea.

Karl Marx categorized peoples as either historic nations or those with no claim to such distinction. To his mind, the Jews were not even a people. Yet he did not wish to consider them merely as a religious group. He wanted them out of both his personal and historico-philosophical system. In his essay on the Jews published in 1844, which he intended as a reply to Bruno Bauer's call to refuse to admit Jews to society unless they converted to Christianity, Marx declared the Jews to be nothing but an economic category of people whose "secular God is money." As such, they were not a problem apart, but part of the problem: capitalism.

Marx's worldview may have been tainted by Jewish self-hatred. (Jewish self-criticism is often classified as self-hatred.) He certainly wished to keep his distance from anything Jewish. The last thing he wanted was to have his doctrine branded as a "Jewish science." (Marxism did better in that respect than psychoanalysis.) Marx blamed the Jews for having, in the words of the Israeli historian J. L. Talmon, "succeeded in instilling their acquisitive spirit into all the pores of Christian society, and turning the worship of Mammon, their only God, into the supreme reality of the modern world."

Marx was by no means the only thinker to hold this view. Moses Hess, before he was transformed into a messianic Zionist, had expressed the same view in even crasser form. In fact, Marx borrowed entire formulations, to the point of plagiarism, from Hess's 1845 essay "On the Essence of Money." Before both of them, Heine had called money "the god of our time." He did not blame the Jews for this development, though he proclaimed Rothschild to be its "prophet." Pierre Joseph Proudhon, too, blamed the Jews for the corruption of the gentile bourgeoisie.

Mark Twain had similar ideas about the role of money in society. It is unlikely that Twain had read Marx, except possibly articles written by Marx for the New York *Tribune*, whose European correspondent he was for some years. In 1871, Twain wrote: "What is the chief end of man? To get rich. In what way? Dishonestly if he can; honestly if he must. Who is God, the one and only true? Money is God." But Twain felt no need to blame the Jews for what with the rise of modern capitalism had become "the supreme reality of the modern world." Money would have become "the supreme reality" even without the contribution the Jews undoubtedly made to its development.

Once capitalism had passed its "Protestant" phase, in which capital formation was achieved through thrift, credit (as opposed to abstention from consumption) became the grist of the economic mill. As a result, the gentile bourgeoisie began to feel the need to differentiate itself from the stereotype of the Jewish moneylender—the more so as its business practices were in fact no different from those of the Jews.

59

Money, a matter of increasing importance to modern society, had to be de-Judaized in order to rid it of its evil, demonic connotations. A very popular literary work, published in 1855, Gustav Freytag's *Soll und Haben* ("Debit and Credit"), thus contrasted the industrious, impeccable life of a German businessman to that of his devilish, devious Jewish counterpart. The Nazis went so far as to coin a new word to replace *Tüchtigkeit* ("prowess"), a perfectly good German word that for some unfathomable reasons had assumed Jewish undertones in their racist ears. The Nazi innovation was *Tucht*, a word that seemed to stand at attention. Besides, it was hewn of the same linguistic rock as *Zucht*, which connotes drill, discipline, and breeding. (Nonetheless, it never caught on, even in Nazi Germany.)

The role the Jews had played in the emergence of modern capitalism was not in itself of concern to the emerging Jewish nationalist ideology—at least not in the internal Jewish context. The "theological" concern of Jewish nationalism was to secularize the notion of divine providence, in the sense of the German rationalist philosophers. The modern Jewish nationalist Golem spoke German.

It is no coincidence that the writings of early Jewish nationalism were almost exclusively in the German language. Leo Pinsker, a Jewish physician and ardent Zionist from Odessa, had to publish his seminal essay "Auto-Emancipation" in German in order to assure it the proper resonance. Herzl unhesitatingly assumed that German would be the language of the future Jewish state (only partly because of its closeness to Yiddish, the language of the masses of East European Jewry). German was for many years the official language of the Zionist Organization, even after its headquarters moved to London during World War I.

The "Germanness" of the Zionist movement evoked political implications, which at times were real. During World War I, the German Foreign Ministry had a Jewish section headed by none other than that unique multinational Zionist and Jewish cosmopolitan, Nahum Goldmann. Goldmann presented a paradox:

he was at the same time an enemy alien and an official of the German Foreign Ministry. The German connection was such a source of embarrassment to British Zionists that, in 1913, Dr. Moses Gaster, the Haham (Rabbi) of the London Sephardi Community, saw himself "forced" to insist "for clear and definite reasons" that Zionism was "not a German movement." "We have," Dr. Gaster emphasized, "had this struggle in London and the rest of England, as well as everywhere else, and we have made it clear that we do not feel and do not think German, English, French, or Russian, but only solely Jewish."

But inasmuch as language informs the way of thinking, and it undoubtedly does, German deeply influenced the thought processes of the young Jewish nationalists. It did so particularly in two areas. In German, the word *Judentum* denotes both Judaism and Jewry, thus further obscuring a clear delineation of the frontiers between the two (assuming, that is, that such frontiers indeed exist).

No less important, in the German language there is a semantic closeness between the words for "solution" (*Lösung*) and "redemption" (*Erlösung*). The tie is made even stronger by the fact that the German prefix *er* denotes the perfection of the task defined by the word it qualifies. In consequence, the German reading of the Zionist proposition for a solution (*Lösung*) to the Jewish problem could be mistakenly assumed to be redemption (*Erlösung*). In this regard, one cannot help noting that the inability to find a solution to the problem of European Jewry eventually led to the tragedy of the *Endlösung*—the infamous Final Solution adopted by Hitler's Germany.

Hannah Arendt diagnosed two "entirely separate" factors that she felt were responsible for the deepening of national consciousness among European Jewry in the second half of the nineteenth century—factors whose "coincidence" produced the Zionist ideology. "The first of these," Arendt wrote in a 1946 essay entitled "The Jewish State, Fifty Years After," "had little to do, essentially, with Jewish history. It so happened that in the '80's of the last century anti-Semitism sprang up as a political force simultaneously in Russia, Germany, Austria and France." In contrast, "the second factor responsible for the rise of Zionism was entirely Jewish—it was the emergence of a class entirely new to Jewish society, the intellectuals, of whom Herzl became the main spokesman... who were not only de-Judaized, [but] also Westernized."

The simultaneous rise of anti-Semitism and of Zionism was surely not a coincidence. Both movements were the result of the failure of the Enlightenment to create a rational human society imbued with the ideals of truth, justice, and brotherly love. For their part, political Zionists freely conceded that the movement was a reaction to the rising tide of anti-Semitism. Herzl even went so far as to define a nation as "an historic group of a recognizable cohesion, held together by a common enemy." The common enemy of European Jewry was anti-Semitism.

Like the survival of the Jewish people, anti-Semitism is a puzzling phenomenon. Some thinkers believed it to be a permanent feature of the Jewish condition, an assertion that comes very close to saying that the two are permanently interdependent. Issac Bashevis Singer, the Yiddish novelist who won the Nobel Prize for literature in 1978, attributed the hatred of the Jew to a hatred of miracles. In a story called "Miracles," the narrator says: "I've long been convinced that there is a hidden Messiah in every Jew. The Jew himself is one big miracle. The hatred of the Jews is the hatred of miracles, since the Jew contradicts the laws of nature." By laws of nature, the author must have meant the nature of history, in which the Jew played a special role because of the "hidden Messiah" inside him. It is the storyteller's way of saying that the Jews are radically different from other nations because their historic destiny is radically different from—indeed at cross-purposes with—that of all other nations.

Freud attributed Christian resentment of the Jews to the son-father tension in the superego. Maurice Samuel out-Freuded Freud in suggesting that anti-Semitism was an outlet for the yearning of Christians to free themselves from the inhibitive yoke of Jewish morality inherited by their faith and to open wide the gates to the pagan, orgiastic "id." At the same time, Samuel proposed, modern man projects the fearsome dark forces lurking in his subconscious onto the Jews, a people he cannot understand and, therefore, fears.

What seems clear is that, for the anti-Semite, self-affirmation is inseparable from the negation of whatever the Jew happens to stand for in his eyes. As Leo Pinsker put it: "For the living, the Jew is a dead man; for the natives, an alien and a vagrant; for property holders, a beggar; for the poor, an exploiter and a millionaire; for the patriot, a man without a country; for all classes, a hated rival."

Since the Jew negates Christ, negating the Jew becomes to some an easy way to affirm Christ. Similarly, the Jewish claim to be the chosen people can be inverted into a claim to be a master race. Negating the Jewish claim establishes the superiority of one's own "race." To Hitler, wiping the self-proclaimed chosen people off the face of the earth was tantamount to asserting the exclusivity of the German people as the master race. (A witness reported that Dr. Joseph Mengele, the infamous Angel of Death of Auschwitz, had told her that the Final Solution was the ultimate struggle for the control of the world between the only two peoples superior enough to vie for it, the Jews and the Germans.)

But while anti-Semitism seemed as old as the Jews themselves, political anti-Semitism was a new phenomenon. All over Europe, the middle class had become disillusioned with the Enlightenment and had turned away from political liberalism. At the same time, socialism began to seem to the bourgeoisie to be a dangerous enemy bent on depriving it of its economic advantages and political power. Not that socialists were free of anti-Semitism. In France, the leadership of the Socialist Party refused to come out in favor of Captain Dreyfus for fear of arousing a negative reaction among its supporters. In Germany, the Social Democratic leader August Bebel (1840–

1913), derided anti-Semitism as the "socialism of the imbeciles."

The masses, which had gained little from the political demise of the aristocracy, were swayed by populist slogans replete with anti-Semitic refrains that resounded in the streets of French, German, and Austrian cities. There was political hay to be made from anti-Semitism. It became an important part of the political platform of many different parties.

No longer was the Jew mainly reviled as the killer of Christ, although the Catholic and other churches never let their flocks forget it. He was now cast in the role of the alien exploiter, the alien competitor, the alien enemy from within. He was *Ahasuerus*, the wandering Jew, condemned to find no peace anywhere. His homelessness and lack of roots predestined the Jew for the role of the threatening alien, a role that in modern times, one would hope, has been taken over by fictional creatures from outer space.

Even if one believes that anti-Semitism is an incurable disease of the gentiles (though it is the Jews who suffer its consequences), its manifestations are obviously influenced by objective factors. A real or perceived increase of the Jewish population often seemed to get the anti-Semitic adrenaline flowing. It appears that a threshold of tolerance of alien minorities has always been operative in nationally and culturally homogenous societies. These days many Western European countries are concerned about the great numbers of unassimilable foreign workers and refugees—unassimilable because of their refusal to dissolve without a trace—living within their borders. Today the problem centers on the Turks in West Germany, Arabs in France, Pakistanis, Indians, and West Indians in England; even tolerant Denmark is leery of a further influx of refugees from Iran and other "exotic" countries. In the nineteenth century, the aliens were the Jews.

In his exploration of the magical background of anti-Semitism, Adolf Leschnitzer, a noted educator who was put in charge of the segregated Jewish educational system in Nazi

Germany (before escaping to teach at New York's City College), suggests that the reason the persecution of witches replaced that of Jews in the sixteenth and seventeenth centuries was that the number of Jews in Europe had declined noticeably. In the eighteenth century, however, the Jewish population of Europe began to grow at a rate equal to that of the general population; and in the nineteenth century, the Jewish population of Europe grew even faster than the non-Jewish one. According to accepted demographic estimates, the number of Jews in Europe grew from 2 million at the beginning of the nineteenth century to 9 million at its end. In the same period of time, the general population increased at a much slower rate.

The 1800s were also a time of strong Jewish migration to urban centers. In France, Alsatian Jews were on the move, mainly to Paris. At the beginning of the nineteenth century, the seven principal cities of Germany were home to only 7 percent of the country's Jewish population. By the dawn of the next century, 50 percent of Germany's Jews lived in the same seven cities.

At the same time, Eastern European Jews were moving westward. Vienna was full of Jews from the Eastern provinces of the Dual Monarchy. Or so it seemed, both to the "genuine" Viennese Jews and to the gentiles, many of whom were themselves relative newcomers to the capital. *Ostjuden*, as the old established German-Jewish bourgeoisie called what they regarded as their undesirable brothers from Slavonic countries, established themselves in growing numbers in Berlin.

In the capitals of Western Europe, anti-Semitic politicians had no difficulty in frightening the populace that "the Jews were taking over." It was mainly fear of competition that made Edouard Drumont's book *La France Juive*, published in 1885, a nineteenth-century best-seller.

By 1900, about a million Jews had made their way to America, where their massive influx was, not coincidentally, met by a wave of anti-Semitism. It was perhaps the principal reason for America's closing its gates to free immigration.

In America, economic considerations played a lesser role than the desire to keep out inferior genetic stock. Eugenics, a pseudoscience that flourished in England and America at the time, furnished the ideological arguments. The U.S. Congress was particularly impressed by the forceful teachings of the American geneticist Charles Davenport, who warned that a continued influx of immigrants from Eastern and Southeastern Europe would ruin the genetic stock of white Americans, weakening the nation's moral fiber.

Although anti-Semitism made life uncomfortable for virtually all Jews, different Jews experienced it differently. In Eastern Europe, the discomfort was primarily physical. Unlike their brethren in the West, the Jews in the shtetl never accepted the value system of the gentiles. They thus had no moral problem reconciling their existence with their outlook on life.

In Central and Western Europe, the Jewish bourgeoisie, down to the lowly "trading" Jew, took refuge in the vastly improved economic opportunities which it eagerly grasped and vigorously exploited. Unlike its gentile counterpart, the Jewish bourgeoisie preserved its faith in liberalism and progress, which it was confident would eventually reduce anti-Semitism to a point where it would no longer interfere with the pursuit, if not of happiness, then at least of prosperity.

It was the class that we today describe by the adopted Russian word "intelligentsia," and which Herzl dubbed "average," that felt morally most uncomfortable in post-Englightenment Europe. Jewish intellectuals felt most keenly the lack of dignity inherent in their ambiguous national self-definition. To them, it seemed self-evident that the Jews were a nation with as valid a claim to national identity as any other nation of Europe. They had no need to exalt some obscure national epic. They had the Bible, which they now presented not as the revealed word of God but as an authentic historic document. They had a language of their own, Hebrew, in which their ancient history had been recorded. If anything, they had an older claim to be recognized as a nation than the Poles, Czechs, Rumanians, Bulgarians, Greeks, and many others whose intellectuals also carried the torch of nationalism.

The nationalist intelligentsia comprised no more than a small minority among European Jewry. But its voice had resonance. The *Maskilim*, whose first preoccupation had been a universal humanistic culture, had within one generation turned to national regeneration as the principal object of their creativity. With the erosion of the religious foundation of their national identity, the Jews were in danger of fragmenting completely—unless they became a nation like all other nations. This was anathema to the Orthodox, to the assimilationists, to the universalists, to the socialists, to the pragmatists, and to the indifferent among the Jews. Only a small minority looked to nationalism as a way out of the Jewish predicament. But then all revolutionary ideas germinate among a small minority. Jewish nationalism was no exception.

V

The New Jew

In an era when Europe believed it was rapidly moving into a New Age, an age of great intellectual ferment in which new scientific discoveries would create a New Society, an age embellished by New Art and New Architecture and the appearance of the New Woman, the emergence of the New Jew fitted perfectly into the new zeitgeist.

Jewish intellectuals participated prominently in the creative process, most explosively in fin de siècle Vienna. But there were also Jewish intellectuals who felt that the Jew no longer had a natural habitat in Europe. These intellectuals were less concerned with European civilization and the place Jews were to occupy in it than with the future of the Jews as a people, as a nation.

The spiritual reservation in which the Old Jew had lived for centuries had virtually ceased to exist. Emancipation was a gift most Jews had readily accepted. But as recipients of a gift, they were placed in a position of inferiority. Rector Kienholt, the gentile antagonist of the hero in Max Nordau's 1899 drama *Dr.*

Kohn, made the point, saying: "After all, you have not wrested equality of rights from us by force of arms. It is, therefore, not a mutual contract. We conceded equality to you of our own accord, it is a gift, and the extent of the gift is determined by the donor alone."

The Hebrew writer and poet Peretz Smolenskin (1842–1885), an early proponent of Jewish nationalism who had a great influence on young Jews in Vienna, where he migrated from Russia, bewailed the assimilationist groveling that he perceived among the Jewish bourgeoisie of Austria. "We have no sense of national honor," he wrote, "our standards are those of second-class people. We find ourselves rejoicing when we are granted a favor and exulting when we are tolerated and befriended." (Proust said the same thing, ostensibly about homosexuals.)

What Smolenskin and likeminded intellectuals wanted was to create a New Jew who would be neither a pariah nor a parvenu. Someone who would be accepted on his own Jewish terms. They soon came to recognize that such a national and social renaissance of the Jewish people would only be possible in their ancestral homeland. In the meantime, until the Jews could become a normal people in a state of their own, they should stop groveling and start thinking of themselves, in both a psychological and a cultural sense, as citizens of a modern nation, albeit citizens forced to live in exile. They were not waiting for the Messiah, they were determined to engineer their own redemption. To the Maharal, that would have amounted to another "incomplete" redemption like the one related in the Book of Esther. But to the restless, frustrated intellectuals of the European diaspora, it looked more than good enough. Theirs was a truly revolutionary idea, and like other revolutionary ideas, it drew much of its force from the refusal to accept adversity passively and from the will to fight its enemy—in this case, anti-Semitism.

To be credible, proponents of a revolutionary or nationalist movement must show that they are ready to fight for their cause—to die for it, if necessary. (In our time, the Palestinians ceased to be a mere refugee problem only when they produced militants ready to die for their ideas.) Herzl put this message into the mouth of the protagonist of his 1897 drama *The New Ghetto*, Dr. Jakob Samuel. Mortally wounded in a duel, Samuel cries out: "Jews, my brothers, there'll be a time when they'll let you live—when you know how to die. [Murmurs] I want to get out...[With all his strength] Out! Out-of-the-ghetto!"

It took quite some time, and millions of Jewish victims, before the Jew was able to get out of Dr. Samuel's ghetto, the exodus from which was Herzl's dream and aim. Only in Eretz Israel did the Jews finally learn how to die for their country.

At the turn of the twentieth century, Jews recognized that the anti-Semites would like nothing better than to get rid of them one way or another. But no one anticipated wholesale slaughter. It was unthinkable that civilized nations would resort to such abysmal depths of barbarism, least of all Germany. Anti-Semitism, although it did have negative practical implications for many Jews, mainly insulted their dignity. Indeed, the very word "Jew" had acquired a pejorative connotation, had become a term of invective and abuse. Jews also generally believed that virulent anti-Semitism was but a passing phase. Anti-Semitism might never disappear completely, but it seemed reasonable to hope that its hold on the gentile psyche would diminish until it became an atavistic echo whose reverberations would no longer be distressing.

Patience and reliance on the ultimate victory of reason were not virtues preached by the nationalist New Jew. Activism was the order of the day; liberation from the indignities to which he felt subjected was the new sacred cause. The ideal was no longer the devout Jew who would rather die than renounce his faith. (Religion was of little importance to the nationalist Jews.) The Maccabees and Bar Kokhba, not the martyrs, were the ones to be emulated. (In 1899, Martin Buber proposed to the Third Zionist Congress that Hanukkah, which commemorates the Maccabean victory over the Seleucid Greeks in 164 B.C., be declared the official Zionist holiday, a proposal accepted with "wild applause," according to the minutes.)

The New Jew was pledged to defend not his faith but Jewish honor and dignity, concepts that were totally alien to the traditional Jew, and defend them with his life. There were not many opportunities to put that pledge to the test. The fight against anti-Semitism could not be conducted in the trenches. Only dueling offered the rare chance of defending Jewish honor against anti-Semitic offenders.

Herzl dreamed of challenging the leading anti-Semitic politicians of his time and country, Vienna's Mayor Karl Lueger and Christian-Socialist Party leader George von Schönerer, to a deadly duel. In his fantasy, Herzl was prepared to die in the knowledge that his death would bring honor to his people. If, however, he were to prevail, his subsequent trial would serve as an invaluable public forum at which anti-Semitism could be forcefully and effectively denounced. Whatever the outcome, the duel would have a redemptive quality as embodied in the code of chivalry, which, in modernized form, Herzl wanted the New Jew to adopt.

The German socialist Ferdinand Lassalle (1825–1864), before he turned *From Maccabeism to Jewish Anti-Semitism* (the title of a biographical essay by Edmund Silberner), expressed the longing for Jewish dignity in youthful, romantic prose. In 1840, at the age of fifteen, Lassalle wrote in his diary:

In fact, I believe that I am one of the best Jews in existence, although I disregard Ceremonial Law. I could—like that Jew in Bulwar's *Leila*—risk my life to deliver the Jews from their present oppressive condition. I would not even shrink from the scaffold, could I but once more make them a respected people. Oh, when I yield to my childish dreams it has always been my favorite idea to see myself sword in hand, leading the Jews, to make them independent.

Lassalle's dreams were childish, while those of the New Jew were definitely adult dreams. But the underlying sentiments and frustration of both were identical. Like Herzl's fictional Dr.

71

Samuel, Lassalle scolded the Jews for not defending themselves. Forty-four years before Herzl wrote *The New Ghetto*, which by his own admission was the germ of the *Judenstaat*, Lassalle confided to his diary the following reaction to the 1840 Damascus pogrom: "Cowardly people you deserve no better fate! The trampled worm will turn, but you only bow your head lower! You do not know how to die."

Lassalle, the socialist, died as a result of wounds received in a duel. He had fought to defend not Jewish honor or socialist ideals but a lady's reputation. Although long estranged from his people, he was buried in the Jewish cemetery of Breslau. (His writings never earned a meritorious place in German literature, but Vladimir Ze'ev Jabotinsky, the Russian Zionist whose radical nationalist and militaristic ideas are gospel to Israel's political right, knew them by heart.)

Jewish university students, including Herzl, were in the forefront of the defense of Jewish honor. In June 1897, Berthold Feiwel wrote in the fourth issue of *Die Welt*, the Zionist weekly that Herzl founded and he edited: "Jewish honor ranks among the highest ideals of the Jewish national student. It is that Jewish honor which the students defend. With the saber." The few who belonged to Jewish nationalist student organizations did just that. And it was they, not the assimilationist majority, who left something to be remembered by. By setting an example of the "young manliness of national Judaism"—a central theme of Zionist cant—they left a mark deeper than the facial scars they proudly acquired in their duels.

Dueling was not the exclusive domain of Jewish students at German-language universities. In Paris, Bernard Lazare fought a duel with the arch-anti-Semite Edouard Drumont at the height of anti-Jewish agitation during the Dreyfus trial. In Algeria, the brothers Vidal and Mardoché Shalom fought some thirty duels with anti-Semites, and spent time in jail for doing so.

Dueling was not a way of life. It was a symbol and a (very rare) demonstrative statement meant to prove that the New Jew was a gentleman. Not the Jewish gentleman who becomes a "yid" (or worse) to his gentile peers the moment he leaves the room, but a true gentleman-Jew who does not imitate but translates the gentile code of gentlemanly conduct into Jewish national terms. He will defend his honor and be honorable. He will practice what Nordau termed "muscular Judaism" in sports associations called Hakoah ("strength"), "Maccabi" or "Bar Kokhba." (In spite of their early Zionist roots, sports have remained one area in which the Jewish renaissance has produced less than spectacular achievements.)

Above all, the New Jew wanted to put the ghetto mentality behind him. "If the Jews manifest a burning wish to create a new Zion," wrote Max Nordau in 1897, "they draw their inspiration neither from the Torah nor from the Mishnah, but from the misery of the times, from the immediacy of their living emotions, from their determined refusal to tolerate the situation in which they dwell amidst other nations."

Zion had no religious connotation for Nordau. It was a name chosen for historic, not religious, reasons. The nationalist movement of which he was a part drew its inspiration mainly from non-Jewish sources and wished to place itself alongside other European national movements of the time. In an article written in 1898 for the Jerusalem weekly *Hatsvi*, Nordau compared the Zionist ideal to that of the Italian *Risorgimento* and the rise of German nationalism in the period between the Wartburger Fest, where in 1817 German students met to demand the unification of their country, and the proclamation of the Empire, when every German felt "like a poet and a hero."

The Italian Risorgimento and the struggle for the unification of Germany may not have meant a great deal to most Jews, but the comparison served to place the Zionist movement squarely into the mainstream of European history. The Jews were thus presented with a new vision that rejected both the anti-historicism of Rabbinical Judaism and the anti-nationalism of assimilation because neither was held to be capable of preserving the Jews as a modern nation.

The desire to begin a completely new era of Jewish history

seemed to many Zionists to demand a radical break with the past. No one expressed that desire more radically than Jacob Klatzkin. According to Klatzkin, Jewish nationalism was defined by "the element of historic commonality and the element of historic will to a common bond and the creation of a commonality in all days to come." Adherence to the Jewish faith was not seen as a central component of Jewish nationalism, not even a necessary one.

Klatzkin went even further in demanding that the demarcation line between the two great eras, the rabbinical and the national, be drawn sharply. "In order to recognize the national idea in its purity and precision," he proclaimed, "we have to renounce also the legacy of *Judaism of the Spirit.*" The misogynist philosopher Otto Weininger (1880–1903), one of the more lugubrious luminaries of fin de siècle Vienna, said the same thing in his book *Sex and Character.* "The Jews must first overcome Judaism," Weininger wrote, "before they will be mature enough to be capable of Zionism."

Not surprisingly, few Zionists were ready to follow this kind of advice. Purity and precision were without a doubt desirable for a new ideology, but the demand that the legacy of "Judaism of the Spirit" be thrown overboard did not recommend itself even to those who were eager to shed the ritualistic shackles of Rabbinical Judaism.

The term "Zionism" itself is hardly free of religious overtones. Zion was the "city of the great King" (Psalms 48: 2)— that is, the city of God as the King of Israel. In the Cabala, Zion is one of the emanations of God. A whiff of sanctity must have attacked Zionist noses even though they no longer were buried in the pages of sacred books. The very claim made by Zionism that it was the answer to Jewish distress had a messianic tone to it. Moreover, the Zionists rang the messianic bell with their usual oratorical abandon, though they always insisted that the bell was secular.

Even as avowed an atheist as Nordau could not avoid blurring the boundaries between the sacred and the mundane. In the

previously quoted article in *Hatsvi*, Nordau identified the attachment to the messianic ideal as the secret of Jewish survival.
In his view, it was an ideal that served for the non-believer as a
"proud symbol, the strength of which lies in its being unattainable." (Reform Judaism also subscribes to that view.)

Nordau was by no means the only Zionist guilty of failing to
enforce a strict separation of the two domains—that is, the solution of the Jewish problem (*Lösung*) and messianic redemption (*Erlösung*)—although he was careful to label the latter an
unattainable ideal. The founding fathers of political Zionism at
least had the excuse that they were living in an era when political messianism as represented by Mazzini, Michelet, Mickiewicz, and Marx was very much part of the European
intellectual climate. If Providence was to work for human redemption through humanity's respective nations—and in the
case of Marx, through the newly created myth of an international proletariat—the Jews surely had a prior claim on the
idea, even if it was now secularized.

When Theodor Herzl became the virtually undisputed leader
of the Zionist movement, he and the new myth he so forcefully
propounded became the target of messianic speculation. Herzl,
who knew the value of imagery long before television politics
and television evangelism turned it into a truism, did nothing
to discourage this speculation. He himself grappled with it, at
time with candid ambivalence, in his intimate dialogue with
his diary.

Was Herzl indeed in the messianic tradition? The noted
American social philosopher Lewis Mumford, a saddened but
sympathetic observer of Zionism, thought so, at least with regard to Herzl's utopian novel *Altneuland*. In a very perceptive
essay, Mumford wrote that Herzl's myth "appeals not so much
to the vague, rational desire for the good society, as to the Jewish myth, and the passion for fulfillment in some concrete form
which has been latent in Jewish myth....Herzl distinguishes
himself, then, by the fact that he proposes to tap a brimming
reservoir of power; on one hand, his utopia gets part of its ini-

tial momentum from the misery of the Jews of Europe; on the other, and this is perhaps even more important, from the perpetuated glory of the Jewish myth." The myth Mumford obviously had in mind was messianism.

Only Herzl's most ardent adversaries accused him of being a false messiah like Shabbetai Zvi who would bring untold calamities on Jewry. Still, the accusation must have stung. Herzl's reference to Shabbetai Zvi in a diary entry made in June 1900 illuminates his ambivalence. Herzl wrote: "The difference between myself and Shabbetai Zvi (the way I imagine him), apart from the difference in the technical means inherent in the times, is that Shabbetai made himself great so as to be the equal of the great of the earth. I, however, find the great small, as small as myself."

The historian David Vital concluded that Herzl neither rejected the analogy with Shabbetai Zvi nor exactly confirmed it. The key to the truth may lie in the way Herzl imagined the seventeenth-century false messiah. Though Herzl does not tell us directly, we can assume that Herzl, who had little understanding of Jewish mysticism, saw Shabbetai Zvis movement in political terms. In seventeenth-century Europe, political and technological conditions were not ripe. Herzl believed they were so in his time. In the seventeenth century, Shabbetai had no choice but to proclaim himself the Messiah. Herzl, who declared himself to be "as small" as the "great" of his world, suffered from no such compulsion. He wanted, and was able to a remarkable degree, to deal with the "great" on terms of equality. He offered them something in return for what he wanted from them: hope for the solution of the Jewish problem—not salvation, but something concrete.

If Herzl was no messiah, was he, then, a modern prophet? Though he never claimed that honor, there are entries in his diaries that have a prophetic ring. "If I point with my finger at a spot: Here shall be a city, then a city shall rise here," reads one entry. On another occasion, Herzl confided to his diary that "perhaps I am solving more than the Jewish question. To wit, *tout bonnement*, the social question." On the other hand, he questioned whether this belief of his amounted to "megalomania."

In *Remembrance of Things Past,* Marcel Proust writes of Swann's conversion to a defender of justice in the Dreyfus affair: "There are certain Jews, men of great refinement and social delicacy, in whom nevertheless there remain in reserve and in the wings, ready to enter their lives at a given moment, as in a play, a boor and a prophet. Swann had arrived at the stage of the prophet." Much deeper than into the life of the fictional Swann, a prophet had entered into that of Herzl "at a given moment, as in a play" (the theatrical metaphor fits Herzl perfectly), a secular prophet who received his call from history, not from God. Or as Herzl himself said in his diary: "I believe that for me life has ended and world history begun."

Prophet or not, without the appearance on the scene of Herzl, Zionism would have in all likelihood remained an intellectual exercise practiced on the pages of perennially struggling publications and in the privacy of associations that were not much more than debating societies whose members rarely agreed on any issue. It was Herzl who placed the Jewish question on the international agenda and who forced Zionism out of the rarefied comfort of intellectualism into the real world of political action.

Even Hannah Arendt, who ranked Herzl with the "crackpots" of his age, admitted that his "lasting greatness lay in his very desire to do something about the Jewish question, his desire to act and solve the problem on political terms." Nonetheless, she would not forgive him for being a "bourgeois reactionary." Herzl was certainly no socialist. But a reactionary he was only in the eyes of those who, in cavalier disregard of realities, deemed the nation-state a dinosaur doomed to disappear.

Herzl was no crackpot. Nor was he a utopian, at least not in his desire to create the political conditions that would enable the Jews to have a state of their own. He vigorously defended himself against such accusations.

In a letter written to a Hungarian friend, Adolf Agai, Herzl wrote: "... an ass your Stephan Uto [in Hungarian the fictitious name "Uto Pista" is a pun on "utopist"] is not, and when we shall perhaps see the day in our life when this utopia will be as real as reconstructed Greece, united Germany, Italy *chi a fatto da se* [which did it herself] and other entities once believed to be fairy tales." To the renowned Danish literary art critic Georg Brandes, he explained that what he meant was to "mentally project into an unknown future that which did not exist but is nevertheless no utopia."

Herzl's own assertions could, of course, be dismissed as being motivated by an understandable need to present his ideas as a real possibility. No utopian will admit the illusory nature of his propositions. It is the judgment of the outside world that attaches the utopian label to certain ideas. In the case of Herzl, these tags were "false prophet" or "false messiah," expressions more appropriate to the strictly Jewish context in which they were applied.

In creation of the State of Israel finally laid to rest the debate about the reality of Herzl's "dream," a debate that raged throughout his lifetime and long after his death. The Jewish state is, one hopes, as much of a reality as "reconstructed Greece, Italy *chi a fatto da se*," and the other now existing entities once believed to be fairy tales. (Ironically, today a united Germany has again become a fairy tale, while undreamt of numbers of "entities" have emerged since World War II.)

What Herzl undoubtedly possessed is what Thomas G. Masaryk (1850–1937), the first president of the Czechoslovak Republic, called "realistic fantasy." (Masaryk, incidentally, had deep sympathies for the Zionist cause. He was the only head of state who came to Eretz Israel in the time of the British Mandate, albeit on a private visit. At the same time, he doubted that the Jewish people would ever succeed in regaining political independence there.) Dr. Marcus Ehrenpreis, an early Zionist who was for many years the Chief Rabbi of Stockholm, had the same idea when he wrote, "His fantasy and his cool calculation fascinated us."

Undoubtedly, Herzl's artistic involvement in the theater helped fashion his "realistic fantasy." Peter Lowenberg, who attempted to draw a psycho-historic portrait of Herzl, pointed out that "Herzl was a man of the theater who brought theater into politics, making drama of politics. He had the capacity to pass from the unreal to the real, to mix the spheres of dream and politics, to transfer the enchantment of make-believe staging to the world of diplomacy and political power."

The greatness of Herzl's achievement becomes even more remarkable when we consider that he acted on behalf of a powerless people dispersed in many lands, and with a clear mandate from only a small majority among them. The majority saw in him a dangerous demagogue at best, a charismatic charlatan at worst.

Virtually everyone who came into contact with Herzl, even those who disagreed with his ideas, admitted that he had an extraordinary presence. Though charisma was not a term in use in his time, Herzl's conversion from a gifted newspaper man specializing in the feuilleton, a personalized piece of journalistic observation, into the "prophet" of a new idea fits what the German sociologist Max Weber (1864–1920) said of charisma. "In the case of charisma," Weber wrote, "the emergence of the revolutionary idea occurs through a subjective process of internal reorientation born out of suffering, conflicts, or enthusiasm," which may then result in a "new orientation of all attitudes toward the different problems and structures of the 'world.'"

In Herzl's case, all three—suffering, conflicts, and enthusiasm—were present, the latter to the point of obsession. Had he been a more successful playwright, he might have chosen to funnel his suffering, conflicts, and enthusiasm exclusively into the theater. His plays clearly show his preoccupation with the ills afflicting his own class, the Jewish bourgeoisie, especially the worship of money. He castigated the shameful self-serving falsity that permeated the overstuffed drawing rooms of equally overstuffed Jewish businessmen and stockbrokers, the very class that ruled the Jewish institutions of Vienna and determined their policies.

Herzl saw Vienna's Jewish bourgeoisie as lacking in dignity and refinement, and blind to the true nature of the growing anti-Semitic threat. It is no coincidence that his pamphlet *Der Judenstaat* (usually translated as *The Jewish State*, although *The Jews' State* would be a more accurate rendering) grew out of *The New Ghetto*, and that both were written in Paris at a time when anti-Semitism, fueled by the Dreyfus affair, had become a potent political force in France, the first country in Europe to have given Jews full civil rights. The year between the writing of the two works marked Herzl's shift from the theatrical scene to that of world history.

Had Herzl not so agonizingly felt the indignity inherent in the situation of Europe's Jewry, he could have remained content to bask in the glory of being a celebrated feuilletonist in the prestigious *Neue Freie Presse*, a position he was forced to keep to earn his livelihood. As a correspondent for the paper in Paris, he enjoyed almost ambassadorial prestige and social privileges, including a coach of his own. Although deeply conscious of the value of prestige—in that, too, Herzl was ahead of his time, as he was in the recognition of the force of propaganda—he knew only too well the difference between political agitation and political action.

The decisive element in Herzl's transformation from a literateur to a man obsessed by the idea of ending "Jewish misery" was provided by his charismatic nature. Herzl acknowledged that the transformation had taken place in a manner he himself could not understand. He first thought of writing the *Judenstaat* in the form of a novel. But, he noted in his diary, "so shatteringly did the streams of thought race through my soul" that he feared he was "going insane." From this point on, Herzl possessed a mission, and the mission possessed him.

Charisma is also a most potent antidote to skepticism and down-to-earth realism of the it-cannot-be-done sort. Herzl put it this way: "Much in these notes will seem laughable, exaggerated, crazy. But if I had exercised self-criticism, as I do in my literary work, my ideas would have been stunted. What is colossal serves the purpose better than what is dwarfed, for anyone can do the trimming easily enough."

In Herzl's thought process, we find not only "realistic fantasy" but also the creation of an action-myth in the sense of the French social philosopher Georges Sorel (1847–1922). According to Sorel, an action-myth "holds the realities of common sense and habit in defiance, and sets before the group some gigantic task or mission which is scarcely this side of possibility. The results of acting upon such a myth will not measure up to expectations, perhaps, of those who throw themselves into it, but it will be measurably above the level of life as it would run without the myth; and this is all the justification needed for its formulation." The myth becomes a psychological necessity. That, in essence, was the strength of the Zionist idea: for many Jews, it had become a psychological necessity, often an unconscious one.

The word "myth" was not in Herzl's vocabulary. There was, however, one entry in his diaries that clearly relegated realism to a secondary place. "Great things need no solid foundation," Herzl wrote. "An apple must be placed on a table, to keep it from falling. The earth floats in midair. Perhaps, similarly, I can found and stabilize the Jewish state without a firm support."

Part of the secret of Herzl's success in being accepted as the representative of the Jewish people undoubtedly lay in his appearance. Herzl was the physical embodiment of the noble ideal of the New Jew, the ideal he hoped all Jews would adopt. His code of behavior and concept of honor were as radically different from those of the ghetto as his dress was from that of a Hasid. The fact that his interlocutors could identify with his bearing and appearance made them more receptive to his proposals. Much in his outer bearing had its roots in Vienna.

In Herzl's time, the Burgtheater, the Imperial Theater of Vienna, exercised an extraordinary influence on the behavioral code of Vienna's "good society." The writer Stefan Zweig (1881–1942) described it in these words:

In the court actor, the spectator saw an excellent example of how one ought to dress, how to walk in a room, how to converse, which words one might employ as a man of good taste and which to avoid. The stage, instead of being merely a place of entertainment, was a spoken and plastic guide to good behavior and correct pronunciation.

It was a code that Herzl, a man of the theater himself, did not have to learn at the Burgtheater, the same theater he so ardently wished would produce one of his plays. (It never did.) There is little doubt that he accepted its aesthetic standards. His belief in this code also helps to explain Herzl's deep attachment to the German language and his benign contempt for Yiddish—"jargon," as it was called by those who spoke proper German (or thought they did) and who saw Yiddish as a "disorderly" language that treated spelling, grammar, and syntax with humorous disdain. "I have adopted a better way of speaking than Jewish German so that he need not be ashamed of me," says the mother of Jakob Samuel, the hero of *The New Ghetto* who bears many traits of Herzl's ego ideal.

Herzl's hopes in this area were never really fulfilled. Of all the Zionist leaders of later years, only Vladimir Jabotinsky was concerned about aesthetics. "We, the Jews, suffer from a lack of sensitivity to forms," he wrote in 1925. Jabotinsky regretted that "the average Jew has no particular charm in his behavior, his dress, his table manners, his relations with fellow men." He would have been appalled to see how feeble an echo his message evokes among Israelis today. Even those who claim to follow in his ideological footsteps show no particular penchant for social graces, with the possible exception of former Prime Minister Menachem Begin.

Herzl never left any doubt that while the ideals and bearing of the New Jew had European forms, roots, and sources, they assumed a particular Jewish character by openly serving Jewish interests. The name of the Zionist weekly he founded in 1897 is a case in point. Herzl called it *Die Welt* ("The World"), a name that evoked no Jewish association. But in the editorial statement in the first issue, he made it clear that it was a *Judenblatt*, a Jews' paper, just as he called his programmatic pamphlet *Der Judenstaat*, "The Jews' State." It was a deliberate choice. In German, in Herzl's time at least, to place *Jude* in front of another noun turned the combined word into a term of contempt and contumely. "We take this word," Herzl wrote in his programmatic introduction to *Die Welt*, "which is meant as a slur and turn it into an expression of honor."

Although culturally he was thoroughly European, Herzl's imposing presence struck many who knew him as "Oriental." Unlike Disraeli, another statesman with a strong sense of the theatrical, Herzl had no need to emphasize his heritage. Disraeli did so deliberately by dressing in ornate suits laden with golden chains so as to remind everyone of his noble Oriental—that is, Jewish—descent. Disraeli's purpose was the opposite of Herzl's. He wanted to prove that his heritage, far from making him a less valuable or less British subject than any English aristocratic blueblood, made him more of one. After all, Disraeli's ancestors had already created sublime values at a time when the British gentry's forebears were still running wild in forests, clad in raw hides and painted blue. Herzl, on the other hand, was out to prove that a Jew could be a perfectly modern gentleman imbued with the highest European values without ceasing to belong to a distinctly separate national collective—the Jewish nation.

Herzl was the quintessential New Jew. As such, he was naturally deemed to stand tall, in contrast to the curbed, obsequious attitude associated with the oppressed Jew of both the ghetto of yore and the new post-emancipation ghetto. This perception even affected appraisals of his physical stature. Though he was usually described as "majestically tall," he actually measured only five feet eight.

It wasn't that he appeared tall only to Jews, who were of

lower average height than, say, the Germanic people. Prince Philipp zu Eulenburg, the Prussian courtier and diplomat who recommended Herzl and Zionism to Kaiser Wilhelm II, noted in his memoirs that Herzl "also made a great impression by his outward appearance: he is a tall man with a head resembling King David's, the prototype of a militant Jewish leader from the age of the Jewish kings, with no particle of the type we call 'trading Jew.'"

This was precisely the impression Herzl wished to make. Not that he believed there was any resemblance between himself and King David, but Zionism wanted to hark back to the glories of Jewish kings and the national rebellions against oppression. It wanted to efface the image of the "trading Jew," grubbing for profit in undignified, unhealthy Galut occupations. This was one area in which the picture of the Jew as drawn by the anti-Semites and that limned by the Zionists came agonizingly close to being identical. In one sense, anti-Semitism and Zionism were two sides of the same coin denominated the "Jewish problem." The anti-Semites, of course, wanted to destroy the Jewish people, while the Zionists wanted to rebuild them. In Europe, the anti-Semites almost succeeded in their criminal quest. The measure of success attained by Zionism still awaits the verdict of that elusive, fickle, and corruptible judge—History.

In addition to his appearance, another "intangible" asset that Herzl brought to the Zionist movement was his uncanny mastery of communication skills. Many fellow Zionists criticized him precisely for his talent in this area. They called him the "great simplificator," implying a lack of depth. The critics, all addicts of intellection, failed to understand that one cannot catch the imagination of the people with highbrow essays or philosophical treatises. If Lenin, in his speeches to the Russian people, had expatiated on Marxist historical materialism and the theory of surplus value instead of dwelling on the single theme of "All power to the Soviets," the Bolsheviks would never have pulled off the October Revolution of 1917.

Herzl understood, before Lenin, that a movement must be

presented with a theme—in other words, a sophisticated slogan. A theme must be emotionally satisfying and strike chords of resonance in both the present-day experience of those to whom it is addressed as well as in their Jungian collective subconscious. And a theme need not always be based on fact. The slogan "A land without a people for a people without a land" is a good example of just such an appealing theme.

The founding fathers of the Zionist movement, and Herzl in particular, were also often criticized for not understanding the Arabs. What these critics overlooked was that the young Zionist movement simply could not afford to understand the Arabs. To have done so would have fatally undermined the Jewish claim to their ancient homeland. Herzl knew only too well that the land he sought for the Jews was not empty. His main preoccupation was how to open its gates and fill it with Jews. (The second half of the problem is still with us.) It would have made little sense to worry about the Arabs before there were enough Jews in the country.

And if Herzl can be called naive for thinking that the prosperity the Jews would bring to a reborn Eretz Israel would turn the Arabs into true friends, as personified by the figure of Reshid Bey in his novel *Altneuland*, so could many later Zionist leaders who harbored the same illusion, either because they wished it to be so or thought it tactically advisable to pretend as much. (Even today the Israeli government never tires of pointing out the progress and prosperity Israeli rule has brought to the West Bank and Gaza, even though no one any longer believes that it will buy Arab friendship.)

Herzl also understood the true nature of propaganda, of the emotional appeal. And he knew their value. "But in truth noise amounts to a great deal," he noted in his diary. "A sustained noise is in itself a noteworthy fact. World history is nothing but noise: noise of arms, and of advancing ideas." "Sustained noise" became the principal weapon in the arsenal of the Zionist movement. (The Jewish people are still articulate and vocal in matters of great concern to them, be it the Holocaust, Israel, or Russian Jewry.) Money was the other big weapon, though unlike words, money was never available in sufficient amounts to achieve everything it could have.

Herzl learned a bitter lesson in his first attempt at making money talk. The interlocutor was to be the Turkish Sultan. Herzl's idea was that the Sultan could be persuaded to issue a charter allowing Jews to settle in Palestine in return for solving Turkey's problems with the International Debt Commission. Whether or not it was ever practical, the scheme certainly had no chance of succeeding without financial backing. Indeed, the intricate and intrigue-ridden diplomatic dance choreographed for Herzl at the Yildiz Kiosk, the Ottoman court, by the Sultan, his Grand Vizier, and other corrupt notables of Ottoman Turkey was principally aimed at finding out how much money could be expected from the Jews. That the Jews had the money, the Turks did not doubt. But while they shared the general (and enduring) misconception about the financial power of "international Jewry," they were rightly skeptical about Herzl's ability to enlist it for his project.

Herzl knew he was in a squeeze. "Without the backing of capital," he wrote in his diary, "political concessions are impossible, and without political concessions, capital is not available." (It was equally unavailable when the "political concessions" were eventually made by the British in the Balfour Declaration of 1917.)

Baron Edmond de Rothschild represented the obvious solution. Baron Edmond was deeply—many millions of francs deep—interested in Jewish agricultural settlements in Palestine, few of which would have survived without his massive financial support. But his approach was philanthropic and paternalistic; anything political was anathema to him. The only aim the Baron shared with the Zionists was his desire to foster the emergence of a new type of Jew, one distinct from the "undesirable" specimen who caused nightmares for the assimilated Jews who had already "made it" in European society.

Baron Edmond wanted the Jewish settlers in Palestine to be

86

exemplary farmers, morally superior to the mainly East-European *luftmensch* and "trading Jew." Edmond wanted to prove that Jews were capable of honest hard work on the land, a phenomenon for which there were hardly any examples in Europe. He also wanted "his" farmers to observe strictly all the Jewish religious laws and rituals that were on the wane among European Jewry, as if the diaspora could in this way acquire holiness by proxy. Religion was also meant to assure the moral edification of the farmers.

Unfortunately, the settlers did not live up to the Baron's (or anybody else's) expectations. They were not paragons of virtue. Indeed, they showed more skill in wresting subsidies from the Baron's pocket than a living from the soil, a state of affairs for which the Baron's administration and an agricultural philosophy ill-suited to local conditions were partly responsible.

Since Herzl estimated that he needed a billion francs for his enterprise, Baron Edmond de Rothschild was the only possible target. (Herzl had already approached another philanthropist, Baron Maurice de Hirsch, but he died shortly after their meeting.) Quite obviously, the Sultan would be more impressed by the Rothschild billions than by Herzl's bearing. Nonetheless, Herzl approached Edmond with deep misgivings. Herzl's father, whose advice he highly valued, warned him not to do it. "You can count the Rothschilds out," Herzl *père* wrote to his son on October 26, 1895, "... because, carried by their conviction that they are indispensable to Europe, they have in fact nothing to fear."

In fact, the Rothschilds were realists, and as such not inclined to believe that they were indispensable to Europe. Rather, Europe was indispensable to them. A Jewish state must have therefore appeared as a dangerous idea in their eyes. True, it was to be a state only for Jews who could not or would not properly assimilate in their host countries. But there was always the question of who would ultimately determine the degree of incompatibility. Would the decision rest with individual Jews or with the host government? Besides, once the principle of national differentiation was established for some Jews, might it not carry over to all Jews—including those, like the Rothschilds, who felt they belonged where they were? Moreover, the Baron considered Herzl a political dilettante, a dreamer who, unlike the Rothschild family, had no solid conception of European political realities, the nitty gritty of which was the Rothschilds' wellspring of wealth.

In addition, Herzl was the wrong type of person to speak to the Rothschilds. To put it simply, he detested the wealthy—not surprising, since his view of them was shaped by what he saw in the milieu of the Viennese Jewish nouveau riche parvenus. Herzl was not a socialist; he said so in letters and in his plays. He favored capitalism with a human, cultivated face. (Another utopian idea?) Still, in a letter written in 1896 to the Grand Duke Friedrich of Baden, Herzl confidentially informed his highly placed sympathizer that besides drawing Jews away from revolutionary movements, the creation of a Jewish state would also "break the power of international finance"—evidently by eliminating the Jews from its circuits—hardly an idea that would recommend itself to the Rothschilds, had they known of it. Though Herzl had faith in the magic of money properly used for a higher aim, he had none in the wisdom of the wealthy. And he had no respect for the rich, an "error" that the Zionist movement and the State of Israel have since amply and assiduously rectified.

If Herzl was the wrong man to speak to the Baron, he was very much the right man for the Zionist movement. Without the "breath of eternity" that the French statesman Georges Clemenceau (1841–1929) discerned in one whom he called "a man of genius, not to be confounded with a man of talent," the Zionist movement would not have been able to launch its ship on the perilous waters of modern history.

VI

Yavneh Zionism

Like all revolutions, Zionism promised too much. Not only would it resolve the problem (and shame) of Jewish homelessness, it would also restore the unity of the Jewish people (though not on the foundations of religion). Though Zionism did not guarantee the millennium, the splendor of the Jewish renaissance it offered looked to many very much like messianic times.

This "miracle" would be achieved by bringing to life an irresistible national will in the best tradition of the nineteenth-century philosophy of the will to power. In the past, religion had been the repository of Jewish national consciousness—a consciousness that, for theological reasons, could not be translated into the language of modernity. Now, however, the core of Jewish consciousness was no longer faith in the living God of Israel but faith in the Jewish nation and its will to build a common national future.

The fact that the unique religious experience of the Jews was —and remained—an integral part of their historic consciousness did not invalidate the central role played by the national will in the Zionist concept. To the Zionists, national revival was the only way to national survival. Just as Moses led the Jews out of Egypt into the Promised Land, so would the Zionists lead the Jews out of the indignity and discomfort of their European bondage into self-determination in a country of their own. Unlike Moses, however, the Zionists neither claimed nor desired divine guidance. At Mount Sinai, the Children of Israel were forged into a nation by an act of God. The Zionists, in contrast, placed their faith in historical evolution.

From the very beginning, the Zionists were at odds with each other over how to achieve the Jewish renaissance. The ideological baggage the delegates brought to the various Zionist congresses was as diverse as the background of its owners. Some Zionists were religious, others hostile to the rabbinical establishment and the forces that supported it. There were liberals and conservatives, socialists and radicals, and many whose ideological mold defied characterization. They all agreed that something had to be done about the Jewish problem in Europe, but unity proved elusive when they came to consider what should be done and what the *Endziel*, the ultimate goal, should be.

Some said they would be satisfied with a state anywhere in the world where a suitable territory could be obtained. Others insisted that only Palestine, the original and only true fatherland of the Jews, could serve the purpose. Still others held that the movement's declared aim shouldn't be a state but the creation of a national home for the Jews in Palestine, or the recognition of Palestine as the national home of the Jews. Some thought that the solution was to be sought in creating a cultural center in Palestine from which a new, secular dispensation would illuminate even the darkest corner of the diaspora. All these notional proposals were the subject of heated debates.

The propensity of Zionists to form groups that would split away from one faction and link up with another, which in turn would split because of those who had just joined, added a great deal of liveliness and divisiveness to Zionist congresses. So did walkouts by factions, protests, back-room caucuses, and other deliciously disruptive parliamentary tactics.

Herzl would undoubtedly have preferred to preside over and represent a movement that behaved less like an unstable chemical compound whose molecules whirled around wildly, forever forming uncontrollable, unstable, and curious compounds. That, however, was to remain a constant phenomenon within the Zionist movement—a phenomenon that was carried over into the Jewish representative institutions of Mandatory Palestine, and eventually to those of the State of Israel. It is the root cause of the proliferation of secular and religious political parties in modern Israel, as well as the country's continuing attachment to parliamentary democracy in general and proportional representation in particular.

Although in Herzl's time no faction or political bloc succeeded in disputing his leadership, from the beginning a gap was nonetheless discernible between what could be called the Viennese school and the Eastern European (mostly Russian) adherents of the movement, a gap that crossed ideological lines. The Eastern Europeans were at heart *Hovevei Zion*—"Lovers of Zion." Before Herzl appeared on the scene, the *Hovevei Zion* had gathered in small groups to muse about the return of the Jews to their ancient homeland, where they would undergo a moral and spiritual regeneration as a result of a cathartic contact with the land they would farm. Their emotional attachment to what Martin Buber called *"das geliebte und gelobte Land"* ("the beloved and promised land") was as manifest as their inability to come up with a program that had any practical prospects. In contemporary Hebrew, though not in the language of their time, *hovev* means "amateur." And indeed, as lovers they were ardent; as activists, amateurish.

A reporter for the London *Jewish Chronicle* remarked in a dispatch from the First Zionist Congress in Basel in 1897 that it seemed to him that Herzl had come to a congress of the *Hovevei Zion*, and not the other way round. The reporter was a vic-

91

tim of an optical illusion created by the presence of so many delegates from Eastern Europe and the fact that many delegates from other countries had Eastern European roots. In fact, the 1897 meeting in Basel was indisputably Herzl's congress. He almost single-handedly convened it, orchestrated it, and dominated it—to the point of forcing everybody into full evening dress, complete with boiled shirt fronts and high wing collars. (The most recalcitrant delegate in this respect turned out to be a Westerner, Max Nordau, whose abhorrence of conventions apparently extended to formal dress. But in the end he, too, surrendered.)

The Hovevei Zion knew it was Herzl's congress to which they had come. They knew, as the historian David Vital wrote, that they were at a "dead end in which they had entrapped themselves," and that Herzl was offering something they sadly lacked—"namely, a continuing strategy of mobilizing external political forces in the Jewish interest."

There were objective reasons for the inability of the Hovevei Zion to formulate a political program. For one thing, they had to be careful not to arouse the suspicion of the Tsarist secret police, who looked on any political activity by Jews as potentially subversive. For another, the *Hovevei Zion* were temperamentally ill suited to political action. True, they were people who had broken with the past in the shtetls of the Jewish Pale of Settlement. But while they had burst the fences erected by Rabbinical Judaism, they had not shaken its predilection for abstract intellectualizing.

Still, they understood full well that a new era had dawned with the appearance of Herzl. They were infected by the enthusiasm he generated, perhaps even more so than Western Jews, who tended to be cerebral where their Eastern brothers were soulful. (Among those who understood that a new era had begun was a young man in Plonsk named David Green who, to mark the new era, began dating his letters by counting the year of the First Zionist Congress as Year One. He kept it up for eight years. Later, as David Ben-Gurion, he would play a pivotal role in the creation of the State of Israel.)

In many cities of Eastern Europe, Herzl was enthusiastically greeted. In Vilna and Sofia, Jews came to welcome Herzl en masse at the railway station. Not so in Vienna, London, or Berlin. True, Herzl was exuberantly received at a popular meeting in London in July 1896, but the crowd consisted mainly of recent arrivals from Eastern Europe.

Nevertheless, there was something about Herzl and what he represented that greatly disturbed the Easterners. They had little use for the virtues of punctuality, precision, and decorous behavior that Herzl so highly valued—values which they deprecated as gentile affectations. (Only one of their own, Vladimir Jabotinsky, whom the Zionist right still venerates as the only legitimate heir of Herzl, preached similar values.) They seemed to grasp instinctively what David Landes explained in his 1984 book, *Revolution in Time: Clocks and the Making of the Modern World*—namely, that punctuality was a Christian invention.

Landes credited Saint Benedict of Nursia, the sixth-century founder of the monastic order that bears his name, with first establishing fixed hours for prayers. Previously, Christians had followed the Jewish tradition of praying in the morning, in the afternoon, and in the evening, though not necessarily at any precise hour. Some Hasidic groups rejected even the vaguest of timetables for devotions, advocating prayers whenever the spirit moved one. Submission to the tyranny of measured time was un-Jewish.

Not that Easterners didn't have watches and clocks. In many situations, they had to pay heed to the time. But it was one thing to look at one's watch in order to be on time for a train, and quite another to elevate punctuality to a quality Jews had to acquire in order to attain national dignity. Such a demand struck the Easterners as symptomatic of the desire of the Western Zionists to look to the gentiles for role models, a desire that certainly existed, be it conscious or unconscious.

In his autobiography, Chaim Weizmann, the Russian-born scientist and Zionist leader who became Israel's first president, noted that Herzl "was full of Western dignity which did not sit well with our Russian-Jewish realism." Underlying that "Russian-Jewish realism" was the conviction that the Jews were a breed apart, a people who could not and should not be forced into a gentile mold. To be sure, the majority of Eastern Zionists were largely westernized. Like Weizmann, many Russian Zionists were graduates of Western and Central European universities. And many, like him, remained in the West. Nevertheless, they kept a mental and emotional distance from the West and its Jewry, whose mores they could not understand or, worse, found unpalatable. (Weizmann himself eventually learned to love the English way of life.)

The principal reason for the Easterner's distance was his nostalgic attachment to the genuine communal spirit that, in spite of poverty, squalor, and stagnation, reigned in the shtetl. This spirit was so strong that Easterners could recreate it almost anywhere, in their own circles, groups, factions, and associations. It was a living force quite unlike the romanticized vision of shtetl culture that has sparked the renewed interest in Yiddish that is currently fashionable in certain parochial circles of American Jewry.

In contrast to the present-day version, there was nothing inauthentic about the communal rootedness of the early Russian Zionists. They carried their communal spirit with them wherever they went, together with their propensity for interminable speeches and endless imbibing of tea (which was always served in a glass—never, heaven forbid, in a cup). They knew Pushkin by heart and could correctly quote Jewish sources. Their emancipated brothers from the West could do neither.

They were also sentimental. They possessed *yiddishkeit*—that special quality that encompasses everything from Jewish lore to Jewish *latkes* (potato pancakes), from Jewish gestures to Jewish genius—in short, all that a Jew is sure to lose when he mounts a horse, as the noted Soviet short-story writer Isaac Babel put it, and all that he is in danger of losing when he takes up even the superficial ways of the goyim (to say nothing of accepting their value system hook, line, and sinker).

In his autobiography, Chaim Weizmann described "the Western conception of Zionism" as "lacking in Jewishness, in warmth and in understanding of the Jewish masses." In fact, Weizmann himself never felt close to the Jewish masses and did not bother to understand them. His strength lay in his ability to present the cause of Zionism to influential people in their drawing rooms, not to move crowds at mass meetings. He certainly nurtured no nostalgia for the shtetl, from which he was happy to escape. Nonetheless, he did possess some indefinable *yiddishkeit*, which enveloped the distinguished scientist-statesman in a uniquely Jewish aura.

The Westerners lacked such rootedness and the spontaneity that often went with it. Instead, they brought to the Zionist movement a sense of decorum and duty, a scrupulous accountability in money matters, and a love for order and proper procedure. The Easterners regarded this as deplorable inflexibility at best, and gentilesque foolishness at worst.

As later developments proved, Zionist organizations and institutions controlled by Easterners were invariably plagued by an endemic disregard for proper procedures and correct accounts. The institutions in Palestine were no exception, though they did provide Easterners with an opportunity to show what their uncanny knack for improvisation could achieve in such fields as the creation of new settlements, self-defense, and clandestine immigration.

On the debit side of the ledger, one must note that these "Eastern" attitudes contributed to the failure of groups like the Jewish Agency both to attract immigrants from America and Western Europe after the establishment of the State of Israel, and to encourage many of those who had come to remain in the country.

It also explains why relatively few German immigrants of the Hitler era managed to attain prominent positions in Israeli public life. It certainly was not for lack of professional qualifications, but because most immigrants from Germany were temperamentally unsuited to the method of work (or rather, the lack of method) practiced in a society largely run by Eastern European Jews. (The Germans' attachment to Western dress and neckties made them the butt of jokes.)

It was not quite like Kipling's "East is East, and West is West, and never the twain shall meet." In Zionism, East and West did meet in a common desire to do something about the plight of the Jewish people. But their hearts did not beat in unison, and their brain waves oscillated at different frequencies. Neither quite understood the other.

At the first Zionist Congress, Max Nordau perhaps unwittingly underscored the difference when he said that "Western Jewry suffers from a moral Jewish misery that is even more bitter than the physical because it afflicts more differentiated, prouder, and more sensitive people." True or not, those from Eastern Europe, who had come to the congress in greater numbers than the Westerners, could have hardly relished hearing themselves described as less proud and less sensitive.

The fact remains, however, that Herzl, too, did not think of Russian Jews as likely devotees of the opera and the other cultural institutions that he imagined would spring up magically in the Old-New Land of Israel once the political conditions for a mass transfer of Jews had been achieved. Herzl was obviously mindful of the Easterners' lack of respect for Western culture when he included in the program of the gala concert at the Second Congress the warning: "Please, refrain from loud talking during the music."

The antagonism between East and West went deeper than matters of form, behavior, sensitivity, aesthetics, warmth, and alleged understanding of the Jewish masses. The Hovevei Zion and their spiritual heirs had an even greater difficulty with another, perhaps more fundamental, aspect of Herzlian Zionism. They could not accept that the new era in Jewish history was not to be linked with what had gone before. They could not accept any discontinuity in what they conceived of as an ongoing evolutionary process, a process that had begun with Abraham and (they felt) should now be entering the phase of a national renaissance. As they saw it, the New Jew could only evolve from the old ghetto Jew. He could not spring full-blown from the philosophical foundations of European nationalism, like Athena from the forehead of Zeus.

Western Zionists, too, valued a sense of history. Indeed, the moment that Zionism put forth the notion that national revival could not succeed anywhere but in the ancient homeland of the Jewish people, the Bible became a valuable source of the movement's legitimacy, for its claim to the land. (It has remained so to this very day, buttressed by the findings of archeologists that bear witness to the historic connection *in situ*, not only in the pages of the Book.) But the Western "political" Zionists had no use for the history of the Exile. They were concerned with the future of the Jewish people, not with their past—with Jewry, not with Judaism. Speaking German, they did not have to make a distinction between the two, both of which are expressed by the same word: *Judentum*.

The Easterners admitted no hiatus. To them, the Exile was no less important to Jewish history than the Biblical period. Indeed, in more than one sense, the Exile was closer to their hearts: their parents were part of it. It was thus important to them to preserve the entire Jewish heritage. However, the zeitgeist of secularization dictated that their heritage be repackaged and labeled "culture produced by the Jewish national genius." There would be room for religion in this new "package," but religion would no longer dominate the nation's spiritual life, let alone be its only criterion of value.

The Western Zionists were too busy looking into the future to pay attention to the cultural ballast of the immediate past. They believed that when conditions were ripe—that is, when a Jewish commonwealth of sorts was re-established—a new culture would grow on its soil as naturally as it had in other nations. Though this new culture would undoubtedly draw on the nation's past, its creative power would be directed to the realization of the humanitarian ideals that the Herzlians saw as the true fulfillment of the Jewish people's destiny. They continued to believe in humanitarianism despite Europe's failure to move significantly closer to these ideals, a failure they only too painfully felt. Indeed, in the best tradition of Prophetic Judaism, as distinct from the rabbinical tradition they wished to relegate to oblivion, they believed that the Jewish people were best qualified to rectify that failure.

The first priority for the Westerners was the establishment of a state for the Jews. Like Giuseppe Mazzini, they held that before a people can dedicate their energies to the establishment of the universal reign of peace, righteousness, and the brotherhood of nations, they must have a country and political power. It didn't really matter whether Zionists interpreted the vision as political messianism of the European brand or as a reformulation in modern terms of the teachings of the Prophets (or both for that matter).

"Gesta Dei per Francos," said Dr. Litwak in Herzl's novel *Altneuland*, adding: "God's deeds through the Jews, say the truly pious today, those who do not let partisan rabbis incite them." The Latin quotation is from Jules Michelet, the nineteenth-century anti-clerical French historian who claimed that his nation had a special mission to realize a larger vision of humanity. Mazzini said the same of the Italians, and Mickiewicz of the Poles. Through Litwak, Herzl applied it to the Jews in their land. The same idea was expressed through the mouth of another character in the novel, Dr. Steineck, who exclaimed: "Liberalism, Tolerance, Love of Mankind! Only then will Zion be truly Zion."

Indeed, this was the central theme of Herzl's concept of Zionism at the time he was writing his utopian novel-cum-blueprint. It can be seen as a recognition that Zion can truly become Zion only when it translates its prophetic meaning into a living reality. In other words, the hoped-for Jewish state could be viewed as simply another version of the European liberal utopia, with nothing specifically Jewish about it, except that the genius of the Jewish people would make it real.

"We venerated him, loved him," Buber wrote of Herzl in

1944, "but a great part of his being was alien to our souls. In a word, Herzl the liberal was alien to us." Buber spoke in this case for the Eastern Zionists, to whom he was in many respects closer than he was to the Westerners, perhaps because of his immersion in Hasidism. Though the Eastern European Zionists recognized Herzl as a charismatic leader, they yearned less for a leader than for a teacher who would guide them out of the spiritual and psychological maze into which they had been thrust by the loss of religious faith and the desire for emancipation. They needed a new *Guide for the Perplexed* that would show them how to create a national future out of their religious inheritance, just as Maimonides in his age had attempted to forge a link between religion and Aristotelian philosophy. They found such a teacher in Ahad Haam.

Ahad Haam's real name was Asher Hirsch Ginzberg. A scion of a Hasidic family who received a traditional Jewish education, Ginzberg adopted his famous nom de plume (Hebrew for "One of the People") when he published his first essay in 1899. An indefatigable autodidact, he taught himself Russian, German, French, English, and Latin, and acquired a vast knowledge of philosophy, history, and science. In 1894, he settled in Odessa and became the editor of *Hashiloah*, the most important journal of Hebrew literature in Eastern Europe.

Ahad Haam offered a philosophical cover for the antagonism between Eastern and Western Jews—an antagonism that Zionism meant to overcome but did not. In 1904, Dr. Arthur Ruppin, a sociologist who played a prominent role in the Jewish agricultural settlement effort in Palestine, predicted that relations between Western and Eastern European Jews would be as antagonistic as relations between Sephardi and Ashkenazi Jews had been during the French Revolution, when the former had strenuously opposed giving civil rights to the latter. As it turned out, Ruppin wasn't far off the mark.

In Ahad Haam's view, the Western, Herzlian Zionists were on the wrong track. To begin with, they were too impetuous in making the creation of a state for the Jews the first and overriding Zionist priority. Worse, the state they desired was not of the right kind. In Ahad Haam's view, Herzl was no better than an assimilationist, in that he advocated the assimilation of the Jewish people as a collective in an entity that would not truly be a Jewish state. That was why Ahad Haam sat among the delegates to the First Zionist Congress in Basel in 1897 "like a mourner at a wedding" (his own words). The Zionist bride had chosen to marry his philosophical rival.

"After a thousand years of untold misery and suffering," Ahad Haam wrote in an essay on the First Zionist Congress, "the Jewish people cannot possibly be content with attaining at last to the position of a small and insignificant nation, with a state tossed about like a ball between its powerful neighbors, and maintaining its existence only by diplomatic shifts and continual truckling to the favored of fortune. An ancient people, which was once a beacon to the world, cannot possibly accept, as a satisfactory reward for all that it has endured, a thing so trifling, which many other peoples have won in a short time."

What Ahad Haam feared was that, in such an essentially ordinary state, the Jewish people could not hope to maintain their uniqueness, let alone their historical-spiritual mission. What was good enough for other nations—that is, "merely" political independence—was not necessarily good enough for the Jews. Certainly not if they wanted to be again a "beacon to the world" (a proposition made even more difficult in our times because the overwhelming majority of the world shows no inclination to look to the Jews for edification and illumination, if indeed it ever did).

Besides, Ahad Haam feared that such a state would be necessarily dominated by Western Jews like Herzl who seemed better equipped than their Eastern brethren to deal with modern politics and to make use of modern technology. Such Jews would inevitably "gentilize" the state until it was Jewish in name only.

Ahad Haam was not impervious to the plight of European

Jewry. He was very much concerned about the persistent viru-
lence of anti-Semitism. But he did not believe that the Jewish
state was a realistic proposition. True, he thought it was a desirable aim as long at it was not considered an end in itself, but
merely a tool for a Jewish spiritual renaissance. The point was,
the creation of a state for the Jews would not in itself bring
about a spiritual renewal. "A renaissance of Judaism that would
be really Jewish," he wrote in a scathing attack on Herzl's *Altneuland*, "...cannot be achieved in one breath, not even
through shared companies and cooperatives...an historical
ideal requires an historical evolution, and it moves slowly."

In this, he echoed the sentiments of many Zionists of his
time. However, he went further in holding that the creation of a
state was not something one need or should actively work for.
There were other, more urgent, more realistic, more spiritual—
and therefore more Jewish—aims to be accomplished in the
here and now (that is, in the diaspora). The most important of
the tasks Ahad Haam called on the Zionists to undertake was
to redefine in modern terms the spiritual vocation of the Jewish
people, a vocation that had hitherto found expression exclusively in religious tenets and teachings.

True to his evolutionist creed, a kind of spiritual Darwinism,
Ahad Haam tended to look at the faith in a living God that had
preserved the Jewish people in exile as a manifestation of the
Jews' indomitable will to survive. Faith had been severely eroded in his time. European nationalism had created a new political and social environment. The Jewish people now had to rise
to that new challenge; as a species, they had to adapt to changes
in their environment or perish. The point was, the Jews could
survive only by responding in an exclusively Jewish way—
namely, by asserting, or rather reasserting in secular terms,
their moral credentials.

Ahad Haam's views were very close to those of his contemporary and friend, the historian Simon Dubnow (1860–1941). "In
philosophical opinions we went along together," Dubnow remarked in his autobiography, "because we were both evolution-

ists of the English school and attached ethical criteria to the phenomena of social life."

Ahad Haam parted with Dubnow in one essential point. Dubnow held that a nation that had lost "its natural homeland ...becomes dispersed and scattered in alien lands...loses its unifying language [yet] creates an independent existence [and] reveals a stubborn determination to carry on its autonomous development"—in other words, a nation like the Jews—has reached "the highest stage of cultural historical individuality." Ahad Haam disagreed, maintaining that the Jewish people needed to be sovereign in their own country, Eretz Israel, in order to take the place in world history that was rightfully theirs.

For all practical purposes, however, both Dubnow and Ahad Haam advocated cultural autonomy for the Jews in the countries of their residence. It was just that Dubnow saw autonomy as an end in itself, while Ahad Haam saw it as a necessary step in the long evolutionary march toward the Jewish state. (Ahad Haam moved to Tel Aviv in 1922. Dubnow refused to leave his brethren, and was killed by the Nazis in 1941 during the mass slaughter of the Jewish population of Riga.)

Dubnow also rejected Zionism on practical grounds. "What effect did the new messianic dreams of a return to Zion have on the solution of the worldwide Jewish problem?" he asked rhetorically. All Zionism had to show for itself was a few "insignificant" colonies that had to be continually bailed out by Baron Edmond de Rothschild.

Ahad Haam, who had visited Palestine in 1891 and 1893 and looked at the settlements and the settlers with sharp, critical eyes, found them equally wanting. True, in Palestine the Jewish settlers had shed the "loathsome traits acquired through commerce"—a positive sign, in Ahad Haam's eyes, of renewal through love of the soil and physical labor. But the settlements were a far cry from the community imbued with the "prophetic spirit" that Ahad Haam saw as the motive force of the collective national will to survive. (Ahad Haam would have happily agreed with the Catholic historian Ernest Renan that a "nation is a spiritual principle resulting from the profound complication of history, a spiritual family.")

The farmers in Rishon LeZion, Zikhron Ya'acov, or Petah Tikvah were hardly cut out to be the part of the Jewish people that Ahad Haam expected to attain "a natural and free life there," who would "constitute a center for our national life as a whole and exert a spiritual or moral influence on all other parts of the people, those remaining in foreign lands, cleansing them of the filth of their inner slavery and uniting them into a single national body with a single spirit."

He had no illusions on that score. "A single properly ordered settlement, one that would be capable of arousing the Jews' love for the Land, is better than the rickety settlements which only [our] love for the Land can excuse," he wrote in the introduction to the first edition of his 1895 essay "On the Crossroads." The Zohar promised redemption if only a single Jewish community would repent wholeheartedly. But mysticism can propound such miraculous transformations. For a rationalist like Ahad Haam, the proposition was objectively inadmissible.

Ahad Haam had a profound belief that spiritual evolution could be helped along by a moral elite. With this in mind, he founded in 1889 in Odessa a secret society modeled on the Freemasons, complete with secret rituals. Many men who played prominent roles in the Zionist movement, including Chaim Weizmann and the poet Chaim Nachman Bialik, were among its members. So were the founders of Rehovot, today the home of the Weizmann Institute of Science.

This same belief was behind Ahad Haam's conviction that the first task of Jews in Eretz Israel should be the establishment of a cultural or spiritual center there. (He made no distinction between cultural and spiritual.) This, he felt, should be done even before the Jews became a majority in Palestine or had created any political structures through which the center might act. His reasoning was clear: though he agreed that a Jewish state was a historical necessity, he wanted to make sure that the "cultural" nature of that state would be shaped in advance along the lines of his philosophy. The early establishment of the kind of center he had in mind would do just that.

Such a center would also be needed to achieve his primary Zionist priority: a national, spiritual, and moral revival in the diaspora. Though he recognized, in principle at least, that it would take a Jewish majority in Palestine to support a national culture, he saw no inconsistency in placing national work in the diaspora ahead of the effort to secure in Palestine the material and political foundations needed to give such work a chance of success.

At the Minsk Conference of Russian Zionists in 1902, in a speech characteristically entitled "The Spiritual Revival," Ahad Haam advocated the creation of a separate organization that would "attract all those who appreciate the value of the national culture." The organization would be open to all—even those who were not officially Zionists. In this, Ahad Haam was obviously thinking of the advocates of cultural autonomy, both of the socialist and non-socialist variety. Most important, Ahad Haam insisted that the new organization "must neither be subservient to the political organization [that is, Herzl's World Zionist Organization] nor be dependent on its opinion."

No cultural or spiritual center arose in Palestine during Ahad Haam's lifetime—except to the extent that his large following, which included prominent personalities such as Chaim Weizmann, saw such a center in his person. (In today's parlance he would be called a "guru.") The only practical incarnation of his idea of the cultural center appeared in the form of the Hebrew University, founded in 1925. At its conception, the university was, like political Zionism, intended as a remedy to the specific *Judennot* of Jewish students who found the portals of higher learning shut in their faces, or at best only slightly ajar.

Weizmann first thought of founding the university in Europe, preferably in Switzerland. But it soon became evident that to be truly expressive of the spirit of the national renaissance it could only be placed in the Land of Israel. And it was in this spirit, in order to emphasize the integral role that "cultural" (as opposed to "political") Zionists assigned to the revival of the Hebrew language, that it was called not the Jewish but the Hebrew University.

Great hopes were placed in the Hebrew University. In 1902, Chaim Weizmann proclaimed that it would "be a nursery fostering the living national language, the focal point of Jewish creativity in the field of literature, the arts and the sciences— in a word, a cultural center whose spirit will radiate in all directions, a center for Jews and for Judaism." All the tenets of Ahad Haamism reverberate in these words of his disciple. Now over sixty years old, the Hebrew University in Jerusalem has developed into a respected institution of higher learning. It is not, however, a center of Judaism.

Norman Bentwich, a prolific writer on Zionism and Israel who served as the first Attorney General of British Palestine (he resigned in 1931 in protest over British policies), called Ahad Haam the "first philosopher of Zionism." He was most influential as the progenitor of a substitute for religion as the national bond that held the Jewish people together. Instead of the old-time religion, he advocated what an American rabbi, Samuel Schulman, cleverly called "Ethical Culture on the basis of Jewish national consciousness."

Ahad Haam's message was appealing and appeasing to every Jew who was disturbed by the Zionist idea that Jewry had to become a nation like all other nations and that Jews had to make a clean break with their Exilic past.

Ahad Haam reassured Jews that there was no break, that secular Judaism (an apparent oxymoron that is alive and well today in both Israel and the United States) was, on the contrary, the successor to and the legitimate heir of the faith of Israel. Indeed, Ahad Haam insisted, secular Judaism had cultural roots that went deeper than the religious practices of Rabbinical Judaism. The feasts and holy days of Judaism were merely reflections of national culture—reflections that could but didn't have to be given a religious meaning. The Bible, in short, was the national epos of the Jews.

Ahad Haam's secular theology was exemplified by his reaction to Nordau's suggestion that, in the Jewish state-to-be, the day of rest could be shifted from Saturday to Sunday. He fulminated from Odessa:

> Not one word escaped the mouth of this Zionist sage [Nordau] which would testify that his heart rebels against the cancellation of the Sabbath, because of its *historical and national* [emphasis added] value. The whole question in his eyes is purely religious and therefore he excludes himself from any direct commitment. He, the freethinker, will have his own appropriate day of rest, bereft of any religious intent, and he does not care whether the Sabbath, the Queen of Judaism, exists or not.

For Ahad Haam, the "religious intent" of the Sabbath was beside the point. It was not a matter of keeping the Fourth Commandment. Ahad Haam's Sabbath Queen had nothing to do with the "Bride of Sabbath" of Jewish mysticism, with whom the worshipper sought to be united in a religious-erotic union as expressed in the hymn *Lekha dodi likrat kallah* ("Come lover meet thy bride") composed by the sixteenth-century Safed cabalist Solomon Alkabez. (This hymn has become part of the contemporary Friday night liturgy, though in some American prayer books, the word *dodi*—"lover"—is chastely bowdlerized into "friend.") Ahad Haam's Queen Sabbath was, rather, a folkloric figure glazed in sugary sentimentality. In this, she resembled Heinrich Heine's "Princess Sabbath," which that rueful convert to Christianity celebrated in a poem of the same name. Of course, Ahad Haam would have denied any kinship between his "Queen" and Heine's "Princess." (So presumably would have Heine.)

To Ahad Haam, the Sabbath was part of the Jewish national patrimony that Zionism was called upon to preserve. So too was the belief in the election of the Jewish people and their universal mission. And so was the belief in the coming of the Messiah. All were sublime expressions of the Jewish national genius that set it apart from any and all other nations of the world.

The same held true for the teachings of the Prophets, to which Ahad Haam gave a purely rational, ethical interpretation. Instead of looking at the Prophets as God's messengers, he saw them as inspired knights of morality. Ahad Haam saw himself, and was seen by his followers, as just such a knight. His universe, built on the seemingly solid foundations of rationalism, still needed Judaism, but not a God. God had become unnecessary.

It was as a bearer of a new secular Judaic dispensation that Ahad Haam had founded his secret society in 1889. He called it "Benei Moshe"—"Sons of Moses." However, more than spiritual heirs of the Prophet/Law-Giver of Mount Sinai, its members were meant to be the spiritual sons of Ahad Haam, the new Moses from Odessa.

As Ahad Haam saw it, the moral message of Judaism should be used not only to guide the individual but also as the foundation of the future Jewish state in keeping with the Prophetic tradition. Ahad Haam rightly saw in the Prophets the guardians of a particular kind of Jewish nationalism. Of course, according to the Prophets, the Jewish nation had no right to exist unless it fulfilled God's purpose of justice and righteousness. Ahad Haam did not care whether the nation served God's purpose or not. What mattered to him was its ability to safeguard the Jewish national culture. As far as Ahad Haam was concerned, that was the point of Zionism: not to create a mere political entity, a nation-state like any other, but to establish a unique and special homeland that would assure Jewish survival as he understood it. "The Jewish people will be saved by prophets not by diplomats," he proclaimed after the First Zionist Congress. The diplomat was obviously Herzl; the prophet, none other than Ahad Haam himself.

The primary task was therefore the moral and intellectual re-edification of the Jewish people in the diaspora—above all, those in Eastern Europe. First, spiritual Zionism had to take root among the people. The rest could wait. Ahad Haam was less concerned about the distressing situation of European

Jewry than about the crisis of Judaism. His priority was moral, not political.

By focusing virtually all his efforts on the diaspora, Ahad Haam effectively shifted the goal of Zionism from political emancipation in Palestine to psychological self-emancipation in the diaspora. It seemed an attractive proposition, especially when the political efforts appeared to bear little fruit. Besides, it did not require the individual Zionist even to consider an actual move to the ancient homeland. One could be a good Jew and a good Zionist right at home in the land of one's fathers, not in the faraway land of one's forefathers. There was also a very down-to-earth political side to this brand of Zionism: it strived to gain control of the Jewish community institutions. Thus was born the ideology of diaspora Zionism.

This essentially cultural Zionism was meant to be the ideology of the Eastern European Jewish masses. A network of Hebrew day schools would replace the traditional *heder* and Talmud Torah. Ahad Haam insisted that the students in these new Jewish schools—schools that were to imbue them with the secularized values of Judaism—must not "lag behind European students in their general knowledge, manners, and all other attributes of modern culture."

In fact, few such schools were ever established. The Jewish masses turned out to be more attracted to the kind of cultural separatism preached by the Bund, the Jewish Social Democratic Party that was founded in 1897, a year before the establishment of the Russian Workers Social Democratic Party.

Unlike Ahad Haam's cultural Zionism, the Bund had no use for Prophetic Judaism. It placed its hope for the creation of a just society in the collective ownership of the means of production. Its language was Yiddish, the *mamme loshen* ("mother tongue") of the Jews of Eastern Europe. The Bund promised separateness, not chosenness—a comforting notion to a Jewish proletariat that hardly had any contact with its non-Jewish counterparts. The sweet smell of *yiddishkeit* saturated its rank and file like the odor of gefilte fish wafting through a good Jewish household on Sabbath eve.

Ahad Haam's cultural Zionists made far greater demands on Jewry than the Bund. "Our entire existence in the diaspora is possible only as long as we feel ourselves to be a 'historical aristocracy,'" wrote Ahad Haam. This was not the kind of appeal likely to move the masses, who were naturally more interested in bettering their lot than in becoming a spiritual aristocracy and learning Hebrew, as Ahad Haam demanded. In fact, neither Ahad Haam nor his followers were close to the masses, notwithstanding the literal meaning of the pseudonym Ahad Haam: "One of the People."

The fact was, the Zionists of Russia and Eastern Europe were virtually all urbanized and westernized. Though they may have looked on the poor Jews of the shtetls with sentimental compassion, they had mentally removed themselves from any real connection with them. They consciously formed an intellectual elite, and it was to that elite alone that Ahad Haam spoke with any authority or lasting effect. It was also this elite that he expected to become the repository of his teaching. He wanted them to emulate the Pharisees, who twenty centuries earlier had preserved Judaism by moving their sages and teachers away from Jerusalem, the embattled political hub of the country, to Yavneh. In this small town, halfway between Jaffa and Ashkelon, a rabbinical center was created with the permission of the Romans. When Jerusalem was sacked, Yavneh—and, through it, Judaism—survived.

The cultural center Ahad Haam wished to create was to have a similar function. Just as the Pharisees had met the challenge of the loss of Jerusalem, so would his cultural center defend the values of Judaism at a time when the Jewish religious world was in danger of dissolution.

In extolling the historic role played by the Pharisees in preserving the Jewish people, Ahad Haam overlooked the fact that without the benevolence of the Emperor Vespasian, Yavneh would not have been spared. The Jews of Ahad Haam's day could not count on similar luck. The Sultan in Constantinople was as unlikely to allow the establishment of a Jewish cultural

109

center in Palestine as he was to grant a charter that would open the territory to Jewish settlement.

The ambiguity of Ahad Haam's pseudo-religious cultural gospel was reflected in his ambivalent attitude to the use of the Hebrew language. As far as he was concerned, Hebrew was to be reserved for the written word, not for ordinary daily speech. Ahad Haam initially opposed, and never quite reconciled himself to, the use of Hebrew for banal, mundane purposes. On his visits to Palestine, he refused to speak Hebrew even when addressed in that language. He even refused to address in Hebrew the guests at a dinner given in his honor in Jaffa in 1900, in spite—or perhaps because—of the presence of Eliezer Ben-Yehuda (1858–1922), the man who did more than anyone else for the revival of Hebrew as a modern spoken language. (Among other things, Ahad Haam accused him of not speaking it fluently.)

His attitude paralleled that of the ultra-Orthodox who still reserved the use of Hebrew exclusively for the sacred, which has to be strictly separated from the mundane. Of course, Ahad Haam's concern was not the desacralization of the language. Rather, he feared the vulgarization that would inevitably accompany its common use. As Tudor Parfitt, a lecturer in Hebrew at London University, put it: "He viewed the Hebrew language in almost mystical light as the receptacle of the national spirit. One can understand, therefore, that he would have felt a certain distress at hearing it spoken indifferently."

When Ahad Haam moved to Palestine in 1922, spoken Hebrew was a fait accompli, energetically propagated by the leaders of the Yishuv, the collective Hebrew term for the Jews settled in Eretz Israel. He avoided distress "at hearing it spoken indifferently" by consorting mostly with people who did not, such as his close friend the poet Chaim Nachman Bialik. (He would suffer greatly if he could hear how Hebrew is spoken in Israel today. Like any other living language, it is spoken sloppily, peppered with slangy expressions, and "polluted" with foreign transplants.)

By placing themselves between the political Zionists and the Jewish autonomists, the cultural Zionists, whose prophet Ahad Haam was, deliberately chose to operate in a political limbo. They did not believe that a political solution to the Jewish problem was possible through mass emigration to Palestine. By 1902 the faint chance that the Sublime Porte could be induced by massive bribery and pressure from other powers to permit massive Jewish immigration to Palestine seemed to have totally vanished. It is impossible to judge whether things might have been different had there been widespread agitation among the Jewish masses of Eastern Europe for a political solution to the Jewish problem. Whether or not such a course was ever really possible, the cultural Zionists—and most of the Russian Zionists at least flirted with Ahad Haamism—never even considered it.

They also rejected national autonomy within the diaspora, both in the form advocated by Dubnow, who believed that a Jewish nationality could thrive in any multicultural democratic state, and in that propagated by the Bund, which thought it possible in a social-democratic state only.

But if Ahad Haam rejected both autonomy in the diaspora and political Zionism, how did he envisage the future of Jewry? Reduced to its core, Ahad Haam's dream was to create an elite of such moral superiority that it would inevitably bring about the birth of the new Jewish state as a result of having engendered a new secular Judaism of irresistible spiritual force.

The concept had its philosophical attraction as a mutation of the idea of chosenness. It may even have appeared plausible, given the absence of any real forward movement in the effort to obtain a charter from the Sultan and the lack of significant growth in the number of Jews settled in Palestine. At a time that saw a mass exodus from Eastern Europe, less than 3 percent of Eastern European Jews chose Palestine as their destination. The mainstream of emigrants went to America, whose portals were then still wide open. A minority went to Western Europe. The smallest number emigrated to Palestine.

Nonetheless, Ahad Haamism had a far-reaching influence on the future shape of the Zionist movement. It diverted the energies of the Russian Zionists, who alone were capable of becoming the movement's mainstay, toward internalized goals. What was originally conceived of as a mass movement for the self-determination and eventual national liberation of the Jewish people became an introverted effort of an intellectual elite whose impact was in the end mainly psychological. As the historian David Vital tells us, "Ahad Haam was a major perennially looming moral and intellectual presence whom none of the central, full-blooded activists and office holders could manage to shake off—if, indeed, they ever tried to." Whether his presence served the Zionist movement well is another question.

In fact, his elitist approach remained the bane of the Zionist movement in the crucial period of the 1920s. Selection of the "right" type of immigrant was uppermost in the movement's considerations. Such elitism, with less rigidity, continued to be practiced even when the situation in Europe made it imperative to bring to Palestine as many Jews as possible. By then, alas, it was too late. The British had all but shut the gates to Palestine to significant numbers of Jewish immigrants. Soon the only open gates would be those overarched by the insidious inscription *Arbeit Macht Frei* ("Work Liberates"), the slogan of the Nazi extermination camps, whose mission was to liberate the inmates from the burden of an ever more unbearable life.

Looking back, it would appear that cultural Zionism helped keep the flame of Zionism alive in the period between the death of Herzl in 1904 and the Balfour Declaration of 1917, a period during which the movement faltered and seemed doomed to suffer the fate its adversaries had long wished it. In this sense, Ahad Haam and his followers did in fact play the role with regard to Zionism that Yavneh's Pharisees had played for Judaism nearly two thousand years earlier. The role of the secular prophet, however, eluded Ahad Haam. Modern society offers little fertile ground for the prophet, even a secular one, who castigates the iniquities and moral shortcomings of both the rulers and the people. The Prophets of the Bible left a spiritual legacy of great force. Ahad Haam left only a modest collection of essays of interest mainly to scholars.

VII

A Faltering Flame

On a sweltering July day in 1904, Theodor Herzl's funeral cortege wound its way from his home in Marcus Aurelius Street in the center of Vienna to the distant Jewish cemetery in Döbling. Five hundred carriages followed the hearse, and six thousand more mourners made the lengthy trek on foot. Rarely, if ever, had a private funeral so resembled a state occasion.

Delegations came from all over the world. Thousands of messages of condolence were received, including one from the King of Italy. There was even a message from a Jewish resident of Zanzibar. Dr. Chaim Weizmann, who a few years later was to occupy Herzl's position in the World Zionist Organization, remained in Switzerland. His condolences were noted by *Die Welt*, the official organ of the Zionist Organization, as part of a long list of Jewish names identified only by place of residence.

Forty-five years later, a real state funeral was held for Herzl in Israel, where his remains (along with those of his parents and sister) were solemnly reinterred in accordance with Herzl's will. He never doubted that the day would eventually come when his wish to be buried in Eretz Israel could and would be honored.

The Jerusalem burial was not an occasion for mourning. Rather, in the words of then Prime Minister David Ben-Gurion, it was "a march of triumph symbolizing the victory of a vision fulfilled." Some 400,000 people turned out for the ceremony. Another 150,000 had filed by Herzl's coffin while it lay in state in front of the Knesset (Parliament), which at that time still sat in Tel Aviv. In all, more than half of Israel's Jewish population paid their respects to the founder of political Zionism. Once again, however, Chaim Weizmann missed the occasion; now President of Israel, he was away in Switzerland, for reasons of health. This time, though, his message was prominently printed on the front pages of all the local newspapers.

Herzl's death at the relatively young age of forty-four captured the attention of the world far more than the publication of his programmatic pamphlet *Der Judenstaat* had ten years earlier. Even the *Neue Freie Presse*, the prestigious liberal Viennese daily on whose senior staff Herzl served with great distinction and which in his lifetime never allowed the word Zionism to appear in its pages, was obliged to acknowledge that there were "many thousands who honored him not only as a writer and a man, but also as the leader of the Zionist Party."

It must have taken a lot for the paper's two assimilationist Jewish publishers to break their own rule and acknowledge that their former star feuilletonist had gained worldwide reputation as the creator of political Zionism. For years, they had done everything they could to dissuade Herzl from what they considered a dangerous madness, and they were by no means the only Jews to hold that opinion. They wanted Herzl to stick to literature and journalism. But it was Zionism, not Herzl's literary career, that figured most prominently in the obituary notices.

Perhaps the most moving epitaph was written by Felix Salten, a colleague of Herzl's at the *Presse*. Salten was the paper's theater critic, a writer of some renown, and like Herzl a native of Budapest. Writing in the literary weekly *Die Zeit*, Salten noted: "It is the greatest glory of Theodor Herzl that he did not want to be smaller than his idea, weaker than his word; that he undertook not only to conceive the last act of the Jews' drama, but also to stage produce it."

More typical of the obituaries that appeared in the world press, particularly in Jewish papers, was the one published by the Prague German-language daily *Prager Presse.* "The enthusiasm with which Herzl was met...wherever the Zionist idea had taken root," the Prague paper said, "was so widespread that it is possible to assert that the title of King of the Jews which he was given in jest was not devoid of a serious justification."

The King was dead, but the traditional cry of "Long live the King" was not heard in the Jewish street. There was no heir and successor. There never was to be one—not of the same stature, of the same breadth of vision, of the same ability to transform myth into political action. "Zionism without Herzl," commented the non-Zionist London *Jewish Chronicle,* "appears as unthinkable as Zionism without Zion, as a monarchy without a throne."

Martin Buber thought Herzl had died at "the best possible time," as he wrote to his wife, "before all the unavoidable events, disappointments, and decline...at the height." He added: "What shape the movement will now take cannot yet be foreseen."

Obviously, it would not be the same. Although he had a mandate from a minority only, Herzl had spoken for all the Jewish people. His genius transcended the movement and the organization he himself had created. Indeed, after his death, the World Zionist Organization gradually transformed itself into an establishment with a bureaucracy that came to assume an increasingly important role.

Of course, Zionism had been changing even before Herzl's death. Among other things, it had been coming to grips with the fact that, despite Herzl's efforts, there was virtually no chance the Ottoman ruler would grant a charter for the creation of a Jewish homeland in Palestine. Without the kind of massive financial backing needed to tempt the debt-ridden Sublime Porte, those chances had never been robust. It was only Herzl's personal diplomacy, much derided by his opponents (including Chaim Weizmann, who was later to excel at the same game), that had kept the option open at all. Still, even though Herzl had been unable to secure a charter, he had nevertheless succeeded in placing the question of a Jewish homeland in Palestine on the international agenda.

In the decade after Herzl's death, however, as Europe moved ever closer to the cataclysm of world war, the Jewish paragraph slipped lower and lower on the international agenda. As a result, the Zionist movement found itself with little choice but to concentrate on small-scale support of settlement in Palestine and on work in the diaspora—precisely in the areas on which a sizable number of Zionists (perhaps a majority) had wanted the movement to concentrate in the first place. Those like Ahad Haam who insisted that before any political moves could bear fruit, the Jewish people must first undergo a spiritual transformation, became the preponderant ideological voices of the movement.

The Herzlian vision of a Jewish state thus receded beyond the horizon of most Zionist leaders. The national home was increasingly conceived not as a safe haven where the suffering Jewish masses would build a new normal existence in freedom and dignity but as a place where elite groups would create a new communitarian society and revitalize Jewish cultural and moral values, which would in turn irradiate diaspora Jewry and perhaps the world.

The chimerical (or messianic) nature of such a proposition had early on become clear to a young agricultural worker by the name of David Green who had come to settle in Palestine from Plonsk. In a letter to his father in 1909, the future Prime Minister of Israel wrote that he "came to recognize deeply that the people who are settled here only for the sake of an ideal are not capable of living here, save for exceptional individuals for whom the 'ideal' is not an 'ideal' but a necessity... the meaning of their life and the center of their desire. For such people, work is a purpose in itself, but these are singularly inspired individuals, like the thirty-six righteous... the normal person, the average person, demands first of all a purpose for himself, a possibility for material existence."

From his hard, literally down-to-earth experience as an agricultural worker in Palestine, Ben-Gurion had learned as early as 1909 that if the national home was to fulfill its promise to European Jewry, mainly East European Jewry, it had to be built by ordinary people. Yet, after Herzl's death, the ideological trend in the Zionist movement veered in the opposite direction, toward elitism.

Paradoxically, the movement toward elitism was led by Eastern European Zionists, the very people one might have expected to be most concerned with the misery of their fellow Jews in the shtetls. That they seemed less worried about anti-Semitism and the material conditions of life in the shtetls can be explained by the fact that, in spite of misery and squalor, the Jews of Eastern Europe did not feel degraded by oppression and poverty. Indeed, in more than one sense, they thought of themselves as superior to their largely illiterate neighbors as well as the government officials who executed the oppressive policies, often with malice aforethought. Their rootedness in the Jewish past, their sense of community, and their acceptance of their unchangeable other-beingness was by far deeper and more secure than that of their brothers in the West.

Most Western Jews had willingly—often enthusiastically—traded these attributes for economic opportunities, the gifts of European culture, and the lure of civil rights. What brought Western Jews to Zionism was the recognition that the bargain had not only pushed them into a quagmire of ambivalence and ambiguity, but had also produced the "Jewish problem" and virulent anti-Semitism.

The strongest argument against political Zionism undoubtedly was how unlikely it seemed to achieve its aims even partially. The settlement work in Palestine was going nowhere.

The existing villages were in a state of almost perpetual crisis, kept from disaster only by the generous, if paternalistic, intervention of Baron Edmond de Rothschild's millions. Immigration, meanwhile, continued at a trickle. The Ottoman authorities had no desire to see the number of Jews in Palestine grow. Nor did things improve when the Young Turks overthrew the Sultan in 1908. Many Zionists had hoped that the enlightened Turkish revolutionaries would have a greater sympathy for the aspirations of the Jewish people than the corrupt retrograde despotism they replaced. In fact, they were even more hostile to Zionism. They had no use for yet another national group whose political demands would have to be accommodated. Turkey had enough such groups already.

Ben-Gurion noted at the time that there were five Arab deputies from Palestine in the Turkish parliament who never ceased to complain about, attack, and denigrate the Jewish settlers. In contrast, the two Jewish deputies, Emmanuel Carasso from Salonika and Masliah from Smyrna, never rose to the settlers' defense, let alone to advocate opening the doors of Eretz Israel to more Jews.

Only a Bulgarian deputy from Turkish Macedonia, Dimitri Vlachov, voiced any sympathy for the Jews. Bulgarians seemed to have a soft spot for the Jews even then. (This sympathy was expressed resoundingly in World War II, when the Bulgarians refused to follow the Nazi policy of genocide; as a result, Bulgarian Jewry survived the war virtually unscathed.)

The only major accomplishment of Zionism in the period between Herzl's death and the outbreak of World War I was the founding of Tel Aviv in 1909. Those concerned with security could also point with pride to the establishment in the same year of Hashomer, a small group of mounted watchmen dedicated to the defense of Jewish villages, which eventually evolved into the Haganah, the clandestine predecessor of the Israel Defense Forces.

Initially, at least, World War I was a heavy blow to the Yishuv. With the entry of Turkey on the side of Germany and Austria,

Jewish settlers in Palestine who had kept their Russian citizenship became enemy aliens. A number of them, including David
Ben-Gurion and Yitzhak Ben-Zvi, who was to become Israel's
second President, were expelled. Others fled to neighboring
British-ruled Egypt, where they lived in refugee camps. Some
opted for Ottoman citizenship.

But though the situation was desperate, it was not hopeless.
Help was sought and received from the United States, whose
neutrality the Turks had every reason to respect and to accom-
modate. Especially invaluable to the Yishuv was the presence
in Constantinople of U.S. Ambassador Henry Morgenthau, who
was always ready to use his political and diplomatic clout to
help his fellow Jews.

Perhaps more significant, changing geopolitical realities were
breathing new life into Herzl's old dream of securing a charter
for Jewish settlement in Palestine. Within a few months after
the outbreak of World War I, the idea was being embraced by
many who had once opposed or ridiculed Herzl's "diplomatic
Zionism" as little more than "super-swindling charlatanism,"
as Weizmann had once called it. By the end of 1914, even Baron
Edmond de Rothschild was professing to see great merit in the
idea of a charter—an idea he had dismissed with cold hauteur
when Herzl presented it to him fifteen years earlier. Weizmann
reported to the Zionist Executive, the governing body of the
movement, that the Baron had told him that the time was now
ripe to begin pushing the idea. It was a task Weizmann was to
undertake with enormous skill, tact, and charm—though without enough urgency to satisfy his critics (and even some of his
friends).

Pragmatism was Weizmann's forte. Heroics he viewed with
bemused suspicion. He viewed politics and diplomacy as the art
of the possible. Weizmann wouldn't even dare probe the outer
limits of the possible, much less try the impossible—and in his
view, the establishment of a Jewish state was in the realm of
the impossible. He thus spent much energy attempting to prove
to his critics that the idea of the Jewish state had actually been

abandoned at the First Zionist Congress: the program adopted there, known as the Basel Program, did not mention a "Jewish state," only a national home.

In retrospect, it was Weizmann's admiration for and trust in the British, no less than his gradualist, pragmatic approach, that eventually brought the Zionist movement to the brink of political bankruptcy. Warning voices, some quite shrill, had been heard all along the way, but Weizmann was always able to prevail. "At congresses," wrote Dr. Robert Weltsch, an old-time Zionist journalist who was by no means unsympathetic toward Weizmann, "the majority was against his policy, if not against his person, and finally they had no choice but re-elect him as there was no alternative candidate." By the time Weizmann finally resigned in 1931, time had run out for a radical change in Zionist policies.

In 1917, however, Weizmann was the right person at the right place at the right time. No one can doubt that it was his dedication, perseverance, charm, and understanding of the British that midwifed the Balfour Declaration, which established the Jewish people's right to a "homeland in Palestine" (though not to the reconstitution of Palestine as a Jewish state).

Nahum Sokolow, a pioneer Hebrew journalist and translator of Herzl's *Der Judenstaat* who served for many years as General Secretary of the World Zionist Organization, is also due considerable credit for the achievement. It was Sokolow who persuaded the French not to oppose the Balfour Declaration.

In any case, Weizmann's rise to the top of the World Zionist Organization—he was elected its President in 1921—was mainly due to his role in obtaining the Balfour Declaration. Indeed, in his memoirs, Ben-Gurion expressed the view that this was the only reason for Weizmann's ascendance to leadership.

Weizmann's accomplishment is in no way diminished by the fact that the British wanted to grant the Declaration as much as the Zionists wanted to get it. Why they wished to do so is a matter of dispute. What is clear is that long-term imperial interests, as well as short-term ones dictated by the war, must have weighed in the government's decision.

For one thing, Britain wished to encourage America to enter the war on the Allied side. The War Cabinet believed that a gesture in favor of Jewish national aspirations would help, especially as many American Jews were loath to support Russia, and America's influential German-Jewish "crowd," with its family ties and its sentimental attachment to German culture, found it difficult to see Germany as an enemy.

What's more, there were some British politicians who seemed to feel that a pro-Jewish gesture might persuade Russian Jews, many of whom played a prominent role in the October Revolution, to influence the new Bolshevik government to remain in the war. This may well have been yet another case of overrating Jewish influence, a not uncommon belief the Jewish people can ill afford to discourage.

The British also felt that supporting a Jewish national home would strengthen their hand in the tug-of-war with France over spheres of influence in the Middle East.

Lastly, there was the matter of securing the way to India. It was argued that a Jewish national home, by dint of its unquestioned loyalty to its British benefactor and its proximity to the Suez Canal, would comprise a valuable strategic asset. (Although Weizmann rejected this argument in public, he used it privately in his dealings with the British.)

Geopolitics aside, there can be no doubt that many of Britain's leaders at the time felt that to give the Jewish people a national home would be an act of historic and poetic justice sanctioned and sanctified by the Bible, an act Britain would have no reason to regret.

When the Balfour Declaration was published, Weizmann reportedly told his friend Norman Bentwich that he "heard the steps of the Messiah." If so, it was a case of wishful hearing. To translate the intent of the Declaration into political reality would have required above all an act of national will, faith, and readiness for sacrifice on the part of the Jewish people—in terms of massive immigration to Palestine and the expenditure of vast financial resources—that they were simply not prepared to make.

It would also have required the recognition by Britain that the deliberately qualified promise of the Balfour Declaration could not be fulfilled unless the British pursued a policy of openly and actively encouraging and assisting the creation of a Jewish majority in Palestine. Whether this had ever been the intention of the British government is doubtful. In any case, the British denied it firmly each time events in Palestine seemed to call for a clarification of policy.

The fact was, the Balfour Declaration represented a watered-down version of what the Zionist leadership desired. The Zionists wanted its purpose defined as "the reconstitution of Palestine as the national home of the Jewish people." What they got was merely a pledge by the British government to "facilitate the establishment *in* [emphasis added] Palestine of a national home for the Jewish people." Nor did it escape the attention of the Zionist leadership that the Declaration also specified that "nothing shall be done which may prejudice the civil and religious rights of existing non-Jewish communities in Palestine."

What, then, did the Balfour Declaration really mean? In theory, a Jewish majority could safeguard civil and religious rights of non-Jewish communities in Palestine. In practice, however, while religious rights presented no problem, civil rights did, for they were generally taken to include the right of national self-determination, which the Balfour Declaration had implicitly given to the Jews by speaking of a "Jewish national home in Palestine." Did the Balfour Declaration intend to deny similar rights to other communities by defining them as "religious" (as opposed to "national")? Or was the British government deliberately glossing over an apparent contradiction?

The Zionists were undaunted by contradictions, apparent or real, in what they regarded as their long-sought charter to Palestine. It was, after all, the inherent nature of documents that used diplomatically worded constructions to bridge incompati-

123

ble positions that they be open to interpretation. In any case, the Zionists were confident of their ability to create conditions that would force the world community to interpret the Declaration the way they wanted.

After the end of World War I, the Balfour Declaration was enshrined in international law by being made part of the League of Nations Mandate that provided the legal basis for British rule in Palestine. Even before the Mandate was ratified, however, the Zionist leadership tried—in vain, as it turned out—to convince the Versailles Peace Conference to expand the borders that had been proposed for Palestine. (The lands the Zionists wanted to add—the fertile Hauran region in southwestern Syria and the southern portion of Lebanon up to the Litani River— were to re-emerge as an object of Israeli concupiscence fifty years later.) The Zionist leadership was unaware that, with the Mandate, it had already bitten off more than the Jewish people were prepared to chew.

From the beginning, the British administration in Palestine made the chewing tough for the Jews. The military government that took charge of Palestine after the country's conquest by General Allenby virtually ignored the Balfour Declaration, adopting measures that clearly reflected its pro-Arab, anti-Zionist—and anti-Jewish—bias.

The Zionist leadership hoped that this bias would disappear once a civilian government was duly established. And, indeed, that turned out to be the case, at least partly. The British, however, were always in an uncomfortable position as a result of the obligations imposed on them by the League of Nations Mandate. The problem was that the Palestine Mandate did not conform to the League's Covenant—a fact that would have made it awkward for the British to act in accordance with the Balfour Declaration's pro-Zionist spirit even if they had really wanted to.

According to the Covenant, mandates were supposed to be administered for the benefit and ultimate independence of native populations, which in the case of Palestine could only mean the indigenous Arab majority. The wording of the Palestine Mandate, however, implied that its primary purpose was the establishment of a national home for the Jewish people. The Mandate's preamble expressly referred to the Balfour Declaration and to the Jewish people's historic right to Palestine.

The conflict was clear—as were its implications. Among other things, it made it extremely unlikely that the United States would support any efforts to pursue a pro-Zionist policy in Palestine. Not that the American President, Woodrow Wilson, was unsympathetic to Jewish aspirations. (To be sure, he was more impressed by the Zionist convictions of his friend Justice Louis Brandeis than by the 523,048 Jewish signatures on a petition submitted to him in 1919 urging the creation of a Jewish homeland in Palestine.) However, it could hardly have escaped Wilson's attention that the idea of a Jewish national home stood in glaring contradiction to the principle of self-determination that he championed: applied to Palestine, it would have meant majority rule by the Arabs.

The best Britain could hope for was that by keeping Jewish aspirations in Palestine within "reasonable" bounds, the slow progress of Zionist "colonization" would create no more than occasional disturbances. Britain would then be able to administer the country while straddling the nationalist barbed-wire fence across which Jew and Arab confronted each other in what was soon to become a line of battle. The World Zionist Organization, under Weizmann's leadership, was prepared to go along. The Arabs, however, were not.

Much has been written about the failure of the Zionists to understand the Arabs. The implicit assumption is that understanding Arab nationalism would have advanced the cause of the Jewish national home. In fact, the protocols of the sessions of various Zionist bodies prove that at least some leaders were aware of Arab nationalism and brought the matter up in debates. Arthur Ruppin, who came to Eretz Israel in 1908 and went on to direct the agricultural settlement effort for many years, pointed to Arab nationalism as one of three elements working against the Jews. (The others were time and the liquidation by the Bolsheviks of Russian Zionism.)

The question was also raised by such prominent figures in the government as Nahum Sokolow and Menachem Ussishkin. But no one was able to come up with an answer. Cultural exchanges, learning each other's language, offering medical services, agrarian credit, bribes to the leadership—all these were proposed and tried. (The same recipe failed in the 1980s, when Israel tried it with the Arabs of the occupied territories.)

In the socialist camp, Ben-Gurion had in the early days of the Mandate called for a common front of Arab and Jewish workers employed mainly in agriculture to stand against the exploiters of the working class. A few years later, he was forced to recognize that working-class solidarity was as irrelevant to nationalism in Palestine as it was everywhere in the world. The fact was, nothing would induce the Arabs to accept Jewish immigration and a Jewish national home in their midst. Vladimir Jabotinsky proclaimed this time and again. Others agreed at heart, though few would say so out loud, for fear of promoting pessimism and alerting the British, who were always eager to put as much distance as possible between their policies and their promises under the Balfour Declaration.

In the 1920s, and even later, very few among the Zionist leadership were prepared to launch a political struggle against the British in order to remind them of their obligation to support and advance the cause of the Jewish homeland. Instead, they opted for compromise and a gradualist approach. They knew that they had neither the resources nor the manpower for a "maximalist" program, and they had little faith in the movement's ability to create either.

The first anti-Jewish disturbances shook the peace of Jerusalem as early as March 1920. In April of the same year, Arabs attacked Jewish settlements in Upper Galilee. It was there, at Tel Hai, that the defenders led by Yosef Trumpeldor became in death symbols of Jewish determination to fight back. Still, these incidents seemed isolated, of no real import.

In contrast, the widespread riots that erupted in 1921 seemed to have a directing hand behind them. The rioting started on May 1 in Jaffa. It was followed by large-scale attacks on Rehovot, Petach Tikvah, Hadera, and other Jewish settlements, which left forty-seven dead and a hundred forty wounded among the Jews. Among the victims was the noted Hebrew author Y. H. Brenner.

Much to the consternation of the Zionist leadership, the immediate reaction of the Mandatory government was to decree a halt to Jewish immigration. The decision was all the more painful to the Zionists as it was made by British High Commissioner Herbert Samuel, who happened to be a Jew himself.

The same Herbert Samuel had less than two years earlier, on November 2, 1919, in a speech in London celebrating the second anniversary of the Balfour Declaration, called for the promotion of Jewish economic and cultural development in Palestine as well as the institution of the "fullest measure of local self-government, in order that with the minimum of delay the country may become a purely self-governing commonwealth under the auspices of an established Jewish majority."

That was Herbert Samuel the Zionist, not Herbert Samuel the High Commissioner. The latter felt compelled to assure the Arab population that it had never been the policy of the British government nor the intention of the Balfour Declaration to set up in Palestine a Jewish government that would rule over the Arabs.

In a draft of the statement he intended to make in the wake of the 1921 riots, Samuel defined the British government's policy with regard to the Jewish presence in Palestine as envisaging the establishment of a cultural center there, and no more than that. It was as if Ahad Haam were looking over Samuel's shoulder. That was too much—or, rather, too little—even for the Colonial Office, which ordered him to delete the word "cultural." The Colonial Office also quashed Samuel's plan to set up a Christian-Muslim Committee as a gesture of evenhandedness and a counterweight to the Zionist Commission, which was then the official Jewish advisory body to the Mandatory government.

The proposals drafted by Samuel reveal more than his desire to formulate a British policy in Palestine that would do justice to the rights of the two communities as guaranteed in both the Balfour Declaration and the Mandate. They betrayed his fundamental misreading of the nationalist passion that informed the attitudes of the two "communities," Arab and Jewish. To Samuel, "national" meant only cultural and religious particularity.

Herbert Samuel was an Englishman first and a Jew second. He certainly was not a Jewish nationalist. He was philo-Zionist, as opposed to a Zionist, much like Winston Churchill. In 1920, Churchill, then British Secretary of State for War, had written an article for London's *Illustrated Sunday Herald* in which he envisaged a Jewish state in Palestine of some 3 million or so Jewish inhabitants, arguing that such a state would thwart what he believed was a Bolshevik plan to establish a "worldwide communistic state under Jewish domination." (Herzl, too, had argued that Zionism would draw the Jewish intelligentsia away from revolutionary socialism.)

Two years later, in the White Paper of June 22, 1922, Churchill (who was now Colonial Secretary) made it clear that the idea behind the national home for the Jewish people was "not the imposition of a Jewish nationality upon the inhabitants of Palestine as a whole, but the further development of the existing Jewish community, with the assistance of Jews in other parts of the world, in order that it may become the center in which the Jewish people as a whole may take, on grounds of religion and race, an interest and a pride." Samuel could not have agreed more, except that he would not have used the term "race" (which Churchill used as a substitute for "nation"). For Samuel, it was a matter of religion and culture.

The Zionists were shocked at what they, correctly, saw as an appeasement of the Arabs. After all, it was the Arabs who had resorted to violence in opposing the Jewish national home, which the British were duty bound to promote, albeit not at the expense of the "local population."

In spite of the disappointment, the Zionist leadership re-
frained from calling for Samuel's resignation or removal. On the
contrary, the Zionist Executive in Jaffa asked all the Zionist
federations in Europe and America to organize mass meetings.
The circular was accompanied by a draft resolution the Executive wanted the meetings to adopt. It expressed support for Herbert Samuel, protested against Arab violence, demanded the
establishment of a Jewish defense force, and called (as usual) for
increased contributions of money.

It is quite probable that Herbert Samuel correctly gauged the
mood of both the British public and the government, neither of
which seemed prepared to support the use of British military
power to ram a pro-Zionist policy down the throats of an obviously hostile Arab population.

In 1920 and 1921, no Jewish force existed. The British restored order and calmed Arab spirits, temporarily at least. They
did so by introducing relatively mild anti-Jewish restrictions
and by making political gestures toward Arab nationalism and
its leader, Haj Amin el-Husseini, the notorious Mufti of Jerusalem. (The Mufti, a great admirer and political ally of Hitler,
spent World War II in Berlin.)

The Zionists accepted the introduction of what amounted to
quotas for immigration certificates based on the absorptive capacity of the Palestinian economy. It wasn't that unreasonable,
and anyway the official Zionist leadership had always wanted
to maintain a strict quantitative and qualitative control over
prospective immigrants. The devil of the White Paper was not
all that black. There was room for intercession, negotiation,
and therefore hope, all three familiar staples of Jewish lore.

Encouragement could even be drawn from a passage in the
document that read: "That this [the Jewish] community should
have the best prospect of free development and provide a full
opportunity for the Jewish people to display its capacities, it is
essential that it should know that it is in Palestine as of right
and not on sufferance."

In spite of that superb example of British draftmanship,
everyone knew that a dangerous precedent had been estab-

lished. Instead of doing its best to promote the creation of conditions that would favor the establishment of a Jewish national home with an eventual Jewish majority, the British government could be expected to yield to Arab pressure.

As a result, the Zionist establishment came under harsh criticism from such archantagonists as Ben-Gurion and Jabotinsky. In response, the establishment claimed it had no choice. Zionism had not yet succeeded in building a strong enough economic base in Palestine to attract a sizable number of immigrants. The movement was weak—so weak in fact that some historians believe that the British actually saved the Yishuv (and thus the Zionist movement) from extinction in 1921. Be that as it may, it is true that British troops fought the Arab rioters. Most of the Arab casualties—forty-eight dead and seventy-three wounded—were the result of British fire. It is equally undeniable that while a great number of Jews had greeted the Balfour Declaration with enthusiasm, few saw it as a call to pack up and go to Palestine or, at least, to demand to be settled there. The simple fact that the Declaration and the subsequent League of Nations Mandate meant international recognition of the Jews as a nation and their right to build a national home in Eretz Israel seemed to be enough for most Jews, including many of those who thought of themselves as Zionists.

Not that there was any dearth of warning voices, all of which stressed that national rights would remain a dead letter unless the Jewish people, as Ben-Gurion put it, "transform [it] into tangible fact...with body and soul, with their strength and capital." (Ben-Gurion the socialist gave way on the last point to Ben-Gurion the nationalist.)

Those warnings were not heeded. In his farewell address to the Convention of the Zionist Organization of America in Baltimore on June 17, 1923, Chaim Weizmann said:

> The Mandate was ratified [in 1922]. Three stages were necessary for this ratification: the Balfour Declaration, the San Remo decision, and the last stage. And at each stage we all secretly hoped, and you all secretly hoped, that a Messianic wave would sweep

over Jewry from one end of the world to the other, a wave which would converge all forces on the upbuilding of Palestine. We thought it would happen after the Balfour Declaration. We thought it would happen after San Remo. And we certainly thought it would happen when the final vote was cast, after the Mandate.

It did not happen. And there was no one to blame for the failure but the Jews themselves (unless one blamed Bolshevik Russia for suppressing a Zionist movement whose members just might have chosen to come to Palestine if for no better reason than to escape the misery spawned by the October Revolution).

Weizmann was to cry out to the Jewish people often, asking, "Where are you?" He never asked himself, not publicly at least, whether the lack of response might have been the fault of the Zionist Organization and its leadership.

Early critics of the official Zionist policies, both of the left and the right, were insistent in pointing out that the principal failure lay in the organization's inability to turn Zionism into a mass movement. A mass movement, they argued, would pressure the British government into honoring its obligations to the Jewish people. A mass movement would also shake up American Jewry and loosen their purse strings.

"If you will it, it is not a dream" was the motto Herzl had placed on the first page of his utopian novel *Altneuland*. Perhaps he overrated the role national will played in history. In any case, in the 1920s the national will of the Jewish people to return to their ancient homeland and recreate a Jewish commonwealth there was not strongly in evidence.

Worse, no charismatic leader had arisen to take Herzl's place. As a result, the concept of a mass transfer of Jews to Palestine, of the creation of a modern Jewish state there, and of the mobilization of the material and moral forces of the Jewish people all over the world toward this aim became little more than components of a "Herzl myth." It was precisely the kind of *Agadah* ("legend") that Ahad Haam had hoped it would become—a leg-

131

end that, as he wrote to Jacob Klatzkin in 1910, "might contribute more to the strengthening of the national ideal than Herzl was able to do in his lifetime."

When, in 1919, Herzl's early collaborator Max Nordau called for using the honeymoon period following the Balfour Declaration to mount an effort for the immediate transfer of the first half-million Jews from Eastern Europe to Palestine, it evoked hardly any attention. By that time, Nordau was an aging and ailing man who could not have led the effort himself. (In any case, he had always been more of a thinker than a doer.) But no one in the Zionist leadership gave the idea as much as a thought. Weizmann dismissed the Nordau plan derisively on the grounds that Nordau had given no indication as to how it was to be implemented.

In 1919, Weizmann the realist estimated that half a million Jews would come to Palestine over the next ten years. In fact, only 109,000 immigrated to Palestine during that period, while an unknown number left for what they believed would be greener pastures.

In the eyes of many critics, the fire had gone out of the Zionist movement. Yitzhak Grünbaum, the Polish Zionist leader, complained bitterly that the spirit of the "great and holy rebellion" had disappeared. Instead, the Zionist leadership had come to resemble a kind of government without a state, preoccupied with politics, diplomacy, and internal maneuvering, avid for the trappings, however modest, of power and prestige.

Indeed, the movement had spawned a class of professional Zionists who manned (there were very few women among them) what soon became a well-developed—and to its critics, a parasitically proliferating—bureaucracy. Even Nahum Sokolow, the then-President of the Zionist Executive, told his colleagues at a meeting held in Berlin on January 17, 1923: "At times I think that we should all abandon our offices and our work in the European capitals and go to the people, rouse it, and demand from it to fulfill its great duty to its country, its future."

At the first Zionist congress to be held after World War I, the

1921 gathering in Carlsbad, Czechoslovakia, Berl Katznelson, who was to the workers' movement in Palestine what the Rebbe was to his Hasidic followers, asked bitterly: "What have we done at the great hour of opportunity for Zionism in the past three years?" To which he himself answered: "Instead of work, we have placed politics at the head, and creative work has been pushed behind the door."

Another delegate, Eliezer Kaplan, who was to become Israel's first Minister of Finance, complained that "the leadership did not arouse the national forces of the Jewish people, did not sufficiently support Jewish immigration [to Palestine], and failed to use the propitious hour for the upbuilding of the country."

Still, no one could deny that on the political front the Zionist movement had chalked up some impressive achievements. It had gained international recognition of the national rights of the Jewish people. It could speak in the name of the Jewish people as a whole (much to the distress of anti-Zionist Jews). It had some political clout in countries that had recognized Jewish minority status, such as Poland and Czechoslovakia. It had attracted to its ranks an important and articulate sector of the Jewish intellegentsia. In London and in Jerusalem, its representatives were consulted about all matters affecting the national home, and their opinion carried a certain weight.

That the movement's political impact was not greater and more decisive was due to its inability to implant a more impressive economic and demographic seed in the ground of Palestinian realities. The reason for this admitted weakness was clear to one and all: not enough funds. Revolutions, it is said, are fueled by blood; the engine of the Jewish national revolution ran on money. As there never was enough money, it sputtered shamefully.

There was only one source from which the money could come: America. (This is no less the case today.) And America was whence the Zionist movement expected it to flow in abundance. Alas, that was not to be. Justice Louis Brandeis, who realized early in World War I that "the burden has fallen upon

America to maintain the Zionist movement," was confident that the "Jews in America can be relied upon to perform fully their obligation." If they had followed Brandeis, they might have done so. As it turned out, not even the majority of American Zionists followed him, to say nothing of the overwhelming majority of American Jews who were either indifferent or hostile to the Jewish national renaissance.

The American Zionist movement, never very sturdy in the first place, was crippled by a clash between Weizmann and Brandeis. Although Weizmann's supporters portrayed it as an ideological struggle, it was really a clash over control—a power struggle that was aggravated by incompatible temperaments. Weizmann was deeply disturbed by Brandeis's lack of *yiddish-keit*—the same lack he had found so intolerable in Herzl. Indeed, Weizmann may have found Brandeis's version of Zionism even more troubling, since it came wrapped in the American flag. At least Herzl had flown a Jewish flag.

For Justice Brandeis, being a Zionist was the best way for American Jews to perform their duty to their country. But since one could not do one's patriotic duty by emigrating from America, Aliyah (settling in Palestine) could therefore not be a desirable aim. Brandeis went even further. "The Jewish spirit," he wrote, "the product of their religion and experience, is essentially modern and essentially American. Not since the destruction of the Temple have the Jews in spirit and in ideals been, in these respects, so fully in harmony with the noblest aspirations of the country in which they lived."

Weizmann could agree with Brandeis about the relevance of the Jewish spirit to modernity. But to declare it also "essentially American" was anathema to him. To Weizmann, the Jewish spirit could only be Jewish, a meaning he clearly did not restrict to its religious dimension.

In a novel form, the antagonism between Weizmann and Brandeis was a replay of what separated Eastern European Zionists from their Western brothers in arms. In her biography of Brandeis, Philippa Strum quotes an unidentified Hadassah leader who described him as a "new phenomenon—a leader in Zionist life who was a listener instead of a speaker, one who had respect for punctuality, regard for time and precision, a dislike for personal publicity."

The Zionist movement in Europe, in which Easterners had become dominant, especially after Herzl's death, was simply not ready to bow to American leadership. Neither, for that matter, was the American Zionist movement, whose membership was overwhelmingly composed of immigrants from Eastern Europe.

Like the Jewish Agency today, the Zionist Executive was more than willing to spend American money, as long as it could do so in the way it thought appropriate. It was suspicious of what it saw as an American obsession with accounting. Its priorities for spending were also different from those proposed by Brandeis and his supporters. The latter wanted all money to go to Palestine, primarily for agricultural development, including a massive attack on malarial swamps. Weizmann wanted money for cultural objectives, to say nothing of the growing administrative costs incurred by the Zionist apparatus inside and outside Palestine.

Nothing was less justified than the accusations leveled against Brandeis that he wanted only private enterprise to develop Palestine. Yet it was this accusation that was the reason given by Weizmann for his final breach with Brandeis. On the contrary, Brandeis shared with both Herzl and Weizmann a healthy suspicion of unbridled capitalist enterprise, although he would not think of stifling private initiative.

The only valid reproach that could be made against Brandeis was his unwillingness to resign from the U.S. Supreme Court in order to devote all his energies to the Zionist movement. Brandeis felt that such a step would be a disservice to American Jewry. He was probably right in that, too. Nonetheless, Weizmann, who had resigned from the University of Manchester when his service to the cause became an all-consuming task, made much of Brandeis's refusal to follow his example.

Brandeis resigned from the leadership of the Zionist Organization of America after the defeat of his faction at the Cleveland Conference of 1921. We shall never know whether Zionism under the leadership of Brandeis would have become a greater force, one that would have been capable of generating the resources required to settle a substantial number of Jews in Palestine during the short "Balfour Declaration honeymoon." By the time the Brandeis faction was voted back into power in 1930, the honeymoon was over.

By then, the policies rejected by Weizmann and his followers a few critical years earlier were being hailed as the way of salvation. In 1929, Weizmann's plan to get non-Zionist Jews to actively participate in the work for Palestine had been ratified by the Sixteenth Zionist Congress. When Brandeis had first proposed the idea in 1920, it had been violently rejected.

Ten years of opportunities had been lost. In the meantime, Albion had added another chapter to the legend of its "perfidy": it was gradually dismantling its responsibilities for the implementation of the Balfour Declaration and the Mandate. And on Tuesday, October 29, 1929, the New York Stock Exchange crashed, spawning an era of worldwide economic blight.

"Stepping back from the debacle at Cleveland," wrote the historian Melvin Urofsky, summing up the history of American Zionism in the 1920s, "one can see it not only for the tragedy it was by itself, but as a part of a barren landscape dotted by other evidence of the sad plight of Zionism and of Jewry at the beginning of the Roaring Twenties."

In Eretz Israel, the 1920s were anything but roaring. The Yishuv struggled through one crisis after another. "The teachers of Eretz Israel are without pay," Weizmann lamented, "and the *halutzim* ["pioneers"] without work."

It was always the same vicious circle caused by the lack of money. Had more funds been available, there would have been more economic development and more jobs. More land could have been bought and more immigrants brought in—which in turn would have created additional economic opportunities, and so forth.

The British certainly showed little inclination to finance the country's economic development. Although they did provide employment for Jewish labor in public works, mainly road-building, they had no interest in aiding the establishment of industrial enterprises that would compete with their own at home. And for fear of offending the Arabs, they were miserly in placing government-owned lands in Jewish hands. The expansion of agriculture was therefore dependent on the ability of the Zionist Organization to purchase lands from private (mostly Arab) owners. (The Zionist Organization placed less emphasis on industrial development, not least because of its ideological, pseudo-religious penchant for the literal redemption of the land.)

Far more frustrating for the Zionists than the lack of British support was the reluctance of world Jewry to finance the "experiment" with sums large enough to assure its success. Few if any diaspora Jews were willing to risk investing in what today would be called an underdeveloped country. Palestine simply was not a priority for the Jewish communities in the diaspora, particularly those in America. More money was available for the agricultural settlement of Russian Jews in the Crimea, when the project was adopted by the Soviet government, than could be raised for the settlement of the Jewish national home. Diaspora Jews were ready to help individual Jews in distress, but the national distress of the Jewish people left them cold.

Only "emergencies" such as the 1929 anti-Jewish riots that took the lives of 133 Jewish settlers—Hebron alone counted seventy dead and four hundred injured—loosened Jewish purse strings significantly. The phenomenon is well known today to the fund-raisers of the United Jewish Appeal and similar organizations: when Jewish blood flows, Jewish money follows. Perhaps this is so because there is, in Hebrew, an etymological connection between *dam* ("blood") and *damim* ("payments"). Originally, the word meant compensation for spilled blood. Now it is the compensation for not having to spill one's own.

Who was to blame for the lack of response? Critics of the official Zionist leadership cited the movement's timidity. It was impossible, they claimed, to inspire the masses by settling limited, "realistic" goals, some of which had a clearly elitist flavor. Herzl had certainly thought so. The official history of Betar, the frenetic phalanx of Jabotinsky's brand of revisionist Zionism that preached military virtue and violence as the only way to redeem the country and the people, blamed the leadership of the World Zionist Organization for the failure to inspire the masses. The *Book of Betar*, published in 1969, pronounced a clear guilty verdict:

> Following the Balfour Declaration and the establishment of the Mandate, the Zionist leadership headed by Chaim Weizmann showed no faith in the power of the Jewish people and its will to create a state of its own. Nordau's idea for a one-time, all-out immigration campaign angered the makers of the official Zionist policy. Worse: the very idea of Hebrew statehood held no appeal for them, both because they interpreted Ahad Haam's teaching about a "Spiritual Center" with an extreme restrictiveness bordering on falsification, and because they did not dare confront the power entrusted with the Mandate for *Eretz Israel* with great ideas and great demands.

Adolf Boehm, an old-time Zionist and historian of the movement, had a different explanation for the ebbing attraction the Zionist idea had for the Jews. In a 1924 article, he accused Zionism of having failed "to bring immediate redemption to the Jewish poor or to prove with new deeds that it is capable to bring such redemption." Moreover, he felt that "the situation of our people in the countries of persecution has improved, and as has been the rule in our history the hopes of our people to found its existence in Exile grew." Boehm's pessimistic conclusion was that "the flame was extinguished that for a time burned in the heart of the Jewish masses."

Ahad Haam, not surprisingly, blamed the failure on the unchanged moral condition of the Jewish people. The Jewish people were neither spiritually nor morally ready for a homeland. He had said so in 1897, and he would say so again in 1922. In a letter to Leib Jaffe of Tel Aviv, Ahad Haam wrote: "To me, it appears...that the political victories of Zionism in the last years bear witness to the truth of the view that no 'Charter' and no 'Declaration'...will bring 'salvation,' as long as they are not anchored in the spirit of the people."

For its part, the Zionist Executive pointed to many achievements in the first decade following World War I. More than 300,000 acres of land had been acquired, and tens of new villages and townships had sprung up in Palestine, from Metullah in the north to well south of Tel Aviv. Factories, such as the Nesher cement works, heralded the beginning of a modest industrialization. The decade also saw the founding of the Histadrut, the unified trade-union movement that was to play an important role in the country's economic development, as well as the Hebrew University and the Technion, a school of engineering. The revival of Hebrew manifested itself with increasing vigor and vitality in the realm of culture. There was a lively Hebrew press, some serious Hebrew literature, and two good Hebrew theaters, Habimah and Ohel.

The Zionist establishment did not take credit for the short-lived economic boom that hit Palestine in the middle of the decade—a result of an unprecedented rise in Jewish immigration. After hovering around the 8,000 mark for several years, annual immigration suddenly jumped to nearly 14,000 in 1924. The next year it mushroomed to more than 34,000.

The moving "spirit" behind this wave of immigration, eventually named the Fourth Aliyah, was the Polish Minister of Finance, Josef Grabski, whose discriminatory economic policies threatened the livelihood of thousands of Jewish families in Poland. With the gates to America virtually closed by restrictive legislation, Palestine appeared as the only hope—thus, incidentally, reaffirming the unappealing nexus between Zionism and anti-Semitism that had played such a prominent role in Herzl's conversion to Jewish nationalism.

No one could pretend that the new immigrants were animated by any other motive than the search for a way out of an economic predicament. They were mostly middle class with modest capital resources, determined to make a living in their new homeland as best they could, unburdened by any desire to redeem the land or spiritually redeem themselves.

They were precisely the type of "normal" and "average" people seeking "material existence" whom Ben-Gurion in his 1909 letter to his father had said would be necessary for the building of the homeland. But when these "normal" people arrived in the mid-1920s, he found them undesirable: they were not workers but petty-bourgeois wheeler-dealers. The bourgeois Weizmann did not like them any better than Ben-Gurion.

The newcomers were attracted to the cities, mainly Tel Aviv. A building boom ensued, and so did real estate speculation. Small workshops sprang up, as did small businesses of all sorts. Moneylenders plied their trade freely. Demand for capital grew, especially as a boom in citrus export engendered a stampede to buy even small plots on which the "golden fruit" could be grown—by hired labor, of course. The circumstances were new, but the socioeconomic ethos was a duplication of the Jewish street in Poland's cities, small towns, and villages.

By the end of 1926, the boom was over. Worsening conditions in Poland cut the flow of capital from home. No alternative sources were available to sustain the undeniable, if often unappetizing, growth initiated by the new immigrants. As the Zionist leadership had always looked upon them with suspicion and apprehension, it would not have embarked on a salvage operation even if it had the ability to do so. As a result, in 1927 twice as many people left the country as came to settle, including some socialists who returned to the Soviet Union. That summer, there were 8,000 unemployed Jews in Palestine to testify to yet another apparent defeat of Zionism.

At the beginning of the 1930s, the Zionist leadership was too preoccupied with the aftermath of the 1929 Arab riots to pay much attention to the gathering storm in Europe. In many respects, events bore a familiar mark. The Arabs seemed to have understood that their nationalist aims would best be served by a policy of confrontation with the Mandatory power. Violence against Jews was a deliberate part of this confrontational policy. Not only was the Mandatory power obligated to protect the Jews, it was also committed to further the Jewish aspiration to build a national home in Palestine.

The riots challenged the British on both counts. And on both counts the British tried to give a restrictive interpretation to their obligations. The pattern had been established back in 1920: though Arabs were found guilty of having started the riots, neither proven participants nor the instigators were punished. Instead, Jewish immigration and freedom to acquire land were restricted in the hope that this would appease the Arabs. Since this served Arab interests, though not to their full satisfaction, it is hardly surprising that they resumed their confrontational approach in 1929 and again in 1936.

That they did not try it more often was partly due to the growing defensive capability of the Haganah, the voluntary Jewish defense force. It also had something to do with the proverbial British talent for muddling through. Although by then Arab nationalism had a recognized leader in the Mufti of Jerusalem, the Arab leadership lacked the ability to funnel all of the huge emotional appeal of nationalism into effective political action in the street.

As in 1921, the 1929 riots resulted in a British investigation and a White Paper—published in 1930 by the Colonial Secretary, Lord Passfield (né Sidney Webb, the famed Fabian social reformer). This White Paper further watered down the Balfour Declaration and the Mandatory obligations. Once again, the British aim was to appease the Arabs.

A new element in the 1929 disturbances was provided by the injection of religion into the conflict. The embers started to glow at the Western Wall with disputes over the right of prayer. They were fanned into flames by the Grand Mufti, who evoked the specter of a Jewish takeover of Moslem holy places, a specter that has not yet been laid to rest.

Arab nationalism and Islam have long walked hand in hand, even though the former was originally fathered by Lebanese

Christian Arabs resentful of Ottoman rule. For Jewish nationalism, the event marked the first—though not the last—time
that the Western Wall was to assume the role of a national as
well as a religious symbol.

A raucous demonstration at the Western Wall by a group of
Jabotinsky's followers may well have contributed to the explo-
sion. Ironically, religion was the least of Jabotinsky's concerns.
He was as secularized a Jew as could be found. Indeed, in his
will he asked to be cremated after death, contrary to Jewish
religious precepts. (As it happened, his wish was not granted. In
1963, Prime Minister Levi Eshkol, perhaps the most sensible
politician Israel has produced to date, authorized the reburial of
Jabotinsky's remains in Jerusalem.)

With the exception of Jabotinsky's Revisionists, who called
for active resistance against the Passfield White Paper (including illegal immigration and demonstrations), no Zionist political party or movement advocated a policy of confrontation with
Britain. The Zionist leadership placed its hopes in an updated
version of the time-honored method of *shtadlanut*—that is,
pleading, intercession by sympathetic influential non-Jews,
rousing of public opinion and the press, intervention in political backrooms, and similar nonviolent, though by no means
Gandhian, tactics.

Zionism's most prominent personality of the time, Chaim
Weizmann, firmly and unshakably believed that only through
compromise and accommodation with Britain would the Jews
stand any chance of advancing the cause of their national home.
It was this sincerely held trust in England that eventually led to
Weizmann's eclipse as a political figure in the most critical
phases of the slow march toward Jewish statehood.

Weizmann and his followers were not the only ones opposed
to the radical activism preached by Jabotinsky. The Zionist
labor movement also fought him tooth and nail. As a result, at
a time when the entire Zionist movement should have been
closing ranks in order to combat the rising tide of Nazism and
anti-Semitism, Zionists were concentrating their efforts on the

election campaign for the eighteenth Zionist Congress.

It was a vicious campaign. Labor emerged from it as the strongest party, but the movement was badly splintered. In 1935, the Revisionists left the World Zionist Organization and set up a separate New Zionist Organization, which claimed to be the true heir of Herzlian Zionism.

As Adolf Hitler rose to power in Germany, pressures for immigration to Palestine grew markedly. In 1932, the number of Jewish immigrants jumped to 12,553, a threefold increase from the year before, and that in spite of British restrictions. By the outbreak of World War II, a record number of 235,370 Jews, mostly from Germany, had reached the shores of Eretz Israel, not counting those who had managed to enter the country illegally. It was a far larger number than the Mandatory government deemed the country capable of absorbing. (Of course, the official estimates of the country's absorptive capacity disregarded the opportunities that immigrants created.)

As a result of the 1934 "Transfer" agreement between the Jewish Agency and the German authorities (an agreement that served as the basis of the Soviet propaganda ploy about Nazi-Zionist collaboration), German immigrants were able to qualify as "capitalists"—that is, immigrants who brought with them at least one thousand British pounds sterling. At the time, this constituted an important influx of money, in addition to providing the Zionist Organization in Germany with additional funds raised from the prospective immigrants, many of whom would have once been outraged had anyone suggested that they were Zionists, no less that they move to Palestine.

The Zionist leadership understood that more would have to be done to help European Jewry. In the mid-1930s, Weizmann estimated that one million certificates would be needed over the next ten years, and another one million Jews would have to find refuge outside Palestine. He did not find a responsive ear in London.

Like Weizmann, Ben-Gurion proposed the immigration of 100,000 people a year. (True to his style, Jabotinsky called for a mass evacuation of Jews from Europe.) Still, though the Zionist leadership was very concerned about the situation in Europe, they did not believe that the danger European Jewry faced was radically different from the calamities that had befallen the Jewish people in the past. This was an error shared by almost all Jews. In any case, the eyes of the Zionist leadership were trained first and foremost on Eretz Israel.

"After the record immigration figures of 1935," wrote Ben-Gurion's biographer Michael Bar-Zohar, "Ben-Gurion was convinced that the Zionist movement must now storm ahead with all its strength and bring masses of Jewish emigrants (principally from Germany and Eastern Europe), settle them in Palestine, and find sources of livelihood for them. But to achieve this, he needed three instruments: a united and effective Zionist Organization; American Jewry as a source of financial support; and the sympathy of Great Britain." None of the three instruments was available.

The Zionist Organization was neither united nor effective. Its budget was more strained than ever. American Jewry gave no signs of an "outpouring" of funds. And by 1935, Britain had moved dangerously close to the conclusion that the national aspirations of the Jews and Arabs in Palestine were irreconcilable.

The Arab revolt that broke out in 1936 made this clearer than ever. It took the Mandatory government two days to quell the riots, which resulted in sixteen Jewish deaths, a great number of wounded, and considerable destruction of property. And that was hardly the end of it. On and off, the Arab revolt continued for three years, including a general strike that lasted nearly six months before the Haganah and British forces were finally able to put it down. In fact, the revolt was a war of attrition against the Yishuv.

In 1937, the British tried a Solomonic solution in the form of the Peel Partition plan. The plan had logic on its side. If the two "nations" could not live peacefully within one country, then each should be given a part of the country in which it could constitute a ruling majority. Unfortunately, logic held little appeal for either side. The Arabs rejected the plan outright. The Jews were, as always, ready to talk. Ben-Gurion, for one, favored the plan—he hoped that one day, when the Jews were strong enough, the proposed partition borders could be changed in their favor.

King Solomon had an easier task when he confronted the two women who each claimed the same child as her own. Solomon knew there was only one true mother, and he knew he could count on her to yield rather than see her child killed. Lord Peel, on the other hand, was faced with two true mothers—one Jewish, one Arab—neither of whom would yield.

After the failure of the partition plan, Britain drastically downgraded its obligations to the Jews. The emerging danger of a world conflict persuaded the British government that it had to gain—or, rather, regain—the friendship of the Arabs. Clearly, that could not be done by opening the gates of Palestine to Jewish refugees and thus bringing the establishment of their national home closer to fruition.

What "stormed forward" was, alas, not the Zionist movement but the Nazi juggernaut. Back in 1921, Arthur Ruppin had remarked wistfully: "I don't know whether our children will not reproach us that we missed the only opportunity for the creation of a new homeland." By 1945, most of the children who could have spoken such words of reproach were dead, murdered in the Holocaust.

VIII

The State

To mark the hundredth anniversary of Theodor Herzl's birth, a richly illustrated, English-language, coffee-table edition of his utopian novel *Altneuland* was published in Israel in 1960. Besides honoring Herzl, the republication of his work was aimed at illustrating (literally) that, as the publishers' note put it, "the resemblances between Herzl's ideas and those of the planners of Israel of today are so close often to the point of detail that they give this essay in prophecy an historical importance which is not always realized."

The publishers hedged their bold statement by admitting that they did not "claim that this vision of a Jewish State in Palestine which Herzl put out in the guise of a light fiction in 1902 is an exact description of the present State of Israel." That was putting it mildly. Even a cursory glance at *Altneuland* reveals that any similarities between Herzl's dreams and Israeli reality are at best merely semantic. For example, the anniversary volume attempted to link the Histadrut, Israel's federation of labor, to Herzl's idea of cooperation. In fact, the two had hardly

146

anything in common. Herzl's vision was inspired by the mutualist ideas of Bellamy, Hertzka, and the Rochdale and Rahaline experiments. Histadrut had little to do with any of that. Besides being a regular trade union, Histadrut is also the country's largest holding company, controlling industrial plants, housing, contracting outfits, trading firms, department stores, dairies, and financial services, all run according to standard capitalist principles. The holding company is only nominally owned by Histadrut's members, and the employees of the various enterprises enjoy neither more rights nor better working conditions than their counterparts in private enterprise.

Similarly, the anniversary book presented the Histadrut-owned department store in Tel Aviv as the embodiment of Herzl's preference for such stores (as opposed to small businesses) as a means to cure "the bodies and souls of our small tradesmen... of certain deeply ingrained unprofitable and undignified forms of buying and selling." But as any visitor to Israel could easily ascertain, by 1960 the country was awash in small businesses, including stalls in produce markets, in much the same way as were Jewish communities in the diaspora.

Some of the parallels drawn by the book would strike anyone familiar with Israeli realities as wryly (if unintentionally) amusing. Pictures of the Dagon Company grain elevator in Haifa port, the headquarters of Solel Boneh (the Histadrut-owned giant contracting company), and the Dan Carmel Hotel in Haifa were chosen by the editors to illustrate the "spectacle of various architectural styles" enjoyed by the fictional visitors to *Altneuland*. All three edifices were actually built in an identical style. Variety is simply not the strong suit of Israeli architecture.

The prize in the category of well-meaning misrepresentations, however, must go to the paragraphs describing the railways. No one who has ridden Israel's railways could ever liken them to those described in *Altneuland*. The trains of Herzl's visionary country boasted "every comfort, ventilation, bright interior lighting, no dust and no smoke, and almost no jolting in spite of high speed," and they ran "from Lebanon to the Dead Sea, from the Mediterranean to the Golan and the Hauran, channeling labor where it is needed." In the real Israel, passenger railways link only Jerusalem to Tel Aviv, and Tel Aviv to Haifa. There is no direct train connection from Jerusalem to Haifa. (In 1986, the Jerusalem–Tel Aviv line was closed down for lack of passengers. It was reopened a year later because of its symbolic value.) The trains are neither speedy nor comfortable. And as for mobility of labor, it is notable in Israel by its absence. The only truly mobile workers are the Arabs of the West Bank and the Gaza Strip, who reach their places of employment by trucks and buses.

Herzl endowed his visionary nation with all the institutions of the modern welfare state. These can, indeed, be found in the State of Israel (just as, in one form or another, they can be found in virtually every industrialized country). But Israel's welfare legislation bears no particular Herzlian—or, for that matter, Jewish—imprint.

The editors of the centenary edition of *Altneuland* were guilty of a singular misapprehension: contrary to their assertion, they were the ones who didn't understand the "historical importance" of what they called Herzl's "essay in prophecy."

In *Altneuland*, Herzl went beyond the nation-state to describe a societal organization based on mutualist humanism in a secular, political reinterpretation of the age-old dream of the millennium. It was a Jewish version of political messianism in which Michelet's *Gesta Dei per Francos* was replaced by *Gesta Dei per Iudeos*—"God's deeds through the Jews."

Lewis Mumford, in his 1923 essay on *Altneuland*, regretted that Jewry did not see the truly revolutionary possibilities inherent in Herzl's vision and thus failed to convert the vision into a "live program which might have regenerated Jewry throughout the world." Whether or not this was ever a realistic possibility, Mumford was certainly right when he wrote:

> It was, alas! easier to cling to the letter of the Jewish myth, all the more since it demanded no personal effort and no personal adjustment on their own part; just as it was easier for those who

had been educated under Western influences as violent nationalists to transfer their balked nationalist complex to the Jewish
State. So the romanticists wove their dreams, the realists pulled
their political wires, and between them all that was fresh and
original in Herzl's *Altneuland* was lost; and only the conventional skeleton of his inspiration has been perpetuated.

Like Herzl, Mumford believed that a truly humanitarian society could only be built on the ruins of the nation-state. But
Israel's raison d'être was precisely to *be* the Jewish nation-state,
a state in which the Jews would exercise sovereignty in exactly
the same way as other nations did in theirs.

In the wake of the Holocaust, Zionism's most urgent concern
was to place a Jewish state on the map of the world. The utopian ideas the movement had generated in the past could be left
to impractical dreamers and academics to play with.

In the first two decades of Israel's existence, the debate that
had long raged among the philosophers of Zionism over
whether the Jewish state should be an end in itself or a means
toward a higher, eschatological aim seemed to have been decided in favor of the first concept.

Max Nordau had long ago stated that when it came into existence the Jewish state would, like any other state, have but one
ultimate aim: to survive as a civilized entity. Vladimir Jabotinsky, too, never looked beyond the philosophical boundaries
of the nation-state. And neither, if one judged them by their
deeds and not by their rhetoric, did the leaders of the State of
Israel, among whom Ben-Gurion occupied a place of primacy.

Even Herzl knew that the real Jewish state would be nothing
like the one he had envisioned in his essay "The Jewish State,"
let alone the utopia he dreamed up in *Altneuland.* And, indeed,
when the state emerged, it was precisely like the one Ahad
Haam had rejected as unsatisfactory, as "a thing so trifling,
which many other peoples have won in a short time."

In 1948, however, the Jewish people seemed quite happy
about the turn of events. All that mattered was that a Jewish
state had at long last become a reality. It was small, perhaps
trifling, but it was their own, and it was recognized as such by

149

the majority of the world's nations. As the spokesmen for the new state never tired of emphasizing, there was after two thousand years once again an independent sovereign Jewish entity on the map of the world. What made it a *Jewish* state first and foremost was the simple fact that Jews constituted a majority in it. It was the only country in the world with a government of Jews, by Jews, and for Jews. It was a miracle perhaps, but a man-made miracle, like the one related in the Book of Esther.

What had happened to the Zionist dream of creating not simply a Jewish state but a model nation imbued with a new form of ethical nationalism that would go forth from Jerusalem as a new Law? To put it simply, the dream had inevitably yielded to harsh realities and the exigencies of realpolitik.

Many Zionist leaders had recognized the likelihood of this early on. In 1918, Martin Buber, in a letter to Professor Shmuel Bergmann, expressed the fear that Zionism would follow the path of Europe and pursue an "unrestrained nationalism wedded to realpolitik." With that in mind, a number of leading personalities in the Zionist world, including Buber, the poet Chaim Nachman Bialik, Nahum Goldmann, Jacob Klatzkin, and Chaim Arlosoroff, got together in 1921 and founded the Jewish Society for International Understanding. As explained by Professor Paul Mendes-Flohr of the Hebrew University, the society's manifestly noble aim was "not simply the elimination of strife between peoples through *Nichtkrieg* ["absence of war"] but the establishment of a new type of relationship between nations based on mutual respect for the integrity of each." Power politics was to be replaced by "a powerful fidelity to reality and religious power, the power of faith and the pristine religious ideals of justice and mercy."

Not surprisingly, this synthesis of Prophetic Judaism and the kind of ideals that populate the preambles of international charters failed to influence the course of world history. It had little currency even among those who, in Palestine and abroad, worked hard to advance the cause of the Jewish state-to-be.

Still, the Jews have always been a stubborn and stiff-necked people, and they have found it difficult to relinquish their role as a beacon to the world—in spite of ample evidence that the world remains unreceptive to the light that the Jewish people wish to lavish upon it.

In a revealing contribution to the *Israel Government Yearbook of 1951*, the then Prime Minister, David Ben-Gurion, wrote:

> The State of Israel will be judged not by its riches or military power, nor by its technical skills, but by its moral worth and human values. We must make one more tremendous and concerted effort to become like all other peoples. To be that and no more, a normal vigorous, free and sovereign nation, is not easy, but by setting up the state we guaranteed the principal condition of fulfillment. Each one of us, however, is entitled to cling to the conviction that merely to be like all other peoples is not enough. We may pridefully aspire to bring true the words of the Prophet: "I the Lord...give thee for a covenant of the people to the Gentile."

Ben-Gurion left open the question to which category he himself belonged. In spite of his deep interest in Judaism, he was not an observant Jew, and he never thought that the Jewish state could or should be governed on *halakhic* precepts. Nonetheless, he strongly felt the tug of Judaism, and he was not averse to adorning his pronouncements with Biblical references, blurring the boundaries between the sacred and the secular, a common failing of Israeli politicians and public figures.

Thus, on November 7, 1956, after the victorious first Sinai campaign, Ben-Gurion opened his speech before the Knesset with the words: "The standing at Mount Sinai has been renewed in our times through the heroic sweep of our army." It was an egregious example of wrapping a religious mantle around a classical use of military force, however justified the use of that force may have been. As it happened, the 1956 Sinai campaign was not a renewal or reassertion of the sacred act at Mount Sinai, but a hapless conspiracy with France and Britain aimed, in nineteenth-century gunboat-policy style, at toppling

151

President Nasser of Egypt. (In the process, Ben-Gurion had hoped to redraw the map of the Middle East—in Israel's favor, of course.) Political realities dictated that on the very same day of his Knesset speech, Ben-Gurion had to assure President Eisenhower that all Israeli troops would be withdrawn from the Sinai as soon as a United Nations buffer force could be stationed there. The "standing at Mount Sinai" of the Israel Defense Forces was over. (It was to be renewed in 1967, but this time the Biblical oratory concentrated on Jerusalem.)

Politicians were not the only ones to abuse the sacred in the service of the mundane. Professor Yigael Yadin, for example, presented the purchase of the Dead Sea Scrolls, which had been illegally smuggled out of Jordan, as a divinely inspired act. "Destined from above" was the way he expressed it at the time.

For all the deliberate mixing of the sacred with the secular, however, care was taken not to give the new country a name that had any religious meaning. Ben-Gurion, whose influence at the time was predominant, rejected the idea of calling the new state "Zion," precisely because of its religious connotations. (He opposed the proposal to call the country "Judea" on the grounds that part of Biblical Judea lay outside the boundaries of the new state.) He chose to call the new country the State of Israel in order to emphasize that the Jewish people—or, at least, part of it—had again come into possession of a distinct sovereign national Jewish territory: Medinat Yisrael—the State of Israel. (It also means the State of the Jews, in the sense that Israel is a synonym for the Jewish people.)

The name "Israel" first appears in Genesis (32:28), when God tells the patriarch: "Your name shall no more be called Jacob, but Israel for you have striven with God and with men, and have prevailed." Indeed, "yisrael" means "one who has striven or wrestled with God." (Of course, the sages saw an additional meaning in the divine change of name. The root of the name "Ya'acov" ["Jacob"] is related to the word for "crooked," while "yisrael" is related to "straight.")

It may well be that the connotation of righteousness that the

152

sages read into the name "Israel" made the name even more attractive to the founding fathers of the newly independent country. Zionists had always dreamed of making the Jewish state into a state of righteousness, and they believed in their ability to create a perfect society. If so, they were harboring illusions about the nature of the modern nation-state.

That is not to say that the Israeli leadership was amoral in its pursuit of power and of the public good as it saw it. After all, the preservation of the state's independence and security was obviously a moral aim of primordial importance. Israel's leaders were guilty of nothing more than applying the kind of morality Max Weber defined as "ethics of responsibility," as distinct from the "ethics of conscience." Anyone who chooses politics as a vocation, Weber warned, "contracts with diabolical powers."

Indeed, there has yet to arise a state that is demonstrably governed according to the principles of Judeo-Christian morality and teaching—or on the basis of any other moral ideal, for that matter. Although such claims are often made, the record of history shows that without power, ideals cannot be realized; and once power is gained in their name, ideals are generally relegated to a spectral rhetorical existence. The ethics of politics are "the ethics of doing evil," noted the American philosopher Hans J. Morgenthau. Israel cannot be expected to escape that rule, much as some might have hoped that it could and would.

When Ben-Gurion took power as the first Prime Minister of the fledgling State of Israel in 1948, the survival of the state was his single-minded preoccupation. For all practical purposes, he accepted the Hegelian thesis that the nation-state was the highest moral organizational structure in which a nation could be united to lead a common life and build a common future. And although, like all of Israel, he hoped for peace, he knew that more strife lay ahead. Israel did not want war, but it would not avoid it, if it deemed the price of peace too high.

One of Ben-Gurion's favorite philosophers, Plato, taught that the division of mankind into distinct and often competitive units is a given of nature, and is thus unalterable. In the eighteenth century, when the enlightened concept of a unified mankind, a single *humanitas*, became the ephemeral lodestar of Europe's intellectuals, the German philosopher Johann Gottfried von Herder echoed Plato, warning that division not unity, strife not harmony, characterized the nature of mankind.

Surrounded by the seemingly implacable hostility of the Arab world, Israel found it difficult to dispute that notion. The fact is, however, the philosophy of Judaism has no room for such a view of mankind. Indeed, the Jewish philosopher Maurice Samuel deplored what he called the "deflecting forces" within the Zionist movement that professed the "un-Jewish faith that force, and force alone, is the intelligent directing principle in human relations."

In Samuel's view, it was the Holocaust that gave these forces "a scope and drive they had not possessed before." As he saw it, by "pushing the growth of the Jewish homeland beyond a natural pace," the Holocaust "obscured the purposes of the Zionist movement," deflecting it (only temporarily, he hoped) "from its historic, religious, moral and cultural identity with eternal Judaism."

In rejecting the Platonic conception of the state, Maurice Samuel wrote:

> In such a competitive world, the first business of the state is to be strong, in the combative sense. Therefore as long as he inhabits the planet, man must subordinate himself to the conditions that produce the strong state. His faculties, dreams, potentialities, God-visions, must serve that purpose; at worst, they must not interfere with it.... That is why poets must be excluded from Plato's Republic; that is why the lie is a proper instrument of state policy.

To be sure, poets were not excluded from Israel. On the contrary, they have flourished there. Nonetheless, the lie has always been considered a proper instrument of state policy—or as George Bernard Shaw put it in the preface to *Heartbreak House:* "Truth telling is not compatible with the defense of the realm." In any case, from the beginning, virtually the entire leadership of the country, along with the overwhelming majority of its people, subscribed precisely to the view of the state's business that Samuel deplored as un-Jewish. That may have been un-Jewish, but it was un-Jewish in a Jewish way: it was meant to protect the Jewish state.

In the context of Israeli politics, differences constantly arose over what in a given situation would best serve the interests of the state, but until 1967 hardly anyone argued whether one course was more in harmony with "eternal Judaism" than another. It had always been the principal aim of political Zionism to establish a normal state inhabited by a Jewish people who were themselves normalized precisely because of Jewish statehood. When this aim was achieved in 1948, Zionism could take pride in the knowledge that, except for the fact that it contained a Jewish majority, the State of Israel was, in many ways, a country like other countries. It had, and adored, all the trappings of sovereignty: its own flag, its own army, its own president, its own legislature, executive, judiciary, and whatnot. It controlled entry into its territory and egress from it. Ambassadors came to present their credentials, and Israel sent envoys abroad. It was a member of the United Nations and its subsidiary organizations. It was recognized by a majority of the world's nations. Its ships plied the oceans and its national airline flew wherever the skies were friendly.

With its goal of establishing a Jewish state accomplished, Zionism could now dedicate itself to the creation of an ideal society and to the ingathering of the exiles. In fact, neither goal was ever achieved. The first task Israel never so much as attempted. The second ran into an unyielding wall of diaspora reluctance. Diaspora Jews simply did not want to move, except into yet another diaspora. (In the 1950s, Polish Jews went to Denmark; in the '70s, a great majority of those permitted to leave Russia eventually chose the United States as their Promised Land—

after glasnost widened the gates of emigration only 10 percent of Russian Jewish emigrants went to Israel—and in the '80s, South African Jews looked toward English-speaking countries, not Israel, to shelter them from the future racial cataclysm they feared.)

The fact was, there were "abnormal" aspects to Israel's existence. The very act of its liberation departed from the pattern established by the process of decolonization that exploded after World War II. Israel was the only country born in war against its neighbors, the only country whose very right to exist was denied by other member states of the United Nations.

For most of Israel's first twenty years, its leadership refused to regard these "abnormal" aspects as being inherent in Jewish fate or as resulting from the Jews' unique spiritual destiny. If Israel had in a sense become the Jew among the nations, a nation that had to struggle for survival and acceptance like no other nation in the world, then its obvious task was to do its best to make these abnormalities disappear, and the sooner the better. In fact, the Israeli leadership manifested a great deal of optimism in the matter.

After the War of Independence ended with an Israeli victory, a victory that surprised many military experts, the energies of the government and the country were naturally focused on the formidable task of strengthening the state. Under the circumstances, little if any attention could be paid to spiritual questions such as the renewal of the Jewish people. They certainly were not high on the government's agenda.

Security was the top priority then, as it is today. Not surprisingly, measures taken in the name of security did not always meet the highest humanitarian standards. Nobody, least of all the Israelis themselves, expected this from a small nation that had been set upon by the armies of seven Arab states acting in crass contradiction of international law. Thus, no voice was raised in protest against the forcible removal of Arab civilian populations. Nor was the public unduly disturbed by the systematic destruction of abandoned Arab villages or by the relocation to a specific quarter of Haifa of those of its Arab inhabitants who chose to remain in the city. (In Haifa, the Jewish authorities actually went to great lengths in trying to dissuade Arab inhabitants from leaving.)

A la guerre comme à la guerre. No one had any illusions as to what would have happened to the Jews had the Arabs been the victors. For the Israelis, it ultimately boiled down to the question of who would be the dead and the displaced: the Jews or the Arabs. Naturally, the Jews decided to do everything in their power to make sure it wasn't them. It was also obviously in the interest of Israel to have more territory and fewer Arabs within the borders of the Jewish state. Any other nation would have behaved similarly, if not worse.

It wasn't just in terms of national defense and security that the exigencies of realpolitik required the new State of Israel to depart from its idealistic Zionist roots. Harsh political and economic realities also forced Israel off the Zionist road in terms of domestic policy—nowhere more so than in regard to the Labor Zionist goal of making the new Jewish state an egalitarian workers' society.

There had, of course, long been an elitist strain in the Zionist movement. Indeed, it had always been the movement's ambition to select as candidates for immigration those whom it thought best capable of contributing to the Yishuv's needs and future development. This was particularly true of the pioneer movements that insisted on preparing the *olim* for communal life in the kibbutzim.

Some leaders of the Zionist left found it difficult to suppress their elitist nostalgia after 1948. They saw selectivity as the only possible way to build the ideal society. They may have been right, but it was not a way the Jewish state could follow.

The streams of immigrants flooding the country, now that the locks placed on its gates by the British Mandatory administration had been blown open by independence, presented the fledgling state with a gigantic human and economic problem. All were welcome, of course. To deny entry to any Jew who wished to come would have undermined the very fundament on which the argument for a Jewish state had been built.

After all, the Jewish state was not created only for those Jews already living there. On the contrary, the international community was infinitely more moved by the need to find a home for the survivors of the Holocaust (who felt they had nowhere to go but to Eretz Israel) than by the desire of the 600,000 Palestinian Jews to become independent of foreign tutelage.

But while Israel wanted all Jews to come and settle in the Jewish state and lend their arms, aptitudes, and ambitions to the strengthening of their old-new, definitive, and unambiguous fatherland, some immigrants were more welcome than others.

Not that anyone except the mentally ill and certain categories of criminals was refused entry. But it was no secret that the Yishuv would have preferred to see larger numbers of young, healthy, well-educated, highly motivated, and cultured immigrants. Such immigrants were undoubtedly better equipped to contribute to the growth and strength of the new country. They also were supposed to be more likely to perpetuate the pioneering élan that had brought Israel to where it was when independence dawned. They also were more likely to be Ashkenazi Jews.

With American Jews unwilling, and Russian Jews unable, to go to Israel, the displaced persons camps in Germany were the only source of significant numbers of Ashkenazi immigrants. The problem was that most Ashkenazis who had ambitious visions and talents, or merely an aggressive entrepreneurial spirit, looked toward greener pastures than the Jewish state could offer. (Among these were some 30,000 displaced persons who remained in Germany and became quite prosperous there, many by less than admirable methods.) Another drawback, in terms of social Darwinism, was the process of negative selection that took place in the DP camps: the less capable, the older, and the more feeble were the most likely to choose to go to Israel. After all, they had little chance of being admitted by any other country.

The overwhelming mass of new immigrants—overwhelming

in more than one sense—came from an unexpected source:
Arab countries. Though Zionism had never struck strong roots
there, the hostility of the Arab states toward Israel created an
atmosphere of insecurity and real danger among their Jewish
inhabitants, turning them into Zionists overnight, as it were.

The Zionist movement had never paid much attention to
these Oriental Jews, as they were known. Occasionally, the
wretched condition of Moroccan or Persian Jews was mentioned in a speech. And Herzl had wanted to have some Oriental Jews in colorful costumes on the dais of the Second Zionist
Congress, mainly for theatrical effect. But that was the extent
of it. As a distinctly Europocentric movement, Zionism did not
consider the Jews living in Moslem countries a source of Zionist potential. (After World War II, Zionist emissaries did work in
Moslem countries, mainly in Iraq and Morocco.)

On the contrary, as far back as 1891, in his report "Truth
from the Land of Israel," Ahad Haam remarked in a footnote:
"Many people in Palestine think that the Yemenites are not
physically strong enough for hard work, and their level of culture and their mentality are so different from ours that the
question inevitably presents itself whether an increase in their
number would not change the whole character of the settlement and whether the change will be for the better." In the
1950s, that question did "inevitably"—and with dramatically
amplified intensity—present itself to Israel, which found itself
dealing with masses of newcomers from many Moslem countries, not just with a small number of Yemenite immigrants.
(As it happened, virtually the entire Jewish population of
Yemen wound up coming to Israel.)

It was not so much a question of the Oriental Jews' ability to
work hard, but rather of their "mentality" and the cultural gap
that separated them from the European immigrant, the recent
as well as the old-timer. Since Israel had no choice but to accept
them, the answer was thought to lie in an effort to "bring them
into the twentieth century" by acculturating them to the European values and style Zionism had always professed. It was not
quite the mission Max Nordau had in mind when he declared,

in his speech at the First Zionist Congress, that it was "our intention to come to Palestine as bearers of civilization and to push the moral borders of Europe up to the Euphrates." Nordau never foresaw the need to "civilize" Oriental Jews. Nor did Herzl. Oriental Jews were conspicuously absent among the prototypes populating his novel *Altneuland*.

Whether such acculturation was ever a realistic possibility is a question that cannot be answered. But the methods used to absorb the masses of immigrants from Moslem countries, now imprecisely but flatteringly called Sephardim, nullified whatever chance there might have been. Placing them in a position of dependence that destroyed their self-esteem and sense of self-reliance did not help either.

The absorption apparatus regarded the newcomers as "development fodder" in the service of the country's needs. In true, callous bureaucratic fashion, the preponderantly Ashkenazi authorities were not prepared to countenance any manifestation of personal choice on the part of their wards, which the newcomers were for all practical purposes. Since security considerations demanded that strings of agricultural villages be founded along the borders and in areas vacated by Arabs, that is where the new immigrants were sent—despite the obvious fact that they had no experience or interest in agriculture. They would have to learn. After all, other immigrants before them had had to adapt to new occupations. (Quite a few moshavim—cooperative villages—are still learning in the sense that they are still economically unable to stand on their own feet. On the other hand, many kibbutzim are still deeply in debt, too.)

The Oriental Jews would also have to learn how to part with their old cultural patterns. They were actually expected to do so eagerly. It was generally believed that even the modest amenities Israel had to offer were superior to what they had had in the "old country," to say nothing of the higher cultural level of Israel. (In fund-raising campaigns especially, much was made of Moroccan Jews who were presented as cave dwellers from the Atlas Mountains.)

The protests of the new-baked Israelis were ascribed to the well-known immigrant syndrome of claiming that "back home" the family had been well off and lived in a mansion. (The syndrome now haunts the Palestinian refugees, most of whom have never seen the homes they continue to claim as theirs.) In most cases, this was, indeed, a factor. But there was no denying that the immigrants had felt at home in the old country; in their new surroundings, they did not. In any case, they preferred living in the cities, which is where most of them eventually ended up.

The rapid settlement of large groups of immigrants necessitated their concentration in locations established according to a master plan of sorts. In these locations, they had hardly any opportunity to mix with the old Yishuv, or even with newcomers of European background, and thus absorb Western culture by osmosis, so to speak. But even if that opportunity had existed, culture shock would probably have made the Sephardim unreceptive, the more so as their resentment of the Ashkenazim kept growing. Not that the latter were eager to invite them into their living rooms. Absorption was a matter the Ashkenazim thought should be left to the proper authorities.

This was equally true in rural areas and planned development towns as it was in housing developments built in or near the major cities. In the latter, integration was hindered by the policy of making one type of housing available to immigrants from Arabic countries and another to those of European background, who were deemed to be entitled to better housing irrespective of their educational level. It was a form of culture-based discrimination, and it was rigidly applied. (The Foreign Ministry, for example, was unable to persuade the housing authorities to provide a better type of housing to André Semama, the Israeli correspondent of the prestigious Paris newspaper *Le Monde;* as an immigrant from Tunisia, Semama was, according to the rules, required to live in the inferior housing reserved for immigrants from North Africa.)

To make matters worse, lack of qualifications forced the new

161

immigrants into the lowest paid and least desirable occupations. At the beginning, employment mainly existed in public works and forestation. Over time, employment opportunities also opened up in the growing—some would say wildly proliferating—bureaucratic apparatus, the lower echelons of which have since been preponderantly occupied by Sephardim.

The absorption authorities considered all this as only natural. Objectively, there was not much hope that the first generation of immigrants would be able to adapt to a new way of life. They would thus have to be sacrificed, like the desert generation that left Egyptian slavery with Moses. The next generation would be different. It was, but not in the way the social engineers of Israel envisaged.

In the first decades after independence, reverence for "primitive" cultures and respect for desert ecology had not yet become entrenched in Israeli society. Deserts were to be transformed into blossoming stretches of cultivated land, and the Oriental Jews into a kind of darker-skinned European. They might not necessarily listen to Bach and Beethoven (preferable as this might be to their habit of swamping their neighborhoods with high-volume broadcasts of Arabic music), but they would be literate, clean, respectful of other people's privacy and property. In short, they would behave like "civilized" people.

In both areas—reclaiming the desert and reculturalizing the Sephardim—Israel's achievement fell well short of its aims. The Negev Desert remains largely undeveloped to this day, and the cultural gap between Israelis of European descent and those from Arabic backgrounds still persists. The gap has been narrowed by the movement of the Israel-born generation of both groups toward a common center that now characterizes the Israeli man and woman in the street, the cultural amalgam of which is most successfully manifest in the emergence of a genuine Israeli pop music. It is a process that some decry, not entirely without reason, as Levantinization.

The Sephardim, who now make up a bit more than half of the population, are still heavily underrepresented, not only in government, but also in higher education (both as students and teachers), science, technology, and the arts and letters. Ashkenazim are dominant in the upper echelons of the larger enterprises, the banks, financial institutions, and the officer corps, and they dominate the list of recipients of the Israel Prize, which is given every year to outstanding personalities in the arts, sciences, and letters.

In short, Sephardim constitute an underclass that has become known as the "Second Israel." Not surprisingly, they don't like it. However, when the first stirrings of Sephardi dissatisfaction with their inferior status emerged (and sometimes burst) onto the purportedly egalitarian Israeli social scene, the "old" Yishuv reacted with incredulity and surprise at their apparent lack of gratitude.

It took nearly three decades for Israel's leadership to recognize that it had mishandled the absorption of the immigrants from Moslem countries. One of the first signs that the message was getting through came in 1976, when the then Minister of Education, Aharon Yadlin, introduced a program designed to integrate the traditions of Oriental Jews into the high school curriculum. As Yadlin himself pointed out, the proposal amounted to an admission that regarding the immigrants from Arabic countries who streamed into Israel in the 1950s as a "generation of the desert" that had to be written off was a "fundamental sin which caused a spiritual crisis for them." Even so, one suspects that the Labor Party's rather sudden surrender to the tenets of cultural equivalency was motivated more by electoral considerations than by genuine respect for the culture of Jews from Arabic countries. (Mr. Yadlin, for one, was a member of a kibbutz, and kibbutzim were notorious for considering Oriental immigrants to be largely unassimilable to their standards.)

The doubts raised by Ahad Haam in 1891 with regard to the impact an influx of Oriental Jews would have on the Yishuv may have still been in the air in 1976, but there was no longer anything that could be done about them. By then, it was clear that, in the absence of any reasonable hope for massive immigration by Ashkenazi Jews, the Sephardim and their native-born descendants would soon constitute a majority of Israel's inhabitants—and voters.

As the largest player in a political system in which financial resources and patronage were distributed strictly according to the relative strength of each party, the ruling Labor Party enjoyed a huge advantage in wooing the majority-to-be. Labor would eventually lose the support of the Sephardim as they developed an agenda of their own in the mid-1970s; but in the '50s and '60s, Labor enjoyed their staunch loyalty. And no wonder. Not only did the highly politicized, Labor-controlled absorption machinery steer the new immigrants toward Labor, but the Sephardim revered Ben-Gurion as a contemporary patriarch. In addition, the masses of new immigrants fitted well into the Labor movement's ideological scheme of things.

Back in 1925, in an article bearing the revealing title "The National Mission of the Working Class," Ben-Gurion had played a variation on a Marxist theme and tried to prove that the interests of Zionism and those of the working class were one and the same. By the 1950s, his—and his party's—ideology had evolved into what was known as *mamlakhtiut*, a Hebrew term coined by Ben-Gurion for his brand of statism. *Mamlakhtiut* had nothing to do with socialism. Though the etymological root of the word is in *melekh*, Hebrew for "king," dictatorship was never part of Ben-Gurion's political lexicon, least of all the dictatorship of the proletariat. (He held the Soviet system in abhorrence.) Ben-Gurion was an undogmatic social democrat who relied on democratic methods, or what was accepted as such in Israel, to keep his party (and himself) in power. In any case, in Labor's eyes, the unpropertied newcomers were part of the proletariat, a group whose interests—along with those of the state—would be best served by *mamlakhtiut*. If it happened that the Sephardi immigrants displayed no trace of the working-class consciousness called for in Labor's script for *mamlakhtiut*, there were institutions and organizations that could instill in them the proper values.

Perhaps the most important institution in this respect was the Israel Confederation of Labor, the Histadrut. The Histadrut was the first Israeli institution to give the new immigrant something tangible: in this case, a membership card. Induction into the Histadrut was as standard a part of the processing routine for newcomers as the X-ray screening for tuberculosis; it was something everyone had to undergo. (It did not occur to anyone inside or outside the reception camps to raise the question of whether this obligatory induction violated the immigrants' rights.)

The Histadrut card—a small red booklet with the member's picture on it—was a passport to employment. (It also provided health insurance.) However, just as a real passport is necessary for travel abroad but in itself does not guarantee the voyage, so the Histadrut card alone could not guarantee work; it was only a prerequisite for finding it. Connections—*protekzia* in Hebrew slang—were, of course, far more valuable. (They seem to be so in every society and at every level.) In this, the Ashkenazi immigrants had another clear advantage over the Sephardim: they could turn to relatives, friends, or friends of friends who had preceded them to Israel and gained positions of influence.

In any case, the Histadrut had always been more interested in creating new job opportunities than in pushing a particular social agenda that might conflict with Israel's national economic interests. Thus, it did not object when the Labor-led government decided, in effect, to sacrifice Israel's vaunted egalitarianism on the altar of economic development. In the 1960s, in an effort to attract the kind of private capital and entrepreneurial verve that it felt the economy needed, the government embarked on a policy of favoritism toward private enterprise—a policy that included low-interest loans that, in conditions of constant inflation, amounted to virtual giveaways. The inevitable outcome of such policies was even greater social differentiation—the well-connected Ashkenazim prospered, while the "alien" Sephardim languished.

As a result, the Israeli social pyramid—the normalization of which had been one of Zionism's most cherished aims—increasingly came to resemble those found in European countries. It had its peculiarities, of course: its lowest stratum was almost exclusively made up of immigrants from Moslem countries and their descendants, while its upper class was almost exclusively composed of nouveau riche Ashkenazim.

The same was true of Israel's political culture. In its political mores, Israel could rightly claim to be fundamentally no different, for better or for worse, than most other more or less enlightened societies. Israeli governments routinely denied what proved to be facts, lied when they felt the truth would harm the country's interests, covered up transgressions or mishaps of its agents—in short, behaved much like any other government.

It could, of course, be argued that the government would have done none of these things had Israel not been forced to live, from day one of its independence, in a constant state of war with the Arabs. But that presupposes a disregard of the philosophic fundaments of the nation-state and its government —a disregard that, in Martin Buber's words, is based on the "Occidental dualism that sanctions the splitting off of man's being into two realms, each existing in its own right and independent of the other: the truth of the spirit and the reality of life." The "reality of life" demands that, in statecraft, the *raison d'état*—that is, the state's interest as understood by those called upon to defend it—must prevail over moral considerations, over the "truth of the spirit."

Ben-Gurion, whom many Jews considered a kind of philosopher-king, was by no means free of that dualism. Indeed, the opposite would have been surprising. Thus it was Ben-Gurion who, in the wake of a 1953 Israeli army raid on the Jordanian village of Kibya, in which a greater than expected number of civilians were killed, insisted that the government issue a statement to the effect that the attack had not been mounted by the Israeli army, but by unsanctioned border settlers enraged by terrorist attacks from across the Jordanian frontier. (Like their counterparts in other countries, the Israeli military habitually present the supervisory civilian authorities with plans for military actions that appear to be within reasonable bounds, which they plan beforehand to breach, planning even the excuses for the "inevitable" escalation. In this respect, too, Israel appears to be a normal state.)

Since 1953, many more serious scandals have rocked Israel, to say nothing of the problems, moral as well as practical, that have malignantly grown out of the Israeli administration of the West Bank and the Gaza Strip. Often, it was not so much the failure or misdeeds of any arm of government but, just as happens in other democratic countries, the government's attempt to cover them up that caused the uproar. And it is, perhaps, a fitting irony that Ben-Gurion's final resignation from government in 1963 was prompted by the refusal of the majority of his Cabinet to accede to his demand that a judicial committee investigate the role played by former Defense Minister Pinhas Lavon in an ill-conceived and ill-fated plan to sow discord between the United States and Egypt by bombing American institutions in Cairo. The Labor leadership—except for a few like Moshe Dayan who reluctantly followed Ben-Gurion into the political wilderness—would not countenance their revered elder statesman's singular lapse into the "ethics of conscience." The "ethics of responsibility" prevailed, and justice was not done, as it seldom is in such cases—with good reason, as the pragmatists of realpolitik will tell you.

Inasmuch as national normalization was concerned, Zionism had achieved its goal. The Jews had a state of their own, a state in which they were a majority, a state that was as independent as a small—in some respects Third World—country could hope to be. There was now a framework in which the Jewish people could exercise sovereignty—and be responsible for their own deeds.

In the process, however, Israel proved to be more a state for the Jews than a Jewish state. But then Zionism had never had a clear-cut idea of what the Jewish content of the state would or should be. For almost two decades, Israel hunkered down to face the foreign, political, and social challenges as best as it could. It did so without ideological reference to Zionism or a historical-religious mission—until, that is, its victory in the Six Day War of 1967 induced it to change its outlook.

IX

1967

On May 15, 1967, Israel celebrated its nineteenth independence day. To mark the occasion, the Israel Defense Forces
mounted a military show in the stadium of the western campus
of the Hebrew University in Jerusalem. It was a modest substitute for the parade that could not be held in Jerusalem: both
sides of the divided city, the Israeli and the Jordanian, had been
virtually demilitarized under the armistice agreement signed by
the two countries in 1949.

The celebration was presided over by Prime Minister Levi
Eshkol. Soon after it got under way, an unusual amount of com-
ings and goings by military officers was noticeable in the section reserved for VIP's. The Chief of Staff, Major General
Yitzhak Rabin, was seen leaving his seat, only to come back
after a while. Evidently, some important information of a military nature was being conveyed to the Prime Minister in an
impromptu tête-à-tête. No announcements were made, however, and the show went on.

The next day the public learned that President Gamal Abdel

Nasser of Egypt had moved a large number of troops into the Sinai Peninsula and unleashed not his warriors but a barrage of bellicose statements announcing the impending destruction of Israel. The threat was not taken too seriously by Israel. It had heard the tune before blaring from Arabic radio stations to the accompaniment of martial music. Nevertheless, the Israeli government thought it wise to call up a small number of reservists, just in case.

For the next three weeks, President Nasser and his Arab allies, who included for the first time King Hussein of Jordan, continued to escalate the war tension and hysteria. Nasser closed the Strait of Tiran, which controls the entrance to the gulf of Aqaba, and thus access to the Israeli port of Eilat. He also dismissed the United Nations Emergency Force that had been stationed in the Sinai since 1956 to ensure the freedom of navigation in the narrow gulf as well as to prevent infiltration of terrorists across the border between Israel and Egypt. In one fell swoop, all the advantages Israel had gained from its short-lived conquest of Sinai in 1956 were wiped out.

It was back to square one: as in 1948, Israel had to be prepared for a war on three fronts, with other Arab nations helping the three front-line states: Egypt, Syria, and Jordan. Still, the Israeli military were confident that their armed forces would prevail. Their plans were ready. They simply needed some element of surprise that would allow them to launch Israel's best opening war gambit: the pre-emptive strike—though politically hazardous, the best defense for a country that cannot sustain a long period of full mobilization. The flamboyant commander of the Israeli air force, Ezer Weizman, embodied Israel's confidence, voicing the opinion that it was still more dangerous to be an Egyptian combat pilot than a resident of Tel Aviv, which is only a few minutes' flying time from the nearest Egyptian air base.

Though the military were restless, the government thought it wise to give diplomacy a chance, if for no other reason than to provide an alibi for itself and a surprise element for the armed

170

forces. Thus ensued three weeks of waiting for the Godot of international action to make President Nasser backtrack, three weeks during which the people of Israel felt the whole heavy weight of their isolation.

Instead of defying Nasser's illegal blockade of the Strait of Tiran, the maritime nations warned their ships away from the "potential war area." Instead of putting pressure on Egypt, the countries Israel approached for help urged it not to shoot first. Although Nasser had put a knife to Israel's throat, the blade had not yet drawn blood, there was no cut.

Not much trust could be placed in the Tripartite Declaration of 1950, under which the United States, Britain, and France had guaranteed Israel's existence, and even less in the "understandings" and "expectations" enshrined in a series of mealy-mouthed diplomatic documents that had been drafted as a reward for Israel's withdrawal from the Sinai in 1956. Too many Israelis remembered that Czechoslovakia had received even firmer guarantees from France and Britain after its territory was truncated at the Munich Conference of 1938.

The absence of a charismatic leader at the head of the country undoubtedly contributed to the atmosphere of tense expectation, laced with a dose of gloom, that hung like a pall over Israel. To say that is not to fault the policy of Mr. Eshkol. He was a good no-nonsense pragmatic Prime Minister. But the country wanted a strong leader. Thus, to bolster Israel's confidence—or, at least, to alleviate the pangs of uncertainty that had gripped the population—a government of national unity was established, and General Moshe Dayan, an authentic Israeli hero, was appointed Minister of Defense.

At long last, on June 5, Israel struck. After six days of fighting on all three fronts—King Hussein of Jordan having entered the war in spite of Israel's pleas that he stay out—the country that President Nasser had claimed was doomed to be destroyed ended up controlling the Gaza Strip, the entire Sinai Peninsula, the Golan Heights, and all the territory of Eretz Israel east to the Jordan River.

The armed forces of Egypt, Jordan, and Syria had suffered a shattering defeat. Ezer Weizman had been right. The civilian population of Tel Aviv suffered no losses. (As it turned out, the losses among Egyptian pilots were pretty small, too, but only because 391 of their planes had been destroyed on the ground.)

The dark weeks of worrisome uncertainty now gave way to a surging sense of relief at being saved from a fate too dire to imagine. More significantly, it led to the discovery of new dimensions of geographic space and geopolitical strength. A much wider gate seemed to open on a new, brighter, greater vision of the Jewish state.

Indeed, a whole new world opened up to the population. The majority of Israelis had never stood before the Western Wall, the remnant of the Solomonic Temple that had for centuries been a potent religious-national symbol. Moshe Dayan, whom nobody could accuse of being religious in any sense, made haste to appear at the Wall, his head conveniently covered by a combat helmet. Following the practice of the pious (among whom he surely could not be counted), he placed between the stones of the ancient wall a small rolled-up piece of paper on which he wrote the wish he wanted the Almighty to fulfill: Peace.

Another powerful symbol, Masada, the mountaintop fortress built by King Herod, where in 74 C.E. the Zealots made their last stand against the Roman legions, could now be easily reached from Jerusalem through a road running south to the Dead Sea and then along its western shore. Before the Six Day War, a roundabout route had been required. The same was true for access to Kibbutz Ein Gedi, which sits on the site of a rich spring of water where, according to the Bible, young David hid before the wrath of King Saul.

Shorter routes were also now open from Jerusalem to the northern part of the Jordan valley, which had been part of Israel before 1967, and to Beersheba via Hebron, the city where, according to tradition, Abraham was buried. Jerusalem, which before perched on the tip of a narrow corridor thrust out from the rest of the country like a beggar's arm, now occupied a more central location, just as it had in Biblical times.

Israelis quickly discovered the delights of scuba diving in the waters, rich in colorful fish, along the western shore of the Gulf of Aqaba. Many were attracted to the austere beauty of the Sinai Desert and the romantic lore of the Bedouins. Nor did the country disdain the economic boon bestowed on it by the oil fields of El Tur. Dreams of the exploitation of the mineral wealth of the Sinai were condensed, like elusive vapors, in reams of technical studies. And plans were made for military bases as well as urban and rural settlement in those areas the government believed would eventually be officially incorporated into Israel.

Political rhetoric became increasingly laced with the heady word "never." There would never be a repetition of Masada. Jerusalem would never again be a divided city. Indeed, it would now be an even more eternal capital of Israel than when that claim was made for the western half of the city alone. At his very first visit to the conquered Western Wall, Moshe Dayan declared: "We have returned to the holiest of our sites, and will never again be separated from it."

The specter of destruction that Israel's fighters had so forcefully banished could only serve to reinforce the determination that another Holocaust would never again be allowed to threaten the Jewish people. The Six Day War appeared as the ultimate proof—if, indeed, proof was needed—that powerlessness invites catastrophe, while power can prevent it, indeed turn tragedy into triumph.

It was pleasing to Jews to see the country's geographic reach enlarged by the 23,622 square miles of the Sinai peninsula, an area roughly three times the size of Israel before the Six Day War. In addition, Israel gained control of 2,854 square miles of territory in the West Bank, the Golan Heights, and the Gaza Strip. It also "inherited" over a million Palestinian Arabs.

The State of Israel no longer looked like a strangely shaped entity carved out of something larger. It appeared more like a respectable body of land solidly (so it seemed) implanted on the geopolitical map of the Middle East. Little attention was paid to the fact that not a single country in the world was prepared to entertain the idea that Israel's aggrandizement, even if it did come as a result of miscalculated Arab belligerence, was anything more than temporary.

The Israelis were at pains to point out that the West Bank was legally no man's land. Jordan's annexation of the territory in 1948, when the U.N. partition plan collapsed because of Arab opposition, had not gained international recognition, except by Britain and Pakistan. Authorities in international law were quoted to the effect that the Sinai Peninsula had become Egyptian territory only in 1906, and that only as a result of Britain's imperialist designs on Turkish territory. In other words, the Sinai was not an organic part of Egypt but part of the dismembered Ottoman Empire, as was Palestine. So if Palestine could be returned to the Jews, why not part of the Sinai? That the era of unilateral border changes had ended with the ratification of the United Nations Charter was brushed away by the Israelis as so much pious verbiage. Now that, at long last, the Jewish people had gained military power, they were not ready to accept that the spoils would not go to the victor.

Archeologists, the unwitting witnesses to historical claims, could point to ancient Jewish settlements on the Golan Heights and on the island of Tiran at the entrance to the Gulf of Aqaba. Gaza was clearly part of Eretz Israel as was the West Bank, soon to become known as Judea and Samaria in Israeli nomenclature.

Not that the Israeli government was unaware that its claims lacked international recognition and support, even from its closest friend, the United States. It was hoped, especially in the euphoric years between 1967 and 1973, that time would exercise its proverbial healing genius, and the changes would become accepted. After all, no one any longer considered the tortuous borders drawn in the 1947 United Nations Palestine Partition Plan to be a viable alternative to the 1949 Armistice Line. Thus it was believed that, as had been the case with the Partition borders, the memory of the Armistice Line (known as

174

the "Green Line" because it was drawn in that color on the maps attached to the Armistice Agreements) would be buried in the archives. (On newly published Israeli maps, the Green Line was thinned down into near invisibility or deleted entirely, as if in answer to Arab maps that did not show the State of Israel.)

Until the withdrawal from the Sinai in compliance with the 1979 peace treaty with Egypt, Israel was able to fend off all challenges to its territorial conquests. It may be able to do so a bit longer with regard to the West Bank, the Gaza Strip, and the Golan Heights—to say nothing of the unification of Jerusalem, which Israel is determined never to relinquish. (Will this prove to be another of the illusory "nevers"?) Nevertheless, the nation's psyche has not found it easy to digest the fruits of its 1967 victory.

Suddenly Zionism had delivered what few thought it would ever be able to do. Not only a Jewish state but the whole of Eretz Israel was in Jewish hands. (By 1967, even the heirs and followers of Jabotinsky had relinquished the Jewish claim to the territory east of the Jordan River, although the movement's anthem still sings of two banks of the Jordan, both of which are "ours.")

Israel never had any intention of conquering the West Bank. On the contrary, it sent King Hussein urgent appeals through the United Nations and the United States, asking him to keep out of the war. Only when these appeals went unheeded did Israel launch a counterattack. And in the euphoria of victory, the fortuitous circumstances that led to the seizure of the West Bank were dismissed as inconsequential—or adduced as proof that, indeed, the ways of the Lord were inscrutable.

The creation of *Eretz Yisrael Shlema*—the "Whole Land of Israel"—represented the ultimate vindication of the Zionist vision of modern Jewish history. And now that the land was "whole"—in Hebrew, *shalem* also carries the connotation of being at peace with oneself—it was time for the Jewish people also to become "whole" in the Zionist sense. In other words, it was time for them to put an end to their dispersal. It was time for them not merely to heed the call of the new physical frontier but to fulfill their destiny as posited in Zionist theology.

But history stubbornly repeated itself, and not in the way the Zionists would have wished. The Jewish diaspora of Western Europe and America remained deaf to the call. All over the world, thousands of young Jews had volunteered to fight when Israel seemed in mortal danger in the three weeks before June 5, 1967. But few were ready to come and live in the country for which they had been ready to die. The anguished question "Where are you?" that Chaim Weizmann had flung at the Jewish people on the morrow of the formal establishment of a Jewish national home in 1920 remained unanswered in 1967.

That's not to say diaspora Jewry wasn't filled with enthusiasm for the newly acquired status of Israel. This time, it was felt, Israel had not only gained a new lease on life, it had earned a patent of permanence. From the safety provided by geographic remoteness, many Jewish leaders—including the Lubavicher Rebbe, who had never so much as visited Israel—exhorted Jerusalem not to yield an inch of Eretz Israel. The general sentiment was as sanguine as the one expressed by the American newspaper that headlined its front-page report on Israel's victory, "This Time It's for Keeps."

But this enthusiasm, which was matched by an unprecedented swell of donations from Jews throughout the diaspora (and particularly in America), did not beget a notable desire on the part of diaspora Jews (including the avowed Zionists among them) to pull up the stakes of comfort and affluence and go fulfill a destiny that, obviously, was less manifest than most Israelis would have liked it to be. Diaspora Jewry had (and has) an agenda of its own, one that intersects with that of Israel but is not necessarily congruent with it.

The only part of the diaspora where the challenge inherent in the emergence of a "Greater Israel" after the Six Day War led to a revival of Zionist fervor was perhaps the least likely place: in the Soviet Union. The reason may well lie in the anachronisti-

cally anomalous situation of Russian Jewry, a situation not encountered today by any other Jewish diaspora community. (Significant changes are under way for Russian Jewry as a result of
the accession to power of Mikhail Gorbachev. And if the trend
continues, there may eventually be a viable diaspora in Russia,
too.)

In accordance with the Soviet doctrine of nationalities, the
Jews of Russia have long been officially regarded as one of the
ethnic groups that populate the fifteen republics and twenty
autonomous regions that make up the Union of Soviet Socialist
Republics. But unlike other groups, Jewish national identity has
no geographically defined area in which it can be exercised.

Formally, Biro-Bidjan, an area bordering Manchuria, is the official Jewish Autonomous Oblast from which Jewish deputies
are elected to the Supreme Soviet. (It even has its own version
of a "Law of Return," allowing foreign Jews to settle there—
subject to permission by Moscow, of course.) In reality, only
7,000 to 8,000 Jews live there—a small minority in their
"own" territory. They constitute an even less significant minority among the totality of Soviet Jews, who are estimated by
Western Jewish demographers to number 2,620,000. (A 1985 Soviet census listed 1,700,000 Soviet citizens of Jewish nationality.)

The vast majority of Soviet Jews have never looked to Biro-
Bidjan as the Jewish homeland within the Soviet Union that the
authorities meant it to be when the Autonomous Oblast was
established in 1928. In consequence, they find themselves in
limbo, forced by law to declare a Jewish nationality that is
meaningless in the political context of the Soviet Union, that is
not expressed in any kind of territorial or even cultural autonomy (Yiddish culture, once flourishing, is all but extinct), and
that serves only to single them out, as a rule to their disadvantage.

The majority of Soviet Jewry seems resigned to its situation.
Although virtually no Jews can be found in the higher echelons
of government, in the Party hierarchy, or in administrative

posts that carry any degree of decision-making power, Jews are present in disproportionately high numbers in good jobs in civilian industry, trade, science, education, health services, and the arts—all this in spite of the restrictive admission policies of institutes of higher learning in the Soviet Union.

By Soviet yardsticks, Jews enjoy a comfortable standard of living. It is therefore not surprising that the majority of them do not think of leaving the Soviet Union, even though until recently the social barometer predicted little sunshine, and anti-Semitism, though officially outlawed, continues to sprout in various forms from the depths of a Russian national psyche long nurtured on the fare of Jew-baiting.

As is the case among their brethren of the Western diaspora, the Soviet Jewish population is being eroded by a tendency toward mixed marriages. But unlike in Western countries, no internal Jewish forces are at work in the Soviet Union to stem the tide, or at least put communal fingers into the assimilatory dike.

Ironically, it is the Soviet system itself that places obstacles in the way of those Soviet Jews who might want to assimilate. Not only does the system force Jews into the strait jacket of a meaningless Jewish nationality, it also makes it difficult for the offspring of mixed marriages to efface their Jewish ancestry: since 1983, identity cards have listed the nationality of both parents. It seems that it is not so much the Jews who insist on keeping a Jewish identity, but the goyim who desire to set them apart from the Russians.

It is hard to understand why the Soviet authorities would want to make it more difficult for their Jews to fuse into Russian nationality. True, the coexistence under Communism of various distinct national groups is a sacred tenet of Leninism, but its application to the Jews is the reason why of all the countries in the world the Soviet Union alone still has a "Jewish problem." It makes one wonder whether in insisting on a distinct national identification for its Jewish citizens, who enjoy (in official Soviet cant) full rights and an equal footing with all the other ethnic groups, the Soviets are really guided only by the desire to preserve intact the ideological foundations of the Soviet state or whether this insistence is not at least equally conditioned by atavistic anti-Semitic reflexes.

Be that as it may, a solid core of Russian Jews have long regarded as intolerable the identity-card Jewishness forced upon them by the Soviet system. They could not hope to create a framework in which to exercise their natural right of (and headstrong penchant for) particularism. The existing synagogues were not permitted to serve as a fulcrum and a focus for Jewish communal life. (Until recently the Moscow synagogue played this role only once a year, during the celebration of Simhat Torah, the feast of the Rejoicing in the Law; for the rest of the year, it was but a showcase intended to impress the outside world with the tolerance of Judaism by a constitutionally atheist regime.)

A Soviet Jew could thus not cultivate a true national, cultural, or religious Jewish identity without running afoul of the Soviet system. It was the unwillingness to live in a void of national identity that gave birth to a renewed yearning for Zion among Soviet Jews. And it was the "miraculous" victory of Israel in the Six Day War that brought the yearning forcefully into the open and into a fierce conflict with the Soviet regime.

To many Soviet Jews, the 1967 war signified a turn in Jewish history, as it did to most Israelis and to diaspora Jewish Jewry as a whole. The event appeared to prove that, for once, the circle of recurrent catastrophes had been broken. The foreshadowed destruction of the Jewish state—with the apocalyptic consequences such a disaster would have brought upon Jewry—was, through a magnificent feat of Jewish arms, transformed into a ringing affirmation of the Zionist vision. (Whether, objectively, a catastrophe was actually in the offing is entirely beside the point.)

In the hearts of Russian Jews, Israel's victory reverberated even more resoundingly since it was achieved in the teeth of Soviet hostility. The argument that to be authentically Jewish one has to live in Israel thus assumed for Soviet Jews an unprecedented cogency and attraction.

How many Soviet Jews reached that conclusion out of deep conviction is impossible to establish. What is certain is that the number of aliyah activists was small. Numbers, however, do not count. What counted was the heroic disregard for their personal fate that led the activists into a courageous confrontation with the Soviet authorities.

The gates to emigration would probably have remained closed had not the authorities found themselves enmeshed in a struggle with a group of determined people whose idealism and readiness for self-sacrifice, however misguided it may have appeared in Soviet eyes, they grudgingly acknowledged. International pressure, too, was effective, mainly in periods when the Soviet Union felt it would serve its interests to appear conciliatory on human-rights issues. As a result, since the fall of 1968, close to 270,000 Jews have been able to leave the Soviet Union with Israeli immigration visas stamped in their one-way passports. (Some 350,000 more are believed to have applied for Israeli visas, and since Gorbachev came to power close to 40,000 Jews have been allowed to leave.)

However, the Russian Zionist flame began to falter a few years after it was miraculously kindled by the determined struggle of the aliyah activists. From the mid-1970s on, Russian Jewish emigrants officially headed for Israel began, in growing numbers, to drop out along the way (in Vienna) to pursue the American dream rather than seek salvation on Jewish soil. They took advantage of being recognized by the United States as refugees, and thus enjoying preferential processing of their immigration applications. (The United States might have rendered a better service to Israel if such privileges had been extended to Palestinian refugees of the Gaza Strip instead.)

By the end of 1986, only about half of the Jews who had left the Soviet Union were living in Israel. Most of the other half had never even set foot there. (A few did try life in Israel first, but found it not to their taste, while a small number succeeded in leaving the Soviet Union without having to go the tortuous route of ostensible reunification with sometimes remote relatives in Israel.)

As was the case with other diaspora communities, for Russian Jews an emotional or sentimental attachment to the Jewish state did not necessarily translate into the will to make Israel their home. In that respect, at least, Russian Jews were no different from other Jews who preferred to exchange an uncomfortable diaspora for a more promising one. This choice undoubtedly further biased the Soviet authorities against Jewish emigration. The "Soviet Man" could bring himself to understand that a Jew might like to live in a Jewish state, even a "retrograde capitalist" Jewish state. But it did not sit well with him that Jews would turn their back on the Soviet Fatherland merely for a better material life.

Again, Zionism suffered defeat. But it did not admit it. Indeed, Israel continued its exertions on behalf of Russian Jewry, especially the "Prisoners of Zion," the activists who had paid for their idealism by being banished to the Gulag. By February 1988, all were out of prison and elatedly embraced in Israel, together with a number of well-known refuseniks who had been able to escape the brutal arm of Soviet justice.

There was no escaping, however, from the recognition that the "Exiles" in their overwhelming majority refused to be ingathered. Yet to this day the Zionist movement continues to pursue this elusive aim. In this, it is spurred on more by ideological reflex than by any expectation that the effort will bear fruit. In any case, any hope Israel may have harbored that a mass influx of new immigrants would dramatically strengthen its demographic position in the West Bank crumbled before the determination of diaspora Jewry to stay where it was.

Still, the state was in place, and after the 1967 victory apparently more securely so than ever. With the Ingathering of the Exiles virtually postponed sine die, the only task left to Zionism (in theory, at least) was the transformation of Israel into a model state in which the light of social equity, justice, and public morality would burn as brightly as the fires of a lighthouse, a lighthouse that might even help the errant peoples of the world find their way to the right path.

This had always been the ambition of the founding fathers of Zionism. It had also been at the back of the minds of the usually otherwise engaged Old Zionist Guard, which led the country until the 1970s. Realizing that ambition, however, would have required a moral commitment that is rarely, if ever, found among people who choose politics as a vocation. Thus, it is hardly surprising that Israeli politicians, like their counterparts elsewhere, succumbed to the blandishments of power, and did so without regrets.

It was this abandonment of any moral mission that lay at the root of the anguished question "What happened to the dream?" asked by Jewish intellectuals in Israel and the diaspora. It had always been a naive dream, to be sure, but during the struggle for the creation of the state it tallied with reality. After 1967, however, it became glaringly apparent that Israel was not, in the words of former President Ephraim Katzir, "the best country the Jewish people could dream of"—the Jewish people of today, that is, with all their virtues and shortcomings, not the formidable dreamers Jewry had produced in the past.

The seeds of this perhaps inevitable change were sown before 1967. After an initial spell of harsh but equalizing austerity, all dreams of creating a more just society evaporated in the heat of the inevitable race toward industrialization and consumerism. The vaunted egalitarianism of Israeli society was turned into a myth.

The same fate befell the original Sabras. In their pristine patriotism, their remoteness from Jewish tradition, their earthy attachment to the native soil, their imperviousness to material goods, the Sabras had been like the Guardians of Plato's Republic, ready to devote their "strength, power, and courage to the good of the society." They were also the quintessential authentic native "New Jews," and they happened to be Ashkenazi. But by the beginning of the 1960s, Israel's self-image was no longer shaped by the mystique of the Sabra and the kibbutz pioneer. In a society heavily burdened with the task of absorbing vast numbers of newcomers (particularly those from Moslem countries), economic development, and increasingly more sophisticated and costly defense requirements, the kibbutz and the original Sabra were no longer in the forefront of the struggle for Israel's major national objectives.

The kibbutz was too elitist an institution to play a significant role in the absorption of immigrants, and there were few agricultural frontiers the movement cared to conquer. The military effort, in which the Sabra had played such a signal and symbolic role in the days of the Palmach, was now, by necessity, being carried forward by a professional military establishment. The military was patriotic, to be sure, but it came to reflect Israeli society as a whole, and was no longer informed by the Sabra mentality, attractive as it was.

Gone also were the days when a substantial sector of society was in its impulse and import inspired by the desire to serve the common weal. Outside the area of national defense, private interest rather than public purpose began to motivate the mass of Israeli society. This was true also of its leadership. The old generation of leaders had been frugal in habit and outlook. They never worried about how much money they had in the bank (usually very little) or how well appointed their apartments were (generally they weren't). Their successors, however, had no taste for frugality or self-abnegation. They wanted politcal power as well as prestige and affluence. They wanted to, and did, live in villas and penthouses, and they sought ways and means—usually legal, though not always in the best of taste— to cash in on their status, mostly through connections to the wealthy of the American diaspora.

The Zionist dreamers had wanted the citizens of the Jewish state to earn their bread by the sweat of their brow, not by the sound of the cash register, much less by speculation on the Tel Aviv stock exchange. (Herzl would not allow a stock exchange in his notional state. He also wanted to keep the generals in the barracks and the rabbis in their synagogues, in other words out of politics: in modern Israel, both are heavily into politics.) But the religion of labor—above all, labor on the land—preached by the early pioneers lost all relevance when cheap Arab labor from the occupied territories became available.

Urbanization—almost 88 percent of the population now live in urban agglomerations, some of which are just that: mere agglomerations—relegated the religion of labor to that of a cult practiced by a few starry-eyed adepts of alternative lifestyles. Even in the kibbutzim, which could have been expected to keep alive the idea of redemption through work on the land, ideological firmness began to sag.

In contradiction of the ideological prohibition (of Marxist parentage) against exploiting workers and appropriating the surplus value they produce, hired labor is now the rule in kibbutz enterprises. The good life, with the comfort of swimming pools, espresso bars, individual color television sets, foreign travel, and other amenities that the kibbutz buys for its members (on continually rolled-over credit), has become a higher priority than the nation's needs, which the kibbutz movement had so admirably and unselfishly served in the era of the "state on the way." Today, no one finds it shocking if financial managers of kibbutzim play the stock exchange.

If the kibbutz movement, which still constitutes in many respects an elite, got caught up in the consumerist me-first merry-go-round, little in the way of idealism could be expected from the rest of Israeli society. And in fact, the will to create a better society has withered. The last item in the Zionist agenda has disappeared. No one seems willing to implement it.

All these trends and tendencies were arrogantly amplified in the wake of the 1967 victory. Israel was convinced that, as a consequence of the Six Day War, it had not only changed the map of the Middle East but, more important, its place in the region. In the Middle Eastern context, it was—or at least saw itself as—a superpower. The few warning voices that were raised were drowned in the swell of self-congratulation and the enthusiastic applause of the diaspora. The country enjoyed an economic boom that belied its continued record indebtedness and dependence on foreign financial assistance.

In Israel perhaps more than in any other country, the transition from an ideologically motivated to a consumerist society bore a particularly strong American imprint. With the exception of pop music, it could be felt everywhere. Jeans replaced the khaki of the pioneers. Shop signs and brand names appeared in English, and not for the convenience of tourists. The advertising industry followed the American model, as did magazines. Political campaigns were run by media advisers and pollsters. For the more affluent, and often for those who could not quite afford it, weddings and Bar Mitzvah receptions ballooned into huge affairs of dubious aesthetic merit in emulation of the customs of American Jewry.

Car sales soared, as did sales of refrigerators, televisions, hi-fi sets, and other luxuries that are characteristic of the "good life" as it is defined in Western materialistic terms—luxuries that all peoples of the world who are sophisticated enough to "need" them long to possess. Although Israel is a poor country, the author Isaac Deutscher once wistfully remarked, its people are rich (in contrast to the Soviet Union, which Deutscher declared to be a rich country whose people were poor).

Israel never had it so good. Golda Meir said so to Richard Nixon when she visited him in the White House in March 1973, a few months before the outbreak of the Yom Kippur War of October 1973.

The earthquake that shook Israel as a result of the Yom Kippur War interrupted the race for the "good life" for a short time only. It did, however, change the political track on which that race was run. The Labor-dominated government had to pay the price for the scandalous lack of preparedness of the Israel Defense Forces and the public's perception that the country's political and military leadership had this time failed to react with its usual sharply honed decisiveness.

Officially, the blame was pinned on the Chief of Staff, Major

General David Elazar. But nobody in Israel really believed in his guilt. The real culprit was the complacency that had taken hold of Israeli society after the 1967 victory and the conviction that Israel was now a power with whom no one would dare trifle. The Israel Defense Forces, in which discipline had always been (and continues to be) a problem, had become so lax that the unexpected attack by Egypt and Syria caught its tanks with their tracks down, its ammunition stores short of requirements, and its officers momentarily bereft of professional judgment.

However, in October 1973, the Jews were not as abandoned and isolated as they had been in 1967. With massive military aid from the United States, Israel was able to reverse the fortunes of war. The damage to its psyche, which at first seemed profound, was soon repaired (as was the combat readiness of the Israel Defense Forces). The Yom Kippur War was thus not a chastening experience. It did not change the mental landscape of Israel, though it changed the political scene: Labor soon found itself out of power, for the first time since the creation of the state.

It is an irony that Labor's defeat was due to the defection of many of its voters to a party—led by the distinguished archeologist and former I.D.F. Chief of Staff Yigael Yadin—that intended to bring Israeli society back to the austere values it had abandoned over the years. Yadin's success in drawing Ashkenazi votes from Labor opened the door to the assumption of the premiership by Menachem Begin, whose party had been able to attract a great number of Sephardi votes. (Yadin's party soon collapsed, but not before having joined Mr. Begin's government —a move typical of the unprincipled political opportunism so prevalent in Israel.)

The voters from the Sephardi "Second Israel" were no longer swayed by the policies that made up Labor's platform, not even the economic policies, although they were mostly at the bottom of the socioeconomic ladder. They blamed Labor for having misused them all through the years of its stewardship, for having robbed them of their dignity and self-respect, and for having turned a deaf ear to their woes. Labor's enemies—the opposition parties—thus became ipso facto the Sephardim's friends, and being nationalistic, they favored the nationalist right. They were also looking for a leader, a hard-liner in the confrontation with the Arabs, whom they emotionally despised after having lived among them as second-class citizens in their countries of origin. They were clamoring for a *melekh yisrael,* a King of Israel. The populist Mr. Begin fit the job description perfectly.

Mr. Begin's party, Herut, the pillar of a grouping of right-of-center parties known as "Likud," had never paid much attention to social questions. This did not change during his "reign." What satisfaction he gave to his Sephardi voters was not in improving their economic situation. On the contrary, they grew worse off. But they felt better about themselves—in large part because they were no longer at the bottom of the pecking order. That place was now occupied by the Palestinian workers from the occupied territories, who came in their thousands to do menial jobs (for lesser wages) that Jews no longer wished to perform, and on whom the Sephardim could look down.

What the Sephardim wanted (demanded, really) was recognition—"honor," as they called it—and it became politically prudent to give it to them. Maimuna, a folk festival of Moroccan Jewry, became almost an official holiday. The yearly pilgrimage to the grave of a Moroccan-born miracle-working rabbi, the Baba Sali, decried by both the secular sector and the religious establishment as an exercise in superstition, began to attract not only great numbers of venerating pilgrims but pandering politicans as well. Before the 1988 elections, both Likud's Yitzhak Shamir and Labor's Shimon Peres went to the Negev town of Netivot to receive the blessing of the Baba Sali's self-anointed successor, his son Baba Barukh, a convicted felon. (Baba Barukh at least was even-handed; the Lubavicher Rebbe promised his blessing only to those who would vote for the right-wing religious party, Agudat Israel.)

The emergence of the Sephardi factor, however, had little impact on the country's social landscape. As in other capitalist countries, the rich got richer and the poor got poorer. The number of individuals living below the official poverty line kept growing, reaching 500,000 in 1987. They constitute an underclass 85 percent of which is Sephardi, as is 95 percent of the Jewish prison population in Israel.

A report by the Center for Social Policy Studies published in 1985 revealed that the upper 10 percent of the Israeli population reported 35 percent of the nation's total income, while the top 1 percent, composed of some 12,000 families, accounted for 12 percent of all the reported income. By contrast, the bottom 30 percent of families earned only 4 percent of all net income. The distribution of financial and physical assets would, in all likelihood, show similar, if not sharper, inequalities.

Like many Western democracies, Israel has its superrich, many of them arms dealers. (Israel is the sixth-largest exporter of arms in the world, and moral considerations do not seem to have any impact on the issuing of export licenses.) It has its version of jet-setters and café society, its "cosmopolitan collectors of art" (whom the tony American magazine *Town & Country* found worthy of celebrating in its January 1984 issue), its party circuits at which senior government officials and army officers dance attendance, its culture vultures and celebrity hunters, its country club coteries—all with an Israeli veneer.

Not surprisingly, the social gap between Ashkenazim and Sephardim remains wide. Society's underbelly crawls with thievery, prostitution (one field where Arab-Jewish cooperation flourishes, the pimps being mostly Arabs), drug addiction, even organized crime. Here, too, it is business as usual as in industrialized countries.

Social scientists warn about the increase of violence in the Israeli family, psychologists about the increase in teenage suicides. There are hot lines for battered wives. Prisons are overcrowded. Traffic in the cities is snarled. And the military report that Israeli youth is in bad physical shape. It is a picture familiar to Western society.

Adding to all this the propensity of Israel's macho drivers for slaughter on the roads, one gets a near-complete catalogue of all the aspects of normality the founding fathers of Zionism and the Jewish state would have never dreamed was part of the bargain of nationhood. One can find solace in the positive aspects of normality that Israel manifests, and in its undeniable achievements. But while idealists can still be found in Israel, it is no longer they who give the country its imprint.

The Jews of Israel seem to have lost the will to make Israel a model country, a country that is distinguishable from other nations by more than just its Jewish majority. Yet they still show spasms of reluctance to be satisfied with being "simply a nation like all other nations, with the virtues and shortcomings, successes and failures, which national existence seems to entail in the normal world"—a goal rightly hailed as sufficient by Sir Isaiah Berlin, who spoke those words in accepting the Nahum Goldmann Cultural Medal in Jerusalem in January 1986.

This reluctance grows out of an atavistic anti-normality reflex of a people long attached to the vagaries of an anomalous uniqueness. There was no strength left in the old Zionism to respond to that reflex. It was evident that Zionism would not bring on the secular millennium it had dreamed about. Those longing to endow the Jewish state with a higher purpose, one going beyond normal national existence, were therefore led to look for other sources from which to slake their redemptory thirst.

X

The Jewing of Israel

It was the Israeli writer Haim Hazaz who coined the dictum: "When a man cannot be a Jew anymore, he becomes a Zionist." By that, Hazaz did not mean that a Zionist is necessarily not a Jew. Indeed, the Zionist would be the first to resent the implication that by embracing Jewish nationalism—and Zionism is Jewish nationalism—he ceases to be a Jew.

But though the Zionist remains a Jew, the religious part of his "Judeity" is largely superseded by the non-Jewish element of nationalism. Not only is the Jewish content of Zionism devoid of a sense of divine mission, of the Jewish mystique, but the messianic traces it retains are secular. And lacking roots in faith, secularized messianism cannot but become metaphor, a rhetorical embellishment of a political aim to be attained in the here and now.

Rabbi Abraham Isaac Kook, a great Talmudic scholar and mystic who in 1921 became the First Ashkenazi Chief Rabbi of Eretz Israel, warned Zionism (which he called the "great national movement") that it "must drink in from the world of the hidden, from the topmost root where the holy is firmly established with the profane in a single whole." But the pioneers sweating in malarial swamps, the farmers plowing a recalcitrant stony soil under the hostile eye of Arab neighbors, the members of the labor battalions scraping the dusty ground to build the country's roads—in short, all those who were working, on very short rations and in conditions of great hardship, for the realization of the Zionist dream—gave little if any thought to the question of whether their backbreaking toil was part and parcel of a divine purpose, one that only the Jewish people were called upon to fulfill.

The same was true of the political leadership and the swelling ranks of professionals who filled the slots in the organizational chart of the Zionist movement inside and outside Palestine. After all, when the Jewish state came into being, the task of assuring its physical survival, keeping it functioning, and consolidating its gains seemed formidable enough to serve as a worthwhile collective goal for its citizens. Israel may not have been the embodiment of the supreme good, in the sense that Hegel had conceived of the nation-state, but it certainly appeared to be the vindication of all the Zionist movement had fought for.

Nonetheless, there were a small number of thinkers, writers, and poets who were disturbed by what they regarded as Zionism's inadequacy as a substitute for the eclipsed or dying God of tradition. They feared, not without reason, that the nationalist ideology would not be able to create new spiritual values to inform the social and political structures that Zionism was establishing, first in British-ruled Palestine and later in the youthful State of Israel. Zionism might regard the state as essentially an end in itself, but they had a hard time reconciling themselves to the idea that all that the Jewish people were called upon to achieve was to be like other nations, that Israel was nothing more than simply the nation-state of the Jews.

Such feelings were not limited to fringe intellectuals. From time to time, high-sounding speeches by major Israeli politicians betrayed the normally hidden presence of second

191

thoughts. Even Ben-Gurion, who could usually be relied upon to practice the art of the possible, was not immune to the attraction of the unreachable. Thus, in a speech on foreign policy on February 4, 1952, he proclaimed from the rostrum of the Knesset: "We live and die for a messianic ideal, the advance guard of universal redemption." The rest of the speech, however, gave no indication how this ideal would influence Israel's foreign policy.

Normalization, once a cherished aim, raised some ominous questions for Zionism. With its principal aim—the establishment of a Jewish state—achieved, what need was there for a Zionist movement, inside or outside of Israel? And, indeed, it soon became evident that the Israeli population had little use for Zionism, except for those whose living depended on the perpetuation of the Zionist bureaucracy.

In the first decade of Israel's existence, few worried about the Jewish content of what was patently the only Jewish state in the world. To live in the only state in which the Jews constituted a majority seemed good enough; the trappings of sovereignty provided most citizens with a singular source of satisfaction. For a while, at least, it seemed that a new nation had been born: the Israeli nation. Even though it was not the new nation Herzl and Nordau had dreamed about, the Israelis were a distinct species in the family of nations, and surely unlike diaspora Jews.

This view was shared by quite a few thinkers who wished to unravel the confusion created by the restoration of Jewish sovereignty. In a 1965 book entitled *The End of the Jewish People,* the French-Jewish sociologist Georges Friedmann wholeheartedly embraced the notion that a distinct Israeli nation, separate from the Jewish people, had emerged. He wrote:

> There is no Jewish nation. There is an Israeli nation. The state that came into existence as a result of Herzl's prophecies is not a "Jewish state." The Israeli State is creating an imperious national community that is conscious of itself, but does not include in that consciousness belonging to a "Jewish people."

192

Few would quarrel with Friedmann's notion that Israel represents a distinct national community, though many may find his use of the adjective "imperious" objectionable. While it is true that power and arrogance do go together, it is also true that lack of power cannot be the objective of any state, least of all Israel, whose very raison d'être is to end the state of Jewish powerlessness. On the other hand, hardly anybody would claim today that the Israelis have no consciousness of belonging to a Jewish people, as Friedmann wanted us to believe.

How to reconcile the evident Israeli distinctiveness with Jewish peoplehood is at the root of the so-called Israeli identity crisis, a problem that escalated after 1967, when Eretz Israel became "whole." To be sure, it is a crisis that afflicts mainly intellectuals. The vast majority of the population whose identity cards list their "nationality" as "Jewish" have more mundane preoccupations. But though the mere fact of being Israelis provides them with a self-evident Jewish identity, Israelis do have a difficulty with the notion of being Zionists. After all, with the establishment of the state, Zionism had attained its principal political goal, and thus in a sense achieved itself out of business. In many ways, a Zionist in Israel today is very much like an American abolitionist after the Civil War.

True, it could be argued that there remain additional tasks for the Zionist movement to complete as part of the national renewal. Zionist leaders had always preached the need to create new spiritual values, a new culture, new social structures. In the minds of many Zionist leaders, the idea of national renewal was also wedded to a vague millenarianism, a secular variant of the traditional messianism of Judaism that Zionist historiosophy was at pains to repudiate. But as we have seen, these lofty ambitions of the Zionist movement are hardly reflected in Israeli realities.

Since the Israeli cannot be a Zionist anymore, must he therefore, to set Haim Hazaz's dictum on its head, now become a Jew? And if so, what does it mean to be a Jew? This is a question to which there are almost as many answers as there are people who consider themselves Jews. (Only the Orthodox would insist that they alone have the correct answer.)

David Ben-Gurion, whose record of public pronouncements leaves little doubt as to his attachment to the idea of the secular state (his pseudo-prophetic rhetoric notwithstanding), had his feet firmly planted in the soil of Jewish nationalism. Yet his head seemed to reach into supernal spheres. In a letter, dated July 9, 1961, to Professor Baruch Kurzweil of the Bar Ilan University, Ben-Gurion stated that he did not recognize Jewish "nationalism," only Judaism. He made it clear that for him Judaism did not mean the fulfillment of the commandments or rabbinical rule, but a "spiritual-moral destiny."

"I am not a Zionist and not a nationalist," wrote Ben-Gurion, who was generally considered to be a paragon of both, "but a Jew, and only and exclusively a Jew (of course, I am also a human being, because a Jew is a human being)."

The founder and staunch defender of the State of Israel had more surprises in store for the reader of his letter. "As a Jew," he continued, "I know that the concept of a state in the English sense of the word does not exist in Hebrew at all, but only that of a people (and this is a great, qualitative, and characteristic difference)."

Ben-Gurion went on to say that he had "no need for the concept of sovereignty, but [was] in need of redemption and of Israel's freedom." (By "Israel's freedom," he didn't mean the independence of the State of Israel, but that of *Am Yisrael*, the people of Israel.)

Did this mean that Ben-Gurion was ready to sacrifice in one grand, voluntary auto-da-fé sovereignty, political interest, *raison d'état*, statism—in short, the entire arsenal of statecraft that he had relentlessly used during his long political career?

Not really. Ben-Gurion never made the leap into the flames of an authentic act of faith. He did not demand that the Jew be in close contact with the divine, nor did he see any need for the strict fulfillment of the 613 commandments—actions that men of faith deem indispensable if the Jewish people are to inch forward on the way to redemption and thus fulfill their true destiny.

One cannot expect Ben-Gurion even to have hinted, in a letter the purpose of which was to elicit Professor Kurzweil's ideas on religion, how he thought the Jewish people could fulfill their "spiritual-moral destiny." But one thing that comes through clearly is Ben-Gurion's evident belief that it cannot be achieved through the medium of the nation-state.

It is really irrelevant that, as Ben-Gurion found it necessary to point out, there is no word for "state" in the Hebrew language. After all, the nation-state is a nineteenth-century concept, and Hebrew is an ancient language. (It has no word for metaphysics or the stock exchange, either.)

What *is* relevant is that Ben-Gurion admitted that Israel's destiny as a nation-state moved on a different track from that of the "spiritual-moral destiny" of the Jewish people. The destiny of the Jewish state may well be bound up with the spiritual-moral destiny of the Jewish people, but at best the two destinies run on parallel tracks that meet in the infinite.

The impossibility of setting the spiritual switches so that the two tracks merge into one is the source of what some describe as the Israeli identity crisis and others consider to be the sign of deep spiritual disarray in Jewry. Whatever the proper label, it seemed clear in the aftermath of the 1967 war that nothing less than a new *Guide for the Perplexed* would be needed to solve the problem. The original *Guide* had been written by Maimonides in the twelfth century with the idea of bringing the tenets of Judaism into harmony with the principles of Aristotelian philosophy. The new guide would have an even more formidable task. It would have to find an answer to the uncertainties spawned by modernism, where, as Yeats saw it, "Things fall apart; the center cannot hold." With Zionism now largely a dream fulfilled, and there being no signs of a new *Guide,* the vacuum created by the "center [that] cannot hold" attracted one reliable filler for the seemingly irrecoverable old assurances: Orthodoxy.

Zionism had started out as a movement in confrontation with time-honored religious tenets. It was not in itself anti-religious. It was just that except for the small group of religious Zionists of the Mizrachi movement, most Zionists simply had no room for religion in their ideological baggage.

Religious questions were also of little concern to the Yishuv during the Mandatory period. Zionism was a perfectly viable substitute religion (although, for those who wanted them, there was no lack of synagogues and no dearth of opportunities for a religious education for their children).

The Yishuv ran, and paid for, its own educational system. (Although Jews paid most of the taxes, the British Mandatory authorities never spent a single mil on Jewish education; all government-run schools were for Arab children.) As with everything else, educational institutions were organized along party lines. The socialists had their school system, the bourgeois General Zionists theirs, and the Mizrachi, of course, ran religious schools. In addition, the non-Zionist sector maintained charity-supported traditional educational institutions.

It wasn't until 1953, five years after independence, that the government got around to creating a unified state educational system, or nearly so. The General Zionist schools were merged with the Labor-sponsored institutions to become the principal state educational system. However, mostly for political reasons, (specifically the now defunct "historic alliance between Labor and the religious Zionists," which enabled Labor to govern the country for three decades), Mizrachi schools were transformed into "state religious" schools. They were placed under the supervision of the Ministry of Education, which to this day provides their budget as it does that of the "secular" school system.

Eventually, the state also undertook to subsidize the religious schools of the non-Zionist Agudat Israel and other Orthodox groups, although these were not subject to any kind of supervision by the Ministry of Education. It is an arrangement that benefits Agudat more than it does the state. The point is, Israeli taxpayers foot the bill for a kind of religious education that most would be reluctant to subsidize if they had a choice.

The problem Israel began to wrestle with in the 1950s was not so much what opportunities for a religious education should the state provide for those of its citizens who desire such education for their children, but what should be taught about Judaism in the secular school system. Until 1957, when the then Minister of Education, Zalman Aranne, decided to introduce the subject of "Jewish Consciousness" into the high school curriculum, teachers seemed quite content merely to educate Israel's young to be good citizens of the state. This was done with a more or less pronounced bias toward the pioneering ideals, although everyone was aware that only a tiny fraction of the students would ever join a kibbutz. The best one could hope was that they would continue the pioneering tradition in one way or another. By the 1960s, however, that notion appeared as outdated as the motto of the Reali High School in Haifa, which extols modesty, a trait not endemic in the Israeli national character.

The breakdown of the traditional family patterns, particularly among the patriarchal Oriental immigrants, reinforced the already existing tendency to give the public school system an ever greater responsibility for the education of the young, a responsibility the family was either unwilling or ill-equipped to shoulder.

What was to become of the Jewish component of that education, a component that had traditionally been the family's responsibility? Was it conceivable that in the State of Israel generations would grow up and finish school knowing hardly anything about Jewish lore, Jewish customs, Jewish holy days, Jewish religious culture?

By cultivating "Jewish Consciousness" in secular state schools, such a calamity, it was hoped, could be avoided. The initiators of the program rejected any and all suggestions that they had, in fact, introduced religious instruction into secular schools. The program was meant to acquaint the students with their Jewish heritage, teach the history of diaspora, perhaps inculcate spiritual values—all in the name of continuity. Contrary to the assertions of the Herzlian Zionists, who saw a clean break

197

with the past as a condition for national renewal, the Israeli was expected to know where he came from. In any case, "Jewish Consciousness" would be taught by lay teachers, not rabbis.

There was a catch, however: Jewish cultural heritage is religious heritage, the history of at least preemancipation diaspora is religious history, and the spiritual values of Jews are religious values. In an effort to blur the divide between the sacred and the secular, the Ministry of Education's guidelines called merely for the teaching of "respect for Jewish religious observance." In other words, while religious observance could not be taught because that would amount to religious instruction, one could at least teach respect for it. But in the religious schools supervised by the Ministry of Education, no one taught respect for those who chose not to be observant. (No one taught Darwinism, either.)

"Jewish Consciousness" also spread into other areas such as radio and television, both of which were state-run enterprises. There, the topic had no need for camouflage and could be openly presented as religious programming. Such programming had been a part of the broadcast agenda as far back as the time of the British Mandate. Thus, it seemed only natural for the Jewish state to step up the effort in this area, including putting religious shows on the popular radio station of the Israel Defense Forces. When television came to Israel in 1968, the state TV service broadcast a religious program every Friday evening and signed off each night with a reading from the Bible. (That evidently wasn't enough for the religious parties; as part of their price for agreeing to participate in the coalition government after the 1988 elections, they insisted on the establishment of a separate channel reserved exclusively for religious programs.)

Most of the religious radio and TV programs were clearly intended for Israel's more or less secularized audience. Some of them, particularly one popular television show, were (and are) broadcast on Friday night—a time when no observant Jew would switch on a TV set. In short, in the name of historic continuity and Jewish consciousness, the secular state became involved in religious propaganda.

Even the *Jerusalem Post,* that most westernized of the privately owned media, began running a column of homiletics in its Friday edition. The *Post,* like the government, was reacting to what it rightly saw as a religious revival of sorts. It was not that the Israeli leadership decided out of the blue to foist a more religious way of life on Israel's citizenry. Rather, it was responding to an apparent trend, and doing so primarily for political reasons. Still, its actions were hardly neutral: they strengthened the trend, making it more difficult to resist the growing encroachment of religion on the prerogatives of the secular state and the increasing imposition of religious norms on a secular population.

As in other countries, the turning toward religion in Israel grew out of a disappointment with the substitute deities of modernity. Science had failed to deliver the certainty that authentic faith gives the believer. The horizons of scientific discovery widened, but the mystery of life remained a closed book.

During the Age of Reason, vigorous intellectual inquiry undermined the European value system that until then had rested securely on an unquestioned belief in the God-given absolute order of the universe. But the further mankind probed into the frontiers of the cosmos, the larger and darker loomed the shadows that the human soul ached to see illuminated. In more recent times, science itself, notably modern physics, seemed to embrace the supernatural. Modern superstring theory, as proposed by Edward Witten, with its hypothesis that the universe started with ten dimensions, six of which retracted after the "Big Bang," seemed to be taking a leaf right out of the mystical doctrine of *tsimtsum*—God's retraction from the cosmos to allow room for the world—advanced by the Safed cabalist Solomon Luria (1534–1572).

In the meantime, the galleries of failed secular deities, such as liberalism and socialism or the inexorable march of progress, kept growing, and the purveyors of secular millennial promises kept falling into the chasm that separated their visions from reality. Cults appeared as the answer to some, but usually not for long.

Israeli society was not destined to escape these dilemmas of modernity. (Transcendental meditation and Hare Krishna have followers in Israel.) It would have been miraculous if it had. In addition to everything else, Israelis had to deal with the specific failure of the Zionist substitute religion, notably its catechism of nationalism and normality, to serve as an adequate surrogate for Jewish chosenness and a destiny that went beyond the limited one that independent nations cockily claim to have taken into their own hands.

In any case, the state no longer seemed to be the fulfillment of the Zionist dream. It was no longer deemed sufficient that Jews held all the power, controlled the economy, and imposed their political will. It no longer seemed enough that the Jews had their own state in which the President and government, officers and troops were all Jews, the cop as well as the felon, along with the judge, the prosecutor and the defense attorney. It was not enough that industry and trade were in Jewish hands, that the working class spoke through a Jewish trade union organization, that even the prostitutes and their clients were Jews. Even the desecrators of a synagogue, in an incident that occurred in 1986, were Jews. And everyone spoke Hebrew.

In this respect, the state certainly had a Jewish character—which is not to say it had a Jewish spiritual content. Such could only come from religion. The question was whether a secular state—and Israel was conceived as (and still is) a secular state—needed to have a spiritual content, or was capable of having one. To put it another way, what would determine the relationship between state and synagogue in a state that was not a theocracy but nonetheless invoked Jewish religious heritage? The answer could not be separation of state and religion. After all, the Jewish heritage includes the Torah, and the Torah is regarded by the religious as the constitution God gave to the Jewish people.

For many years, a so-called status quo effectively regulated relations between state and religion—or, rather, between the state and that part of the Orthodox camp that recognized the state. In effect, a deal was cut between the secular and religious parties delineating the areas in which religious laws would be given official status, such as in matters of family law governing the personal lives of Israeli Jews (marriage, divorce, child support, etc.) as well as such public matters as kosher food in the army and, most important, the recognition of the Sabbath as the official day of rest for the Jewish population. Religion was a political issue only inasmuch as certain "reasonable" wishes of the religious parties had to be accommodated in order to gain their cooperation in coalition politics.

As long as this status quo was observed, the religious parties did not appear to worry about the Jewish content of the state. They certainly didn't care whether the Prime Minister drove his car on the Sabbath. By and large, the religious—to this very day, a minority in Israel—cared little about the behavior of the secular majority, even if they found some of it rather offensive. Religion only became a burning issue when the debate about the Jewish content and religious meaning of the State of Israel intensified, particularly after the Yom Kippur War of 1973. It was a debate that went way beyond the definition of a status quo designed to enable observant and secular Jews to live side by side without friction. And it quickly moved from the arena of practical politics into the rarefied realm of theology and the spiritual destiny of the Jewish people and their state.

Not that political considerations were superseded by the spiritual. On the contrary, they assumed an even greater weight, if such was possible. Issues such as the future of the occupied territories, or even such minor ones as the sale of pork or the opening of restaurants on religious fast days that were not official holidays, now assumed the significance of milestones on the road to redemption. Secular politicians began to feel obliged to play the religious card more conspicuously. It was a totally different game now. At stake was nothing less than the nature of Israeli society and the meaning of the Jewish state.

Politicians who before never bothered to conceal their predilection for driving on the Sabbath or eating non-kosher food in public now went out of their way to demonstrate publicly their observance of religious law (a law in whose validity or divine origin they did not privately believe).

In January 1987, for example, Foreign Minister (and Deputy Prime Minister) Shimon Peres braved the unusually bitter cold in Rome to make the more than one-hour walk from his hotel to the hall in which the Italian Social Democratic Party was holding its convention in order not to be seen desecrating the Sabbath. (His media adviser saw to it that the Israeli press duly reported the socialist minister's deference to religious law and custom.) Mr. Peres's sacrifice was certainly not inspired by short-term coalition calculations, since the government in power rested on a broad wall-to-wall consensus that excluded only the non-Zionist left. Clearly, he wished to demonstrate a deeper attachment to the religious values that were now in vogue. Mr. Peres also made a point of attending weekly Biblical study sessions held at the private "court" of former Sephardi Chief Rabbi Ovadia Yosef, a theologian known for an Orthodox rigidity more often found among his Ashkenazi counterparts.

In March 1985, Abba Eban, who was not a member of the government at the time (though he was a member of Parliament), found it necessary to defend, in apologetic terms, his widely acclaimed television series, "Heritage: Civilization and the Jews," which had been attacked by American and Israeli Orthodox organizations and individuals. (Eleven members of the Knesset appealed to the Minister of Education to ban the series from Israeli television). The Orthodox had objected to what they called Eban's "attempt to portray Jewish history in historic, literary, and humanistic terms," something that in their view "inevitably leads to a fundamental error in orientation." Instead of proudly admitting the "error" of having, indeed, presented Jewish history in historic, literary, and humanistic terms, Mr. Eban went out of his way to appease his Orthodox critics.

On the one hand, Mr. Eban emphasized that his series did not deal with *halakha*, the creation of the world, and the origin of the

Torah, and thus could not be faulted for having said anything contrary to Orthodox rabbinical views. On the other hand, he hid behind the authority of "authentic and devout scholarship," particularly that of Professor Yehezkel Kaufmann, an eminent scholar and Orthodox Jew who agreed that the "Israelite religion did not, of course, come into the world full blown."

These examples (and a bookful of them could be collected) are symptomatic of the profound way in which religion has come to affect Israeli society. In this respect, the 1988 elections betoken no change. The gains posted by the religious parties, and their subsequent inclusion in the coalition government formed by Likud and Labor, guarantee that the religious agenda is not about to be relegated to anyone's back burner. To be sure, the religious parties may for a time retreat from their more radical—and therefore more controversial—demands. But their clamor for more widespread observance of *halakhic* rules is not likely to subside. They can also be counted on to demand increased financial support for their schools, which have proved to be the most effective instrument for the dissemination of their doctrines. Clearly, the religious sector has made full use of the breakdown of the "status quo."

That policy had worked for many years because religious issues had touched the secular majority only in a peripheral manner. Of course, there were individuals who were personally affected by the impossibility of finding redress from such archaic strictures of rabbinic law as those that made it impossible for a Jew to marry a non-Jew in Israel, or for a *cohen* (a descendant of the priestly caste) to marry a divorcee, or for a childless widow to remarry without the permission of her brother-in-law. But the secular majority had remained by and large unaffected. They drove to the beach on the Sabbath (and still do), found ways to eat non-kosher food, and if they wanted to marry non-Jews, they did so abroad. (The state recognizes such marriages; the problems arise when the parents try to enter their children as Jews in the population register of the Ministry of the Interior, a political fiefdom of the religious parties.)

In recent years, however, the rules of the game have profoundly changed. It is no longer a matter of the secular majority agreeing that the domain of religion should be regulated by those to whom it matters most—namely, the Orthodox. (The politicians of the secular majority have always been ready to sacrifice the concerns of Conservative and Reform Judaism on the unholy altar of expediency. Their followers are not numerous enough in Israel to count, and the American diaspora never went to bat for them with any degree of vigor.) Today, it is the Orthodox camp that defines the perimeter of the religious domain. It is the Orthodox camp that determines which matters can, for the time being, be left to the secular authorities and which ought to be defined in terms of *halakha.* The Orthodox camp thus determines in essence what is Jewish and what is not, with the clear understanding that the ultimate aim is— nay, must be—an Israel in which nothing can exist without the stamp of approval by the appropriate *halakhic* authorities.

In such a scheme of things, there can be no room for Zionism, nor for what is called the prophetic tradition of Judaism as defined in humanistic terms, of which Ahad Haam was the first though by no means the only proponent. And, of course, there can be no room for other values. Orthodoxy sees itself as the repository of divine truth. It follows that everybody else must be wrong. Nor can there be any other culture but religious culture.

The religious camp cannot be faulted for acting true to its convictions. And indeed, the closer it moves to fundamentalism, the more its objectives are in accord with the tenets of Rabbinical Judaism. Religious parties such as Agudat Israel and Shas openly proclaim that their representatives are guided not by the will of the electorate or the party organs but by the decisions of rabbinical luminaries who are elected by no one.

Even the National Religious Party, which has been represented in every government since independence and which professes tolerance and respect for democracy, sometimes seeks guidance from religious authorities. When Golda Meir became Prime Minister in 1969, the leadership of the National Religious Party asked its rabbis whether it would be proper, in view of the clearly inferior status *halakha* assigns to women, for those of its members who were slated to serve in her government to accept Mrs. Meir's authority. (The rabbis ruled they could do so "in secular matters," as if Mrs. Meir, who enjoyed bacon and eggs for breakfast and smoked as heavily on the Sabbath as she did on weekdays, had any interest in dealing with religious matters.)

Not only does the rule of *halakha* have nothing in common with any concept of democracy, it stands in fundamental contradiction to the idea of the sovereignty of the people, which is the philosophical basis of democracy. Anyone who accepts the Torah as God's revealed and thus absolute, infallible truth must reject as heretical the notion that human beings are capable of legislating their welfare outside the boundaries drawn by *halakha* as interpreted by those qualified to do so.

That does not mean that the outward forms of democratic institutions would have to disappear in a *halakhic* state. Judaism recognizes an area of temporal law; in Biblical times, it was vested in the institution of the kingdom. Over—and often against—it, stood the authority of the religious Law. The Bible is full of descriptions of the tensions and clashes between the two. The ultimate authority is, of course, God's word, although in practice the secular power may prevail.

In our days, the religious camp does not call for the renewal of the monarchy or the reconvening of the Sanhedrin. Its aim, instead, is the impregnation of the secular by rabbinical law. In practical terms, this translates into efforts to have the Knesset legislate in the spirit of the *halakha,* or at least not in contradiction to it. In other words, the religious camp tries to enforce religious law through legislative acts of the secular state.

In this endeavor, the religious camp has so far not been spectacularly successful, primarily because the non-religious parties have found it impossible or inadvisable to enforce voting along party lines on legislative proposals that members regard as matters of conscience and not of partisan politics. Until now, the

Knesset has even refused to go along with proposals presented by Orthodox members to amend the Law of Return. That law, which gives every Jew the right to make Israel his or her home, defines as a Jew anyone born of a Jewish mother who has not converted to another religion, or any convert to Judaism. What the Orthodox don't like is that, in talking about converts to Judaism who are entitled to settle in Israel, the law does not specify that conversion must conform to *halakhic* rules. In effect, that means that the law recognizes as Jewish someone who was converted by a Conservative or Reform rabbi. Not surprisingly, the Orthodox reject that possibility, since they deny that non-Orthodox rabbis have any rabbinical authority whatsoever.

But while they haven't made much headway amending the Law of Return, the religious camp and its sympathizers did succeed in knocking the teeth out of a bill that was meant to outlaw racist incitement. After two years of debate in committee and the plenary, what finally emerged was a totally emasculated law that declared that no religious text could ever be considered racist. This loophole allows extremists to protect themselves by presenting their racist statements in the form of cleverly chosen quotations from scripture. (This didn't prevent the Israeli Supreme Court from barring as racist American-born Rabbi Meir Kahane's ultra-rightist Kach party from participating in the 1988 elections. The court based its ruling on a 1985 law that bans electoral participation by parties that are either racist, negate the existence of the State of Israel as the state of the Jewish people, or repudiate Israel's democratic character. It could be argued that the third category could be applied to all religious parties, inasmuch as they are committed to instituting the rule of *halakha;* however, such a ban is not likely to be considered by an Israeli court.

Orthodoxy has been even more successful in stamping its imprint on Israeli life outside the legislative realm. In Jerusalem, this can be easily verified by any casual visitor. For one thing, a greater number of residential quarters are now off limits to private motorists on Saturdays and on holy days, and a greater number of cooperative apartment buildings will accept only observant Jews as tenant-owners. For another, there are many more wearers of knitted skullcaps, many of them young people, than ever before. (Actually, wearing a knitted skullcap is more of a political statement than a religious one. There is no Biblical commandment that obliges observant Jews to keep their heads covered; rather, it is a *minhag*, a custom. In any case, one could keep the custom just as well by wearing any kind of headgear, such as the soft khaki hat introduced by the pioneers. But that would send the wrong ideological signal.)

In the country as a whole, the number of religious educational institutions has grown, as have the sums the government expends on maintaining or subsidizing them. Government funds flow into the *yeshivot* under different rubrics, the largest expenditure being grants that are paid to the institutions on the basis of the number of their students. These numbers have swelled from 18,000 in 1968 to 61,853 in 1985, according to the 1986 budget proposal of the Ministry for Religious Affairs. In fact, there are more rabbinical students in Israel today than could be counted in the whole of nineteenth-century Europe, when rabbinical studies were at their height. The contribution to the nation's common weal of these students—most of whom are exempt from military service—is comparable to that of the Lamas of Tibet, before the Chinese chased them out of their monasteries.

The religious camp continually presses its demands for the introduction of religious education into the secular state schools. The present Sephardi Chief Rabbi, Mordechai Eliahu, called for the appointment of a rabbi to every school. Zevulun Hammer, the leader of the National Religious Party and Minister of Religious Affairs in the coalition government formed after the 1988 elections, declared that the aim was to eventually transform all but 20 percent of elementary schools into *mesorati* ("traditional") schools.

Without any basis in law, rabbinical authorities have also interfered in the medical-ethics debate over organ transplants and the question of exactly when a patient can be considered dead, forcing some hospitals to accept their rulings on a "voluntary basis." "Voluntary" in this instance is a euphemism, for through the supervisory function it legally exercises over questions of kashrut (compliance with dietary laws) the Rabbinate is in a position to apply pressure on hospitals.

Similarly, lawyers and judges are being exhorted to look to the immense body of Jewish law for legal guidance and to apply Jewish law in court. And it was due to pressure by the religious camp that, in 1987, the Minister of Justice defied both the opinion of the Israeli Supreme Court and the practice of most civilized nations by delaying the extradition to France of convicted murderer William Nakash, on the grounds that his life would be in danger in a French prison because his victim had been an Arab.

However, the major ideological success of the religious camp has been its ability to capture the nationalist élan that had been the moving spirit of the Zionist movement in the period known as "the state on its way." Indeed, part of the religious camp did more than merely capture Zionism's élan: it succeeded in claiming for itself a near-monopoly on nationalism. These days in Israel true Jewish nationalism is held to be inseparable from Orthodox Judaism. Any other form of nationalism is necessarily suspect as being tainted by alien sources.

This kind of ideology has always been taught in the religious state schools. Guidelines reissued every school year by the Ministry of Education and Culture have long made it clear that the existence of Israel depends ultimately on the strict observance by the Jewish population of all the commandments. Ministry guidelines also assert that the creation of the State of Israel and the "Ingathering of the Exiles" mark the beginning of redemption, and that the study of the scriptures is "a Jewish national task."

As long as this ideology remained confined within the walls of a religious educational system that reached only a relatively small number of students, its influence on the body politic of Israel was necessarily limited. And until 1967, the contrast was so stark between what the religious establishment considered as the desirable norm for all of Israel and the realities with which it had to contend that the religious impulse was channeled inwardly into the life of the Orthodox community. Before 1967, the religious camp had neither the energy nor the taste for spreading its outlook beyond its ramparts.

That all changed in the wake of the Six Day War as the challenge inherent in Israel's new "wholeness" caused significant shifts in the relationship between state and religion and the delineation of the secular from the sacred.

Secular Zionism had evidently failed to meet the challenge. Had it not failed, masses of Jews would have heeded the Zionist call to abandon the diaspora for the Jewish state. In fact, very few Jews did. It seemed clear from this that, having done its duty (namely, making the state a reality), nothing more could be expected of Zionism. Certainly, diaspora Zionists seemed conspicuously remiss when confronted with the question posed by the conquests of 1967: "To keep or not to keep."

The natural predatory response of the nation was—and, to a large degree, remains—in the affirmative. The motivation for this reaction ranges from the pragmatic to the messianic. Some of those who favor a "Greater Israel" do so on the simple grounds that the new borders are less vulnerable than the old Armistice Line. Others take the view that conquest justifies possession, that only the foolish and faint-hearted give up what they hold. Besides, they argue, the world recognizes only strength, and the Arabs understand only one language, that of force. What better way, then, to manifest Israel's strength than by defending its rights and interests? Many young people had sacrificed their lives in a war that was provoked by the Arabs. (Not that Israel was all that reluctant to be dragged into some wars.) Should their sacrifice be in vain?

Even among those who favor retreat from Gaza and the West Bank there are many who feel that Jews should have the right to settle anywhere in Eretz Israel. For the most part, they advocate relinquishing the occupied territories for the simple reason

209

that either the Jewish character of the state—by which they mean Jewish majority status, not Jewish spiritual content—would eventually be overwhelmed by the surging Arab birthrate, or that by permanently disenfranchising its Arab population Israel would become what its enemies say it already is: another South Africa.

In all this, Zionism plays at best a marginal role as a symbolic point of reference. Whatever ideological impulse is at work is provided by the messianic politics of the nationalist religious camp and its sympathizers, most numerous among whom is the tradition-loving Sephardi population. In this camp, Gush Emunim (the "Bloc of the Faithful"), which was founded in 1974 by several hundred mostly young activists from the National Religious Party, acts as a powerful catalyst whose influence reaches beyond the Orthodox faithful.

Gush Emunim is not a political party. Its followers can be found anywhere right of center. Working through the political system, its aim is to push for more Jewish settlements on the West Bank. Its strength lies not in numbers but in its ability to capture the popular mood and the attention of the government. Continued control of the West Bank still has widespread support. So does the "right of Jews to settle anywhere in Eretz Israel," even if this right is now more often exercised for mundane reasons rather than to further the advent of the messianic era. In any case, Gush Emunim has succeeded in presenting its ideology as the true and perhaps only heir of Zionism, its adherents as engaged in the revival of the old pioneering spirit.

Not surprisingly, the pioneering spirit had been eclipsed and, in a very real sense, made superfluous by the establishment of a Jewish state that demanded nothing more of its people than that they be good citizens. The immigrants who flocked to Israel in the first years of the country's independence did not "come to the land to redeem it and to be redeemed by it," as one of the pioneer songs had it. Rather, they came to build an existence for themselves in a state in which the Jews would be the majority, and not merely a tolerated minority. Preferably, that existence would also be materially superior to the one they had left. The change of the inner man to which the pioneers aspired was not among the priorities of those who made aliyah in the 1950s (as American Jews describe immigration to Israel). Although the word "aliyah" ("ascension") does imply a kind of moral elevation, that was not what most immigrants were looking for. The redemptive songs of the pioneers had no meaning for them. In fact, by the 1970s they were no longer heard. Instead, pop songs adapted lyrics from scriptural texts or conveyed patriotic, pseudo-messianic messages, the most enduring of which were those of Israel Prize laureate Naomi Shemer, whose ultranationalistic musical mirages were wildly popular.

In some respects, Gush Emunim could claim to be doing nothing more than continuing the pioneering tradition. Just as the Zionist pioneers, through the dedicated idealism they deployed in settling the land and defending the Yishuv, brought to fruition the dream of the Jewish state, so can Gush Emunim claim to be doing the same for the wholeness of Eretz Israel.

The pioneers settled amid hostile Arabs. Gush Emunim does the same. The pioneers chose strategically elevated locations. So does Gush Emunim (as a rule, with governmental approval). And if the Gush Emunim settlements are not economically self-sufficient, neither for many years were those of the pioneers. (A great number of them are still incapable of paying their huge debts.)

Ideologically, however, a chasm separates Gush Emunim from the pioneers, and not only because the latter were also socialists. For the pioneers, Eretz Israel was a matter of political necessity and historic justice. For Gush Emunim and the many who share its views, the "wholeness" of Eretz Israel is a religious imperative.

This being so, Gush Emunim and its friends are indifferent to the values of democracy. They will use democratic methods when it suits their purpose. But they do not hesitate to spurn them when they feel that other means are needed to reach their ends. The fact is, Gush Emunim members do not hesitate to take the law into their own hands.

They did it spectacularly in activating an underground move-

ment that committed numerous terrorist acts against West
Bank Arabs. In 1980, members of this underground planted car
bombs that maimed the Mayor of Nablus, Bassam Shaka, and
the Mayor of Ramallah, Karim Halaf. In 1983, three Arab students were killed when three underground members attacked
the Islamic College in Hebron with automatic weapons. And in
yet another act of terrorism, underground members fired a
rocket at a bus carrying Arab passengers in 1985, killing one
and wounding several others.

Though the underground was finally dismantled by police, its
members were sentenced to lenient prison terms. And they
warn that they will take to arms once again should any future
Israeli government relinquish the West Bank and Gaza.

One can understand the aims of the religious camp, both
with regard to the future of the territories and the religious destiny of the State of Israel, even if one disagrees with them. But
the question remains: Why do Israeli secular politicians so
often seek to appease the relatively small religious sector?

Part of the answer undoubtedly lies in the nature of Israeli
politics. Under an electoral system of proportional representation that favors the proliferation of small parties, the small religiously oriented parties hold the balance between the two
major political blocs, Labor and Likud. As a result, they exert
an influence and a power far beyond their numerical strength.

Strictly speaking, their votes were not needed after both
major blocs formed a government of national unity in 1985 and
again in 1988. But politicians are always thinking of the next
election, and the Israeli genus of the species is no exception. As
neither of the major parties can hope to gain an absolute majority of the 120 Knesset seats at stake, they want to leave the
door open to a deal with the religious parties for a narrow coalition, such as was the rule in Israeli politics before 1985.

No less important is the belief, supported by political ana-
lysts and pollsters, that the secular parties need to attract voters
who harbor religious sentiments but do not find the religious
parties quite to their taste, especially as they become increasingly fundamentalist.

In this contest, Labor is at a disadvantage, since the public rightly feels that the rightist Likud is ideologically more akin to the kind of nationalism propounded by religious parties. Indeed, Labor may be fooling itself if it thinks it can attract that kind of voter. Still, it is not going to give up the effort. That means kowtowing to some religious demands. It also means that Labor is not going to repeat the "mistake" of endorsing Jewish religious pluralism.

Between them, the two major parties control enough votes to change the current system of proportional representation to a winner-takes-all electoral system based on constituencies that would all but eliminate the small parties—above all, the religious parties. But it is doubtful that any such proposal for electoral reform will be adopted in the foreseeable future. The major blocs prefer the devil of proportional representation they know to that of a constituency system they don't.

Be that as it may, politics alone cannot be the entire explanation for the greater attention paid to religion in Israel today. Some of the reasons are no doubt the result of the spiritual crisis modern man faces everywhere in the world. Religion's answer to this crisis certainly seems simple enough; at the very least, it has consistency on its side. That is enough to convince many people that it is also the right answer. Religion promises peace of mind and morality, although there is no evidence that religious people are happier or more moral than others. "It is doubtful," wrote Sigmund Freud in *The Future of an Illusion*, "whether men were in general happier at a time when religious doctrine held unrestricted sway; more moral, they certainly were not." The fact remains, however, that the religious camp in Israel is less concerned with true religiosity than with compliance to ritual; with adherence to the letter of the law, not its spirit.

In addition to the dilemmas haunting—or, at least, importuning—modern man, the Israelis are impelled to seek answers to questions only they have to face. They have to ask themselves whether they want to be a people like all other people, a normal people, or whether they want to continue on the path

213

prescribed by Rabbinical Judaism and pursue in Israel the messianic vision Judaism had held to in Exile.

That brings up the painful confrontation with the other claimants to the land: the Palestinians. As a nation in the modern sense, Israel can work toward finding a compromise between the two national claims. However, to do so would amount to a retreat away from redemption in the eyes of those who proclaim possession of the whole of Eretz Israel as a crucial part of Jewry's religious destiny. And that logically raises the question of whether a Jewish state is at all necessary for Judaism's mission in the world, a question most Jews would rather not ask.

What makes the search for an answer even more difficult for the Jews, both in Israel and in the diaspora, is the profound change that has occurred in the nature of the Jewish-Arab confrontation. Until recently, it was a conflict between the Jewish nation-state and the Arab nation-states, a conflict that one could reasonably hope might eventually be resolved in the way such conflicts are usually resolved in the quarrelsome family of nations—through lengthy negotiations that ultimately lead to some sort of mutually acceptable compromise. After all, Egypt did sign a peace treaty with Israel.

But the Jewish-Arab confrontation is no longer simply a conflict between nations. If any proof of this is needed, consider the stones and bottle bombs that have been hurled at Israeli security forces in the *intifada*, the spontaneous uprising on the West Bank that began in December 1987. The fact is, the conflict has assumed aspects of a religious war, a struggle between two sacred claims that can ultimately be settled only by the destruction of one of them. And because of that, the Jewish diaspora is more deeply involved—or, rather, tangled—in this struggle than it was in any of Israel's "conventional" wars.

XI

We Are One

Golda Meir once remarked that just because the Jews have only one God that does not mean they have to have only one friend. In fact, Israel does have more than one friend. Still, no friendship is anywhere near as important to Israel as the one it enjoys with the United States.

The relationship between Israel and the United States is a close one—so close that it is often described as a virtual alliance. But a strong commitment alone does not make an alliance, and it is important to remember that the U.S.-Israeli bond lacks the binding forms of a formal entente. After all, friendships between nations have been known to change as the interests of the stronger partner change. In the 1950s, for example, Israel enjoyed a near alliance with France; in 1962, that relationship evaporated unceremoniously when the French decided to call off their war against the Algerian nationalists.

America, of course, is not France—not least because of the presence in the United States of a vigorous, prosperous, and influential Jewish community. Needless to say, the Israelis are quite aware of this: indeed, it is why they regard America as their only reliable ally. Nonetheless, the Israeli attitude toward the American diaspora is shot through with ambivalence. Israelis tend not to look too kindly on their brothers in "Exile" who refuse to consider themselves as living in exile. The American diaspora may be necessary for the survival of Israel, at least in the style to which it has become accustomed, but that does not inspire the Israelis to respect American Jewry. American Jews are proud Jews, but not in the way Israelis are proud Jews. And it is not only a matter of style. American Jews are a proud minority content to live in a pluralistic society. Israelis are a proud majority with limited admiration for the virtues of pluralism and tolerance.

The commonality of interest in Jewish survival demands that this disparity remain discreetly hidden beneath the bunting of the Jewish people's unity. At times, however, it does erupt. One such occasion arose in 1987, when hardly any American Jews protested the outrageously harsh sentence—life imprisonment—imposed on Jonathan Jay Pollard, a fervent Zionist who admitted spying for Israel while employed as an intelligence analyst with the top-secret United States Naval Investigative Service.

In an open letter published in the *Jersualem Post* on March 21, 1987, Shlomo Avineri, a distinguished professor of political science at the Hebrew University of Jerusalem, harshly attacked American Jews for the lack of courage they had shown in the Pollard affair. He accused them of acting not like the "proud and mighty citizens of a free democratic society" that they claim to be but more like "trembling Jews in the shtetl" or the frightened Jews of Iran.

Israelis also have difficulties with the Americanness of American Jews. If Jews in America adopted American manners and values merely as protective covering, the Israelis would understand it. But it is obvious that American Jews take their American nationality seriously. Among other reasons, this is why American Jews are so perplexed and annoyed when Israelis ask them whether they are Jews first or Americans first.

If that question were asked by a non-Jew, it would be rejected as anti-Semitic. As far as the Jews in America are concerned, there can be no separation between being a Jew and an American, as there is none with regard to other ethnic groups. Rather than being American Jews, they are Jewish Americans. In Hebrew, as distinct from English, "American" is the adjective, "Jew" the noun.

There is no question that the situation of American Jewry is by far the best any diaspora community has ever enjoyed. Not least among the reasons is the pluralistic character of the American nation. Unlike European nationalism, and the Israeli variant as well, American nationalism is not of the blood-and-soil breed. As Theodore H. White, the Pulitzer Prize-winning author and journalist, put it in a posthumously published article he wrote for *The New York Times Magazine* celebrating the Fourth of July 1986: "Americans are a nation born of an idea." What America celebrates on its Independence Day is, in White's words, "the story of how this idea worked itself out, how it stretched and changed and how the call for "life, liberty and the pursuit of happiness" does still, as it did in the beginning, mean different things to different people." All of whom, despite their differences, are Americans.

There is, therefore, nothing incongruous, much less preposterous, about Sima Schapiro, whose given and family name clearly identify her as a Jewish woman, referring in a letter to the *The Times* to "our American forefathers" whose writings she was inspired to "study afresh" by Mr. White's article.

Compare with that the situation of, say, a Danish Jew. Although Danish Jews enjoy both freedom and prosperity, it would be preposterous for them to claim descent from the Vikings. Nor would a French Jew think of Vercingetorix the Gaul as one of his ancestors. But America's founding fathers stand for an idea; they are not linked to any blood-and-soil myth. And though the idea itself may be a myth, too, it is one a Jew can embrace with the same fervor as a non-Jew.

217

American Jews are also very comfortable with the kind of patriotism current in the United States—a sentimental, flag-waving patriotism that does not require (or even request) sacrifices of its citizens. In other times and places, nationalistic fervor has almost always spelled danger to the Jews. But no such thing need worry American Jews today. Even the jingoistic excesses of modern American patriotism, such as were in evidence at the 1984 Olympics in Los Angeles, or are manifested in the popularity of such cartoonlike movie heroes as Rambo, imply no threat to Jews.

As a result, most American Jews are just as ready as their non-Jewish compatriots to proclaim that America is the best country in the world. What about Israel? The fact is, to most American Jews, comparing Israel and America is like comparing apples and oranges. As the only Jewish country in the world, Israel is in a category by itself; no comparison can be validly made. As far as "regular" countries go, America's Jews feel that the United States has been "good to them" in a way that no country has ever been. And in the eyes of many of them, that makes it the best country in the world.

Israelis find this difficult to understand. That's because, having little interest in the history of American Jewry, they are largely unaware of how far Jews had to come in order to attain the status they enjoy in the United States today. Indeed, though the Jewish sociologist and philosopher Emil Fackenheim claims that "the Jewish community in America did [walk uprightly] virtually from the start," the fact is that for a long time the rule among American Jews was not to emphasize their Jewishness in public. While relatively few of them had any thought of actually giving up their Jewish identity, the vast majority perceived the need to become Americanized, to plunge into the melting pot in which all distinctions between American citizens were to be blended into one unified national character. In pursuit of this ideal, which eventually proved to be a fallacy, Jews abandoned Yiddish for English, Anglicized their names, and downplayed any extranational allegiances they might feel.

As a result, even though relatively few American Jews were rigorously observant, most clung to their religious identity. After all, it was the only identity they had. Before ethnicity became an acceptable—indeed, a valued and marketable—commodity in American society, the only acknowledged "right to be different" American Jews had was as a separate religious group.

Why didn't more of these "indifferent" Jews sever their tenuous links with Judaism? Perhaps they felt it would be a treasonable act, a denial of the virtue and value of a long historical past. American Jews may also have had doubts about how a conversion would be received in a society in which belonging and fidelity to one's congregation was held to be the primary vehicle of identification. This belonging also determined to a large degree the social "Pale of Settlement" of each community —for the Jews more so than for others.

Yet at the same time, as Fackenheim notes with evident sorrow, the "Jewish community cast away...quickly and recklessly vast parts of its Jewish heritage, mistakenly believing itself to be merely Americanizing it when in fact it emasculated or even unconsciously Protestantized that heritage."

Whether or not the American Jewish community actually is (or, rather, was) guilty of the transgressions of which Fackenheim accuses it, there is now no need for it to Americanize, much less Protestantize its Jewish heritage. For his part, Fackenheim obviously conceives of Jewish heritage in religious terms. (Otherwise he would not have spoken of it having been "Protestantized.") But the American Jewish community takes a larger view of that heritage, not restricting it to religion alone. So do other ethnic groups, the heritage of some of which, such as the Greeks, also has a religious component. In that, too, American Jews are like all Americans. Karl Kraus's dictum about the Jews doing as the Christians do *(Wie es sich christelt so jüdelt's sich)*, thus receives renewed validation in America.

Jewishness means different things to different Jews. Religion, of course, remains an important point of reference in the American Jew's self-identification. For the Orthodox, it is the only admissible framework. The rest have been Americanized in the sense that their religiosity, if not their theology, has emulated that of their non-Jewish fellow citizens—a religiosity that Michael Harrington has described as a "mile wide and an inch deep." (Alexis de Tocqueville made a similar observation in his 1835 book *Democracy in America*.)

But religion is not the only point of reference. In recent years, ethnicity has become not only acceptable but recognized as a valued attribute of Americanness. Like most other Americans, American Jews have become fascinated with their "roots." That these roots, by virtue of the immigrant experience, invariably lie outside America is in no way perceived as a paradox or as detracting from the seeker's Americanness.

For the Jews, the "roots" phenomenon has manifested itself in recent years in the form of an uncritical, romantic nostalgia for the shtetl and its culture. *Klezmer* music, a variation of Slavonic folk music, has thus enjoyed something of a renaissance. Auction prices for Jewish folk art and other Judaica have soared. Even Yiddish has been restored to a place of honor (though not to the status of a living language).

In short, after decades of being regarded as an embarrassment at best and an outright handicap at worst, Jewishness—in all its varied, sometimes astonishing forms—has become more than acceptable in American society: it has become, like other ethnic identities, a legitimate point of pride. As a result, few American Jews even think of changing their "Jewish" names into English-sounding ones anymore. Few are hesitant, as they once were, about referring proudly in public to their Jewish background. And few are reluctant to demand that their Jewish particularity be taken into consideration in matters of general public interest, such as the scheduling of elections and other public events in which they, as Americans, have a right to participate without getting into conflict with the tenets of their creed.

In 1986, for example, New York Jews raised a hue and cry,

which was taken up by the media, when a crucial play-off game between the New York Mets and the Houston Astros for the National League championship was scheduled to be held on Yom Kippur. Hundreds of Jews protested what they saw as the insensitivity of the commissioner of baseball in scheduling so important a game on a Jewish holy day.

What incensed the Jewish baseball fans was not simply that they would miss the game because of their wish to observe Yom Kippur. It was much more than that: they deeply resented being placed in a situation in which their Jewish particularity conflicted with their Americanness.

After all, baseball in America is not just a sport, a mere game. It is heavily overlaid with symbolic significance as a unifying communal ritual, one that transcends the differences in ethnic origin, religion, and class that form the mosaic of American society. Naturally, Jews do not want to be excluded from such rites, or prevented from participating in them because of conflicting demands of their religion. Any such exclusion would make them less American than they wish to be.

"Not until there is baseball in Israel will the Messiah come," exclaims Jimmy Ben-Joseph, a born-again American Jew who is studying at a Jerusalem yeshiva in Philip Roth's novel *A Counterlife*. Evidently, studying at a yeshiva in Jerusalem does not extinguish the Americanness of even an expatriate. Nothing does. In fact, American Jews who live permanently in Israel do not regard themselves as expatriates. Indeed, the overwhelming majority of them retain their American citizenship. To many of them, living in Israel is a continuation, in a more deeply Jewish sense, of the American Jewish experience.

Of course, Jewishness in America need not be manifested through an attachment to religious rites alone. A figure like Alan Berg represented a compelling example of Jewishness divorced from religion, or at least from religious observance. A popular and controversial radio talk-show host in Denver (he was murdered in 1984 by members of a white supremacist group), Berg saw nothing incongruous in asserting his Jewishness on Yom Kippur by asking gentiles in his audience to call in and explain why they didn't like Jews. To him, as to many other Jews, working on the holiest of Jewish holy days in no way detracted from the authenticity of his Jewishness.

There are many assimilated Jews in America who, like Berg, have fought and found their way back to the texture and tone of Jewishness in one form or the other. But there are equally vast numbers of assimilated Jews who remain outside the "tribe," to whom being Jewish has lost meaning. A perfect example is Judith Resnick, one of the seven astronauts who lost their lives in the space-shuttle disaster of January 28, 1986. Ms. Resnick, who had been on one previous space flight, was never hailed as the first Jewish-American astronaut, the way the first American black in space had been singled out. The fact of her Jewishness was brought out only after her death, and mutedly, in interviews with her relatives.

Ms. Resnick obviously had no interest in showing Jewish colors. Not that her career would have been harmed had she chosen to do so. American society has evolved over the last two or three decades to the point where Jews have real choices. They can be proudly Jewish or quietly Jewish; they can disidentify actively or passively. The point is, they can do whatever they like without fear that their choice will significantly affect their lives or careers.

To be sure, America is not the only society that allows Jews such a choice. Western European countries now do so as well. But unless there is a (highly unlikely) reversal of demographic trends, the Jewish diaspora in Europe is doomed to fade into insignificance. Not so the American diaspora, which as a result is the only diaspora community of significance in its own right.

The fact is, American Jews are solidly in the mainstream of America. In a very real sense, they have lost their minority status—to the nostalgic regret of some Jewish leaders.

In religious terms, of course, they remain a minority—a relatively small group that is distinguished from the Christian majority by the fact that its members reject the deity of Christ. But the Catholic Church no longer accuses Jews of deicide, and its priests do not as a rule nurture anti-Semitism. On the contrary, tolerance is now the trend and dialogue the fashion. It may not affect theology, but it helps coexistence.

What's more, fundamentalist Protestants have embraced Israel, which makes it difficult for them to reject Jews. And in contrast to the Catholics, they have done so for theological reasons.

Indeed, Jews are the only non-Christian religious group of significance in America. There are Moslems in America, and their number is growing, but few would agree with the statement made in 1987 by Dr. M. T. Mehdi, after a meeting of a Moslem leadership group with John Cardinal O'Connor, the Catholic Archbishop of New York, that America "is a Christian, Muslim, and Jewish society."

In any case, Jewish concern is not about the religious attributes of American society. It is about assuring the secular character of the country as such. Jewish organizations spend a great deal of energy and money in combating anything apt to remove even one brick from the wall that separates state from church —or, worse, make America appear to be a Christian country.

Jews will sue to have a cross removed from a Marine Corps base or a Nativity scene from a public square, for the right of an air force psychologist to wear a yarmulke. In August 1986, the American Jewish Committee protested the federal government's plan to give the Christian Broadcasting Network a role in its anti-drug campaign on the grounds that this would single out one religious denomination for a governmental role. (American Jewry does not challenge the observance of Christmas as an official holiday—no doubt because Christmas has become so commercialized—from which Jews profit in no small measure—that its religious character can be overlooked.)

America may be a country the majority of whose population professes Christianity, but it is not a Christian country. Jewish organizations are eager to have this distinction established and enshrined in legal opinion as clearly, and as frequently, as possible. It is a legitimate concern, even if the diligence with which it is being pursued may sometimes appear to be overzealous.

Abe Foxman, the national director of the Anti-Defamation League, once classified Jewish sensitivity on the issue of the separation of state and church as "almost irrational." He should know what he is talking about: the ADL is in the forefront of the battle.

Fortunately for the Jews, a considerable body of legal precedent has been established in the American courts that prohibits government at any level from giving religious norms and forms the cover of secular law. That principle has been repeatedly established, most eloquently perhaps in a 1943 Supreme Court decision that refused the state of West Virginia the right to oblige all students to salute the flag. In that case, as the Court has done in many cases brought before it since, the majority declared: "If there be any fixed star in our constitutional constellation, it is that no official, high or petty, can prescribe what shall be orthodox in politics, nationalism, religion or other matters of opinion."

It is not just the American legal system that protects Jews against any assault on their right to live freely as citizens and as Jews. As voters and members of various organizations, Jews take an active interest in the political process. The percentage of Jews who go to the polls at election time is double the overall figure—which, in terms of election mathematics, means that every Jewish vote carries double the relative weight.

No less important than votes—after all, there are only a few cities in which the Jewish vote is decisive—is the clout Jews wield as a result of their ability to raise and deliver massive campaign contributions. Contributing to campaigns in an effort to influence policy is an accepted American practice, and U.S. Jewry makes full, open, and efficient use of this instrument for making friends with and of politicians.

Overwhelmingly, the organized American Jewish community seeks to use its political influence on behalf of Israel. Indeed, the so-called Israel lobby in Washington basks in its reputation as the most efficacious organization of its kind, even if it is not universally admired.

America's Jews have also profited from the evolution that has occurred in the country's social climate. Not only has the culture come to view itself less as a melting pot than as a multi-ethnic mosaic (a shift that has legitimized Jewish separateness), it has also become more unabashedly materialistic. At no time since Calvin Coolidge first coined the phrase have so many Americans seemed to be so convinced that the business of America truly is business. Given the old cliché about the diaspora Jew's bent for business, the Jews would now seem to be swimming solidly in the materialistic mainstream. After all, how can the Jews be reproached for being obsessed with money when being obsessed with money is regarded as a national virtue? The same is true of sharp business practices and more aggressive competitiveness—precisely the sorts of rude behavior that resentful gentile societies have always characterized as being typically Jewish.

It would be a mistake to think that American Jewry owes its standing in the country only to its economic prowess and wealth. No less important is its contribution, particularly since World War II, in all realms of intellectual and artistic endeavor. Jewish achievement in these areas comprise what sociologist E. Digby Baltzell, author of *The Protestant Establishment: Aristocracy and Caste in America*, calls "the great untold story."

It is a story Israelis would rather not hear, as it is another reminder of the failure of Israel to attract diaspora Jews. There is also the matter of the widely disproportionate number of Jewish recipients of prestigious prizes, first and foremost the Nobel Prize. The prizes enhance America's intellectual and scientific stature, and by the same token diminish that of Israel because the Jewish laureates choose not to live in the Jewish state. The world in general, and the Jewish state in particular, may not think of Albert Einstein, Isaac Bashevis Singer (who writes in Yiddish), or Elie Wiesel (who writes in French) as Americans. But pluralistic America has no difficulty with the idea.

During the Fourth of July celebrations of 1986, when the renovated Statue of Liberty was rededicated with Hollywood-style hoopla, twelve distinguished Americans of foreign birth were awarded the Medal of Liberty in celebration of the "immigrant experience." Five of them were Jews: composer Irving Berlin, former Secretary of State Henry Kissinger (also a Nobel Peace laureate), Dr. Albert Sabin (the inventor of the anti-polio vaccine), the Israeli-born violinist Yitzhak Perlman, and Elie Wiesel (another Nobel Peace laureate).

One is tempted to compare the situation of American Jewry with that of Germany's Jews in the Weimar Republic. There, too, Jews had not only been prosperous but their prominence in the arts and sciences was no less impressive than that of American Jews in the United States today.

But there the parallel ends. While America is firmly wedded to pluralism, the Germans had since Bismarck worshipped the idol of Germanic unity and superiority. German Jews were also reluctant to use the political power they had—and they were not without influence—in favor of their particular interests. They feared that it would set them apart from the rest of the country and brand them as not truly German, a prospect most of them viewed with abhorrence.

Still, there is an Israeli saying that goes, "If things are that good, why are they that bad?" And in Israel as well as in America, the worrying never stops. There are two reasons for this: the persistence of anti-Semitism and the shrinking demographic base of Jewry.

Despite all the self-assurance and the sense of security they manifest, it is nonetheless quite easy to find American Jews who firmly believe that the attitude of non-Jews toward them remains fundamentally tainted by an unalterable (if usually hidden) core anti-Semitism.

Mary McCarthy, the distinguished American novelist, critic, journalist, and social historian, admitted as much. "I am not sure about blacks and Catholics," she wrote in *The New Yorker* magazine in 1986, "but as far as Jews are concerned I suspect that there is a bottom layer of hostility, which then can be top-

226

dressed or overpainted to any desired degree."

A dense network of Jewish organizations works relentlessly to create a climate—through lectures, publications, Christian-Jewish dialogues, and other means—that encourages the process of overpainting. The idea seems to be that while anti-Semitism may never disappear in America, it can be kept within bounds narrow enough to cause Jews no more than some occasional discomfort. By and large, anti-Semitism has thus been privatized; it cannot be manifested in public without subjecting the offender to widespread opprobrium. During the 1988 presidential race, for example, a number of activists from certain Baltic and Eastern European ethnic organizations were forced to resign from the Republican campaign because of their past anti-Semitic associations.

The overabundance of Jewish organizations in America (the Conference of Presidents of Major American Jewish Organizations boasts no fewer than forty-three member organizations plus another twenty-two that enjoy observer status) may well play the role of a safety valve against overanxiety—a need that, in the ghettos of old, was filled by institutionalized psychological defenses and the rigidity of the *halakha*. In any case, these organizations help American Jews feel comfortable in their Jewish-American skin.

Still, apprehensions, misgivings, and suspicions persist. It is difficult to judge whether they are objectively justified. An old Jewish saw teaches that paranoiacs have real enemies, too.

American Jewry may not have *real* enemies, or at least not enemies who present a serious threat. Nevertheless, there are people who dislike Jews and occasionally give vent to their animosity.

Every once in a while a swastika is daubed on a synagogue wall, a window broken in a Jewish institution, even a fire set. These are not acts of organized groups flexing their anti-Jewish muscle; as a rule, they are merely the exploits of youngsters venting their alienation on a group they regard as alien. The Anti-Defamation League keeps a close tab on all such occurrences, and finds most of them to be acts of individual teenage vandalism.

Here and there, one can hear traditional anti-Semitic litanies on radio call-in programs. The old accusations against Jews as exploiters, dishonest merchants, shyster lawyers come up at times. So does the somewhat newer accusation that the Jews manipulate public opinion through their supposed control of the media.

These are relatively rare occurrences, however, and their resonance is limited. The bulk of ingrained anti-Semitism in America has disappeared or gone deeper underground in the gentile American's psyche, or more precisely the white gentile's psyche. All surveys and polls show that Americans today display a greater degree of tolerance of Jews than ever before. This is particularly true of individuals with higher education. Of course, they may not always be honest in replying to the pollsters' questions. But the very fact that they do not wish to be thought of as anti-Semitic is in itself an admission that anti-Semitism is not viewed as a virtue. Not after the Holocaust.

Israelis and American Jews fully agree that the memory of the Holocaust is an indispensable weapon—one that must be used relentlessly against their common enemy, no matter how high the cost to the Jewish psyche. Jewish organizations and individuals thus labor continuously to remind the world of it. In America, the perpetuation of the Holocaust memory is now a $100-million-a-year enterprise, part of which is government-funded. Books with Holocaust themes, documentaries, feature films, TV programs, memorials, and museums are a staple of America's cultural diet.

Whatever comfort American Jews can draw from the decline in anti-Semitic attitudes, the fact remains that close to a quarter of those polled admit to some anti-Jewish feeling. In addition, there is the relatively new phenomenon of black hostility to Jews and Israel.

This troubling development draws sustenance from two main sources that converge into one anti-Semitic flow. On the one

228

hand, Jews serve as convenient scapegoats for the understandable frustration and resentment America's blacks feel at still
being unable to break out en masse from the underclass in
which, as they see it, the white majority has imprisoned them.
Jews are a convenienet target because, having succeeded in
joining the mainstream, they no longer seem to have a common
agenda with the blacks. On the other hand, because of their
identification with Israel, American Jews are also vulnerable to
the anti-Zionist thrust that is part of the Third World agenda
that American black leaders have come to embrace with exasperating enthusiasm. Even if few of them go as far as Black
Muslim leader Louis Farrakhan, who sees the Israel-Arab conflict in terms of a religious war between the Islamic forces of
light and the Jewish forces of darkness, a sense of solidarity
prevents many less extremist blacks from denouncing him. In
this sense, a rise in black political power can only be to the
detriment of American Jews and Israel.

American Jews feel, not without some justification, that
anti-Zionism and hostility to Israel are often only anti-Semitism in disguise. This is clearly the case when the enmity is
directed against what Israel is, as opposed to what it does. But
Jews tend to make no distinctions between the two categories.
In the latter case, it is often the way in which the antagonism is
expressed that raises Jewish hackles.

That was the burning issue during the 1982 Israeli invasion
of Lebanon. Many American Jews, along with a sizable sector of
the Israeli public, were opposed to what has gone down in history as Israel's unnecessary war. Nonetheless, the Jewish public
in America was deeply disturbed by what it saw as a media
blitz against Israel that often seemed to violate the code of objectivity Western journalists are expected to uphold. Some
American cartoonists were among the worst offenders, portray-
ing the Israelis as Nazis (in unwitting emulation of the anti-
Israeli cartoons in the Soviet press) and using religious symbols
to make their satiric points. One cartoon, for example, showed
Prime Minister Begin in an Israeli jet attacking Arab targets

while holding a Torah above his head—a pose meant to evoke the Japanese war cry "Tora! Tora! Tora!"

Israel, too, is concerned about anti-Semitism. Government agencies collect data on anti-Semitic incidents wherever in the world they occur, though they circulate the information in confidential surveys, as if officially ashamed that such things occur. (After all, according to Zionist tenets, anti-Semitism was supposed to disappear with the recovery of Jewish sovereignty.) The Israeli press, of course, informs the public of all such occurrences, as did Herzl's *Die Welt*, which was the first news organ to report them systematically. Whenever possible, Israel intervenes diplomatically to protest anti-Semitic phenomena that seem to be sanctioned by foreign governments.

However, the common interest in combating anti-Semitism is but a marginal fiber in the fabric of the relationship between Israel and the American diaspora. The material support the American Jewish community has long given Israel is naturally of greater importance, even though its value has lately begun to be questioned.

American Jewry has a long tradition of support for needy Jewish communities overseas. Israel, of course, despite the severity of its social problems, is not a distressed Jewish community. And it is the very antithesis of a diaspora community. Still, American Jews send impressive amounts of money to support Israeli institutions for the sick, the lame, the halt, the blind, the old, the orphaned, and the underprivileged. In a separate category are contributions to Israeli universities, scientific institutions, museums, conservatories, orchestras, zoos, sport clubs, trade unions, women's organizations, religious schools, and not-so religious schools. All have "American Friends of..." whose (tax-deductible) contributions help Israel to maintain the panoply of institutions that seem indispensable to a modern society.

Above all these groups towers the United Jewish Appeal. Roughly half of the funds it collects—under the slogan "We Are One"—$740 million for the fiscal year that ended June 30,

1988—help to finance the Jewish Agency, a hybrid (and largely obsolete) institution through whose labyrinthine passages and political blind alleys only the initiated can find their way. UJA money provides 80 percent of the Jewish Agency's budget (a total of $429 million in 1986–87, it declined to $388 million in 1988 and $360 million in 1989, mainly as a result of a change in the priorities of American Jewry). The Jewish Agency in turn funnels funds to the World Zionist Organization and uses a hefty chunk of the money to service old debts.

Still the profusion of financial links between American Jewry and Israeli institutions and organizations alone cannot explain the depth of American Jewry's relationship with Israel. It is no exaggeration to say that Israel has become central to American Jewish life, even if this centrality has different meaning, color, and emotional power to different individuals.

The idea of Israel's centrality burned itself into the consciousness of American Jewry during the Six Day War of 1967. American Jews were profoundly shaken by the shadow of a second Holocaust darkening the life of Israel. The unprecedented flood of emotions ("outpouring" in the local jargon), of fear, of déjà vu, left a massive imprint not only on the checkbooks of American Jews but also on their souls.

Ironically, if Israel had not come into being, American Jewry would not have invented it. True, a significant minority of American Jewry did actively assist in the struggle for the creation of the Jewish state. But the majority did not embrace it until after it became a fait accompli.

If one were to ask in Talmudic fashion, "To what can the relationship between American Jewry and Israel be likened?" the answer would be: "To a marriage in which each partner prefers to live separately—one in America, the other in Israel; one as a minority among the goyim, the other as a majority in a Jewish state, surrounded by hostile nations." (The *yordim*, the Israeli expatriates, are its unwanted children.)

It is not an easy marriage. Misunderstandings abound. They are rooted in the dissimilarity, perhaps even incongruity, of the

American Jewish experience and the changes (some say havoc) independence and sovereignty have wreaked upon the Judeity of Israelis. (The "Jewish revival" vigorously pursued by the Orthodox is trying to undo the "damage." So far its victories have been more political than spiritual.)

The partners do not think of getting a divorce. There are marital fights, constructively called dialogues. It is not a *dialogue des sourds.* Both parties hear each other, and sometimes even listen to each other. The trouble is they do not speak the same language.

Even when the Israelis speak English, as they must when talking to American Jews, they think in Hebrew. Friedrich Nietzsche once made an observation that may explain the difficulties which such a dialogue encounters. "To understand one another," he wrote in *Beyond Good and Evil,* "it is not enough that one uses the same words; one also has to use the same words for the same species of inner experiences; in the end one has to have one's experience in *common.*"

American Jews and Israelis have common experiences, but they relate to the past. They are not lived experiences but memories embedded in the collective subconscious, deliberately dug out from it in a constant self-centered, often self-lacerating effort. They are the sort of national memories of sadness and suffering that Ernest Renan held to be more valuable than remembrances of triumphs "because they impose duties; they command a common effort." Overshadowing all other memories of suffering, of course, is that of the Holocaust.

The absence of a common lived experience is what creates the tensions in the marriage between Israel and the American diaspora. Both groups are part of the same species, as it were. But are they one? The Jew in America lives in an environment created by others, an environment in which he has built a viable Jewish habitat, similar to the ones modern zoos set up for certain animals. Jewish existence in America does not lack authenticity. Yet it is the captive of the non-Jewish environment to which it has had to adapt itself, consciously or unconsciously.

The Israelis, on the other hand, live out in the free, in the wilderness in which nation-states have to survive in a Darwinian struggle for existence. Their Judeity is unmediated; it is self-understood; it needs no institutional props, no defenses against de-identifying assimilation, no dialogues with other religions.

It is the Israelis who do battle in the arena, face the foe, struggle with adverse circumstances (many of their own creation), get hurt, even lay down their lives, while American Jews cheer them on as loyal fans and shower them with gifts in the manner of sports-conscious alumni. For American Zionists who refuse to "make aliyah," Israel is a spectator sport. They may take it very seriously, and to some it is also a substitute religion. But it is the Israelis who consummate the tempestuous love affair with the ancestral land; the pleasure and pain of the diaspora is more like that tasted by the voyeur.

Indeed, as has been pointed out by a number of observers, the very word "freedom" has a different meaning for American Jews than it has for Israelis. American Jews cannot help but conceive of freedom as individual freedom, the freedom of the pursuit of happiness as they see it. The Hebrew word for freedom, *herut*, allows no such interpretation. God never commanded the Jews to seek happiness. The freedom He gave them by liberating them from Egyptian slavery was the freedom to strive collectively to make the Promised Land into a Holy Land. The sacred content of God-given *herut* has become metaphorical in an age in which true faith is rare (despite the religious revival), but the collective connotation of the word remains unchanged.

There is another Hebrew word for freedom: *hofesh*. But *hofesh* implies a relaxation of constraints, an escape from duty, a recess from obligations, none of which is a permissible interpretation of *herut*. The latter is freedom for a common purpose, divine or otherwise. The former is an escape clause for the individual.

Besides semantic difficulties, in its desire to identify with Israel American Jewry finds itself in the uncomfortable position of having to affirm or at least accept conditions in Israel that it would find intolerable in America. In particular, there is the blurring of the boundaries between the sacred and the secular, the intrusion of religion into the legislative and judiciary process, state support for religion—all areas in which the constitutional climate of America differs from that of Israel (if one can speak of a constitutional climate in a country that has no constitution). This forces American Jews to reconcile within themselves the two poles between which Jewish life oscillates. It is thus not a matter of dual loyalty; it is a matter of dual selfhood.

The acceptance of the concept of interdependence raises searing questions. In one sense, American Jewry should be unaffected by what happens to Israel. Even if Israel were to be destroyed (perish the thought), American Jews would remain full-fledged Americans, a brilliant constellation in the firmament of American pluralism. Nonetheless, it can be safely assumed that the overwhelming majority of American Jews are convinced that if anything happened to Israel they would be catastrophically affected. The thought that the collective fate of the American diaspora may depend on events in another country, on another continent, cannot be comforting. If nothing else, it means that American Jewry is hostage to the deeds of Israel, over which it has little influence.

Neither can Israelis draw much comfort from the degree to which their country depends on America—including American Jewry's ability to influence the formulation of United States policy toward the Jewish state. Dependence on American Jewry is more than a source of uneasiness: it damages Israel's virile self-image. In the relationship of interdependence, Israel plays the role of the male partner, American Jewry that of the female. Israel is the fighter, the farmer, the slayer of enemies, the avenger of injustice, and, on a mystic plane, the embodiment of the male principle. (Is this the source of the machismo of Israeli men?) As a caring woman, American Jewry is expected to bring a rich dowry into the marriage. And "she" does so willingly. Of course, in an age of feminism, it is only appropriate that American Jews insist more and more on having a say in how the "dowry" is expended.

As Georges Friedmann aptly observed in his otherwise none too perspicacious *The End of the Jewish People,* the "Judeity [of the American diaspora] is grounded no longer in a similarity but in an interdependence of fate." With interdependence comes not only a deepened interest in each other's fate, but also a right to mutual criticism and a need for mutual respect. All three elements are very imperfectly and asymmetrically present in the relationship between Israel and American Jewry. That they have emerged at all is proof that the American diaspora is the only one of importance. (Israel's relations with Jewish communities in other countries float on the calm seas of uneventfulness.)

For a long time it was possible, even mandatory to overlook contradictions and find devices and formulas that allowed the American Jewish community to pursue its own agenda without tearing holes in the axiom of Jewish unity or allowing serious cracks to develop in the doctrine of Israel's centrality in its life. Not so after the November 1988 Israeli elections. To the intense discomfort of American Jewry (except, of course, for the Orthodox), each of the major Israeli political blocs, Likud and Labor, was prepared to make far-reaching concessions to the four Orthodox parties, which had increased their total representation in the Knesset from eleven to sixteen seats.

What most upset American Jews was the demand by the religious parties that the "Law of Return" be amended so that, in addition to Jews by birth, only persons converted by Orthodox rabbis according to *halakha* would be accepted as immigrants and given automatic citizenship. (Under the existing law, all converts to Judaism were eligible, including those converted by Conservative and Reform rabbis.)

In practice, this proposed change in the immigration law would affect only a tiny number of potential immigrants. Few American Jews come on aliyah to begin with, and among them a mere handful at most are converts. But the change would imply that in the eyes of Israeli law, not merely in the opinion of Israel's religious establishment, Conservative and Reform rabbis had no authority in matters of conversion. In other words, they weren't really rabbis. The change would thus have been another, major step forward in the Orthodox effort to delegitimize Conservative and Reform Judaism. (The Lubavicher Rebbe vigorously supported the change for just that reason.)

In the event, the change in the law was shelved. Likud and Labor agreed to form a broad coalition that obviated the need to yield on the question of "who is a Jew." But the damage was done.

Since the future of the Jewish people now rests on the twin pillars of Israel and American Jewry, Jews naturally worry about how solid the pillars really are. Conventional wisdom says that Israel's ability to survive depends largely on the political course it will steer as a sovereign nation and on its military capabilities. Its geopolitical position remains precarious, just as it was in the times of the First and Second Commonwealth. But in the present international climate the chances that the Jewish state will ere long live in peace are not negligible. They are not a foregone conclusion either.

Whatever dangers threaten the American Jewish diaspora, destruction by outside enemies is not among them. The lingering fear among American Jews that "it"—meaning an American version of Hitler's "Final Solution"—could happen here feeds on the historic fact that Europe's Jews did not believe it would happen to them, either. There is also the gnawing feeling that anti-Semitism is here to stay.

What worries American Jewry most is its diminishing numbers. The birthrate among American Jews is the lowest in the world: a mere twelve per thousand, as compared to a general annual U.S. rate of sixteen per thousand. Much has been made of the growth of the Orthodox congregations among American Jews, a trend that parallels the turn toward more traditional religious frameworks among non-Jews. But though they are forbidden to practice birth control of any kind, Orthodox families are unlikely to produce a big enough crop of children to offset the low birthrate that is expected to persist among the rest.

Disidentification is no less of an enemy. Way back in 1897, Max Nordau warned that a great number of Jews would fall by the wayside if "the defection from Judaism, in order to be fully valid, would not have to be accompanied by conversion to a different creed." This is precisely what is happening in the diaspora today. And not only through mixed marriages.

The demographers make conflicting appraisals about the effect of marriage outside the faith—or the tribe, if you will. The pessimists say it erodes the strength of the Jewish community. Others maintain it strengthens it by bringing in converts.

Pessimists like Elihu Bergman predict that by the year 2076 there will be no more than 944,000 Jews left in the United States. Others claim that the number of Jews will remain more or less stable at some 5 million until the end of the century, and decline to between 3 million and 4 million by 2076. The sociologist Charles Silberman, on the other hand, is all aglow about the Jewish present in America and optimistic about its future —so much so that his book, *A Certain People*, was received with mixed feelings in some Jewish circles. "If indeed we never had it so good," an atavistic Jewish voice whispered in their ears, "is it wise to tell it to the goyim?"

Whatever the actual numbers turn out to be, one thing is certain: American Jewry is shrinking in size. "We are losing," the writer Cynthia Ozick told the *Jerusalem Post* in October 1986. "But that doesn't mean that in the long run I think the Jews are going to die out in America. No. It may be that I'm thinking irrationally, but Jewish history does not take rational turns." Small consolation, indeed.

American Jews do not worry only about their diminishing numbers, they are also concerned about the absence of a true leadership. There is of course the leadership of the United Jewish Appeal, the institution that Emil Fackenheim believes to be the crowning lay achievement of American Jewry in our times.

Undoubtedly, the UJA has become more than a tool for raising funds and dispensing charity. But it cannot provide the kind of leadership for which American Jews yearn. (Rabbi Arthur Herzberg, a prominent Jewish intellectual, has nothing but contempt for the "bourgeois arrivistes" that pass for Jewish lay leaders. To him, they are a monied "macherocracy"—*macher* being a disrespectful Yiddish word for big shot.)

Not that American Jewry is in an acute crisis. But it now has to struggle with the question of its relationship with Israel as never before. To assume Israel's centrality to Jewish life in America is no longer enough. Yet American Jewry must remain conscious of its role as one of the pillars on which the future of the Jewish people rests, a pillar so necessary that its disappearance (even through emigration to Israel) would be a catastrophe for the Jewish people.

Some Orthodox thinkers believe that American Jewry can fulfill its God-ordained role without leaving their homes and going to Israel. The eminent scholar Jacob Neusner, for example, believes that by returning to the safe haven of *halakha*, American Jews will not only overcome their spiritual malaise but be able, through a full religious commitment, to attain a level of moral integrity that will make them into a holy people right among the fleshpots of America. Of course, the present state of morality and religiosity among American Jewry makes such an evolution seem highly unlikely.

What, then, does the future hold in store for American Jewry? The pessimists say that it has nowhere to go but down. The optimists are confident that American Jewry will be able to assume its Jewish responsibilities. And there is no country in the world more optimistic than the United States, which expects each year to be better than the preceding one. It may be even enough to behave as if that maxim were true.

XII

Balaam's Curse

For most of the movement's history there was little the Zionist leadership agreed upon. It was too ideological for that. Factional splits, unholy alliances, chancy fusions, walkouts—all these were standard features of the Zionist road show. (A great deal of it—too much, in fact—was carried over into the political culture of Israel.) In this respect, the Zionist movement behaved like other exile movements, such as the Russian socialists.

The one thing all parties, factions, and groupings agreed upon was that the Jewish state would be a secular democratic republic. Even the religious Zionists had no quarrel with that. They were confident that once the coercive powers of the state were in Jewish hands, Jewish shops would be closed on Yom Kippur and open on Christmas.

The Zionist movement modeled its institutions on those of the parliamentary systems of Europe. Before World War I, of course, most European nations were constitutional monarchies. The Zionists, however, never contemplated any other form of political organization for the future Jewish state than that of a republic. Herzl may have been called the "King of the Jews," but he would have been no more than the ceremonial president of the new nation had his dream of Jewish statehood come true in his lifetime.

The founding fathers of political Zionism had great hopes for the ability of the Jewish people to build a better state, a better, more moral society. Herzl went furthest of all. In *Altneuland*, he extended the general Zionist desire that the Jewish state be a morally superior state into the realm of utopia. Herzl wanted to build a republic ruled by a true aristocracy and tilled by a true peasantry. The fact was, of course, that Jews possessed neither.

The socialists believed that, strengthened by the Prophets' call for social justice, they would be able to create in the future Jewish state an egalitarian society. And it is fair to say that Jewish society in Mandatory Palestine, and in the first years after independence, *was* egalitarian—in the sense that although social differences existed, they were not blatant enough to be offensive.

In its early years, the State of Israel also looked forward to establishing itself as a regular member of the so-called family of nations. Its people greatly relished every sign of acceptance, warmly welcoming every foreign ambassador who set up shop in the Jewish state. Its own diplomats enthusiastically plunged into the prestigious task of representing their country abroad, and endeavored to add their grist to the prolix mill of international meetings, particularly at the United Nations.

In those idyllic early days, Israelis—and Jews in other countries—did not feel that the Jewish state was a pariah state, that the Jewish nation was a pariah nation. Israel did not feel isolated, rejected, or beyond the pale. It did not feel deprived of friends in Europe and the Americas.

However, Israel soon found out that it had no chance of becoming a member of any existing treaty organization or bloc of nations, and not for want of trying. When it set out to enlist the other non-Arab nations of the Middle East, Turkey and Iran, into a new triangular coalition, it quickly hit a brick wall. Both countries were reluctant to offend Arab sensibilities. Turkey wound up downgrading its relations with Israel, while the Shah played the game under a flimsy cover of secrecy, all the time pretending that it wasn't being played at all.

Still, no Jewish voice was raised to proclaim that Israel's "apartness" was ordained by a divinely guided course of history. On the contrary, the net of its diplomatic efforts was cast as wide as possible. And in the 1960s, when Israel finally succeeded in breaking its isolation in the Third World by establishing close relations with Black Africa, the country was jubilant.

Suddenly, Israel had a mission beyond the primordial task of keeping itself alive and well. The country enthusiastically relapsed into the visionarism of the founding fathers of Zionism. Israel was finally a light unto at least some nations. It had something to offer to others. There was, after all, a word that would go forth from Jerusalem. (Of course, it was decidedly not the word of God, and no one pretended otherwise.)

For all that, there was no denying that the relentless hostility of the Arab world had placed Israel in the singular situation of being the only country in the world whose destruction was the avowed aim of some of its fellow United Nations members, the Charter notwithstanding. In addition, there were quite a few countries that could rightly be suspected of preferring a world without a Jewish state, although they would not think of using force themselves to bring about such a state of affairs.

Israel obviously regretted this attitude and tried to change it. Unfortunately, it seemed that nothing could be done with the Arabs. They would have to be taught a lesson by force.

To be sure, there was always talk of Israel's readiness for peace. In practice, however, Israel tended to be suspicious of peace initiatives, especially when they involved any departure from the status quo. The status quo, whatever it happened to be at any given moment, always appeared to be preferable to change. Change, after all, could only mean less territory for Israel—and to most Israelis, less territory meant less security.

This is one reason why Israel has never launched a peace initiative of its own.

Despite Israel's intransigence, it wasn't until after the Six Day War that the movement to isolate, ostracize, denounce, and punish Israel began to gain any momentum in the international community. It wasn't the war itself that changed world attitudes toward Israel but Israel's actions after the war. For the most part, the international community had reacted to Israel's June 5, 1967, pre-emptive strike against Egypt with understanding and tolerance. It had no tolerance, however, for Israel's apparent desire to expand its territory by keeping the land it had managed to occupy during the fighting. The international community was wedded to the dogma that unilateral changes of borders were unacceptable; at most, it would tolerate a few small adjustments in the armistice lines that were for all practical purposes Israel's international borders. This was certainly the view of the United States, whose good will Israel could not afford to jeopardize.

The world's unwillingness to let Israel enjoy what most Israelis and diaspora Jews regarded as the legitimate fruits of its victory had a profound influence on the Israeli mind-set: it was taken as proof that the world's attitude to the Jewish people had not changed. As always, the world seemed to regard the Jews with indifference at best and outright hostility at worst. Fortunately, the Jews were no longer a helpless people. On the contrary, Israel was now a power to be reckoned with in the Middle East, or so most Israelis believed.

Given this interpretation of events, it is hardly surprising that Israel came to view the world's reaction to subsequent events as being motivated solely by a desire to punish the Jewish state for its temerity in establishing military predominance over its neighbors. In short, it was the old "us-against-them" syndrome in new guise. "Them" was the entire world, while "us" was no longer just an individual Jew or an individual Jewish community but the Jewish state as the collective expression of the Jewish people's will to sovereign nationhood.

242

A less apocalyptic view would suggest that Israel's deteriorating international position was less the result of mankind's perpetual hatred of the Jews than Israel's own refusal to recognize new political realities—specifically, its insistence on reaping the fruits of victory in an era in which harvesting the fruits of victory was no longer considered permissible, certainly not for small countries. Wars might still be fought, but the old god of war who saw to it that the spoils went to the victor had been replaced by a new god who jealously protected the territorial status quo. As a result, those who nevertheless insisted on plucking the fruits would sooner or later find that they were poisonous.

None of this has kept Israelis from arguing that their country is judged and found guilty by the international community not only for what it does but because it is a Jewish state. The proof seems clear. No Arab country broke diplomatic relations with France when the latter was engaged in the brutal suppression of the Algerian people's quest for independence. But many countries broke relations with Israel when it fought to preserve its existence. The United Nations does not condemn Libya for its occupation of Chadian territory. But it does harass Israel over its occupation of a territory of undetermined sovereignty. The Vatican is prepared to recognize atheistic states, but not the Jewish state. And contrary to all logic, the United Nations condemns Zionism as racist in an attempt to delegitimize the state sired by the Zionist national revolution.

The perception of persecution created by the international opprobrium that is still being heaped on Israel, most virulently in Third World assemblies, causes Israelis and diaspora Jews to lose sight of the difference between the condemnation of specific acts deemed to be contrary to international law and the comity of nations, and less justified condemnations intended mainly to put Israel under pressure.

Israel, for example, may feel fully justified in bombing to bits an Iraqi nuclear plant in order to save its children from becoming the victims of the nuclear weapons that plant was meant to produce, as Prime Minister Begin declared in 1981. But to claim that the raid amounts to nothing more than legitimate self-defense as defined by the United Nations Charter overtaxes the imagination of all countries, except Israel. The ill-conceived and ill-fated 1982 invasion of Lebanon is another example of an egregious misinterpretation by Israel of its right to defend itself, irrespective of whether or not the campaign was capable of eliminating terrorist attacks on the Galilee.

There is, of course, a reason why the international community treats Israel differently from other transgressors of the international code of behavior: Israel is thwarting Palestinian aspirations to nationhood. Needless to say, a majority of Israelis feel that Palestinians are not entitled to statehood—or, if they are entitled, then prevented by historic circumstances from realizing their aspirations, as are the Kurds and a number of other national groups that would rather be independent. (The Lithuanians, Letts, and Estonians certainly fall into this category.) Unfortunately for Israel, while the international community cares little for the Kurds (and dares not do anything about the Baltic people under Soviet rule), it happens to care a lot for the Palestinians. It does so not because the Palestinians' adversaries are Jews who must be taught to know their place, but because it considers the Palestinians' claim to the land to be no less legitimate than that of the Jews—which is why the United Nations decided to partition Palestine in the first place.

Israel preferred to reject this notion. As far as it was concerned, the wholeness of Eretz Israel supersedes any claims the Palestinians might have. This doctrine may seem self-serving, but it became an accepted policy as a result of Israel's fortuitous conquest of the West Bank in the 1967 war.

It is the pursuit of this doctrine that is largely responsible for Israel's isolation in the world. But that hasn't stopped Israelis from looking for metaphysical reasons for their pariah status. After all, why accept a mundane and unpleasant explanation for your woes when a loftier one may be available? And for the Jews what better place than the Bible to seek the answer to why

Israel seems fated to remain a pariah nation, its aspirations misinterpreted, its eschatological goals misunderstood or rejected? Chapter and verse in this case are Numbers 23:9, the blessing of Balaam, the only non-Jewish prophet of note in the Old Testament: Israel is a "people [that] shall dwell alone, and shall not be reckoned among the nations."

That may sound more like a curse than a blessing. And indeed, before the Lord made him bless Israel, cursing Israel (at the behest of King Balak of the Moabites) was Balaam's original intent. (Talleyrand held that a man's first intentions are always his most sincere.) On the face of it, of all of Balaam's pronouncements this one about Israel's isolation being its fate is the most ambiguous. The rabbis always had a bit of difficulty with Balaam.

All seem to agree that Balaam predicted (or prophesied, if you will) the "aloneness" of Israel. That in itself is not surprising, for what distinguishes the Jews from other people (in their eyes, at least) is not principally their language and culture, but the fact that they have been chosen as the instrument of a divine purpose. No other people claim to have a Covenant with God, nor does anyone so jealously guard the privilege in the face of such overwhelming evidence that neither side is keeping it. (The majority of Jews certainly do not honor the Covenant, and the Holocaust raises serious questions about God's justice.)

One should note that Rashi, a towering eleventh-century exegetic authority, takes a different, more positive view of Balaam's curse. To him, it means that the Jews will not be numbered among the nations when God finally makes "a full end of all nations." Rashi refers to Jeremiah 30:11, which reads: "For I am with thee, saith the Lord, to save thee: though I make a full end of all nations whither I have scattered thee, yet will I not make a full end of thee..."

It is unlikely that the nations among which the Jews were scattered had Jeremiah's prophecy in mind when they tried to expunge the Jews from their midst. Neither could Rashi have envisaged a situation in which the Jews would have a state of their own—no less one in which, rather than the Jews living scattered among other nations, another nation lived scattered among them.

Whatever the correct interpretation of Balaam's curse, after 1967 it was cited by religious nationalists as proof that Israel's isolation was preordained, and therefore was not the result of any "sin" of commission or omission of which the Jewish state might be guilty in the eyes of the world. "Dwelling alone" was thus hailed as the normal condition for the Jewish state—though it surely was not the kind of normality Zionism's founding fathers had in mind, nor what the Yishuv had worked so hard to create.

In a sense, this way of looking at things raised to the collective level of the state the question asked by the distinguished American-Jewish sociologist Nathan Glazer—namely, whether the "peculiar distinctiveness" of the Jews was a reaction to the outside world's attitude or whether the sense of "an overwhelming aloneness" was created by an "inner urge."

The answer is probably a bit of both, each of the elements supporting the other in the construction of a worldview based mainly on a general distrust of the gentiles. Certainly, the relationship between the Jews and the (gentile) world has long been one of "us against them." In recent times, of course, the gentile world's attitude seems to have changed somewhat for the better, mainly as a result of the lessons of the Holocaust. But the "inner urge" leads the Jews to minimize or discount these changes.

With every anti-Semitic—or apparently anti-Semitic—incident, the "us-against-them" worldview is reinforced. The Pope, for example, receives Kurt Waldheim, the champion prevaricator and President of Austria who has come to symbolize to Jews that a man can not only get away with his Nazi past but be honored in spite of it. (The more suspicious would say *because* of it.) In beatifying a nun who was gassed at Auschwitz, the Vatican conspicuously avoids mentioning the fact that she wasn't killed because of her faith in Christ but because she had been born a Jew. In Japan, an anti-Semitic novel becomes a best-seller. North Korea, in announcing moves to make the country more open to visitors, makes it clear that Jews (not just Israelis) need not bother applying for visas. The 1988 Templeton Prize for Religion, which bestows both honor and a $369,000 stipend on its recipient, goes to Dr. Inamullah Khan, the Secretary General of the World Muslim Council, whose anti-Israel and anti-Jewish activities are a matter of record. And it remains a fact that, even before Yasir Arafat was received by the 1988 U.N. General Assembly as the head of the Palestinian state whose existence he had just proclaimed, the PLO enjoyed formal diplomatic relations with more countries than did Israel. (By May 1989, fully ninety–six countries had formally recognized Arafat's newly proclaimed Palestinian state, despite the fact that it is not international legal practice to recognize presumptive political entities.) There is no dearth of such examples, all of which are carefully noted by the Jewish people—perhaps too carefully.

Not every incident of this sort reflects authentic anti-Jewish prejudice. Nonetheless, the "us-against-them" syndrome such indignities provoke is inextricably linked to the notion that anti-Semitism is an immutable feature of Jewish existence. Indeed, they both seem so eternal that it is hard to say which came first. In any case, whether it is a cause or an effect, the "us-against-them" syndrome clearly seems to serve the interests of both religious and political leaders in Israel. The aims of Orthodoxy may differ from those of the politicians who thrive on the syndrome, but for the time being at least both seem to have become comfortable bedfellows.

The new brand of religiously tinged chauvinism that has made its appearance in Israel imputes the worst possible motives to the gentile world. None of the gentiles can be trusted, it preaches, except to plot Israel's destruction, generation after generation, as the Passover Haggadah reminds Jews who read it at the Seder. If this is true, then Israel has nothing to gain by being the "good guy"; rather, it should do whatever serves its interests, without worrying about its image. In any case, Israel is alone. Balaam's curse—or blessing in disguise, as theologian Emil Fackenheim calls it—thus becomes a self-fulfilling prophecy.

The more extremist among the religious nationalists go beyond merely defensive goals. They believe that the greater Israel's isolation, the sooner the Jewish people will be redeemed. Rabbi Meir Kahane preaches that aloneness is the only route to redemption. "The more isolated the Jew," he wrote in 1980, "the greater the sense of awe and sanctity in the victory of the Almighty."

Perhaps Balaam's curse should be read somewhat differently. Instead of Israel not being reckoned among the nations, Israel should not reckon *with* the nations. (In Hebrew, no change in consonants is needed for either reading.) After all, had not Ben-Gurion held that the important thing was what the Jews did, not what other nations thought? In that sense, aren't the religious Zionists then only guilty of carrying the idea further than Ben-Gurion the realist cared or dared to do?

The perception that the Jews will be condemned and hated whatever they do has deep psycho-historic roots. This suspicion of gentiles is by no means limited to people with ritually untrimmed beards who eat only kosher food. The memory of the Holocaust naturally reinforces Jewish distrust and suspiciousness of gentiles. In this respect, the relentless preservation of Holocaust memories is obviously counterproductive—unless, that is, the Jews, and Israel, want to persevere in the "aloneness" that has in the past caused rivers of Jewish blood and tears to flow. (In fact, there is ample proof that the Jews really don't want to be isolated. How else can one explain the enthusiastic reception by the Israeli public of every improvement in relations with the Soviet Union and other Eastern European countries? And why do so many diaspora Jews still bask in any good word a prominent gentile may have for them?)

In the first years of independence, Israelis were not particularly afflicted by Holocaust memories. At first sight, this may appear surprising, as there was virtually no Ashkenazi family that did not lose close relatives in the Nazi death camps. Moreover, the country was flooded with large numbers of Holocaust survivors—the very people in whose name the Yishuv had demanded a Jewish state. But the survivors kept their memories to themselves. And though it was sympathetic, the rest of the old Yishuv had a hard time understanding why European Jewry had allowed itself, in Ben-Gurion's words, "to be driven like sheep unto the slaughterhouse." The Yishuv was not victim-oriented.

Before the Jewing of Israel, the Holocaust was mostly a matter for private grief; for writers, artists, and historians, all of whom tried to understand what cannot be understood. But when it became part of the national ethos, the sheep had to be transformed into martyrs; suicides and futile gestures, into acts of resistance; Jewish collaborators in the Nazi death machine, excused; the belated last-stand revolts of desperation, glorified. (Had not the first Gerer Rebbe, Isaac Meir Alter, noted in reference to Haman's planned slaughter of the Jews of Persia, that being killed does not make you a martyr unless your death has served a holy purpose?)

It was no longer enough simply to mourn the victims. The Holocaust had become a national treasure, a valuable legacy that was (and is) constantly evoked to remind the gentiles of their indifference or, worse, their complicity in the destruction of European Jewry. At the very least, the demand for moral reparations seemed to stand on firm feet: if gentiles were still not prepared to help Israel, they should at least abstain from harming it. (When Jews speak of gentiles, they think of white Christians.) At the same time, the perpetuation of Holocaust memories served as a warning that the Jews would never again passively endure any such calamity, a bark that has now a nuclear bite.

The exterioration of the Holocaust memories might have come about spontaneously as historians, writers, artists, philosophers, and theologians finally managed to address the horror.

In fact, the process was triggered in Israel by an action under-
taken by the state in 1961: the abduction from Argentina, and
the subsequent trial in Jerusalem, of Adolf Eichmann, the chief
executive officer, as it were, of Hitler's deportation and destruction enterprise.

Although the Eichmann trial was conducted according to the
rules of law as understood in civilized society in the light of the
Nuremberg war-crimes trials, and though Eichmann clearly deserved the death penalty he received, his was in a sense a show
trial. In putting Eichmann in the bulletproof glass dock, Israel
was demonstrating that the Jews were now capable of wreaking
justice upon their enemies.

The trial also signaled that the prosecution of the enemies of
the Jewish people and the preservation of the rights as well as
the memory of their victims anywhere was now the legitimate
concern of the State of Israel. Thus it was in 1987, that Israel
put Ivan Demjanjuk on trial after he was extradited by the
United States. Demjanjuk had been accused of being "Ivan the
Terrible," a Nazi prison guard so called by the inmates of the
Treblinka death camp because of his cruelty. Once again long
lines of spectators sought admission to the proceedings, eager
to get a refresher course in the horrors of the Holocaust. It was
surprising to see ultra-Orthodox youth among them, considering that Orthodox theology teaches that the Holocaust was
God's punishment for the sins of Israel. Did they want to get a
glimpse of one the instruments of God's will? The Orthodox
had shown little interest in Eichmann, who in his career never
so much as personally touched a Jew, much less killed one with
his own hands.

Perhaps the intense interest reflected the extent to which
Demjanjuk, who was not a German but a Ukrainian, served as a
symbol for the complicity and indifference of the world to the
fate of the Jews. Indeed, relatively few gentiles lost any sleep as
a result of the deportation and eventual destruction of the Jews
of Europe. Very few asked themselves what had happened to
their Jewish neighbors who one day simply seemed to have dis-

appeared. And even fewer regretted their departure. Poles interviewed by Claude Lanzmann for his shattering documentary *Shoah* did not conceal their feeling that they were better off without Jews; most even admitted having cheered the Jews on to their deaths in the inferno of Treblinka.

The men and women Lanzmann interviewed were not a representative sample of the Polish people. Others may not have been so pleased about the disappearance of the Jews. But few shed any tears, not only among the Poles but also among other peoples under German rule. They were preoccupied with their own lives, with their own survival in a political environment that exacted a very high price for any act of dissident courage or conscience or humanity.

To be sure, there were gentiles, quite a few of them Poles, who did save Jews at great personal risk. Over a hundred have been honored as "Righteous Gentiles" at Jerusalem's Yad Vashem, the shrine erected both to commemorate the 6 million victims of Hitler's war against the Jews and to keep alive the lessons of the Holocaust.

Those determined to keep alive the memory of the destruction of European Jewry fall into two main categories. A minority takes a universalist attitude. The most eloquent among them is the Nobel laureate Elie Wiesel, who wants the Holocaust remembered "for the sake of victims everywhere who suffer," in the hope that the existential despair the Holocaust arouses—or, at least, ought to arouse—in humanity will prevent a repetition anywhere of the ungraspable Hitlerite crime.

The majority of Holocaustodians, however, see the Holocaust as an exclusively Jewish concern. They insist on a Jewish monopoly on suffering. The purpose behind this is twofold: to prod gentile consciences in order to bend them to Jewish purposes and, perhaps more important, to strengthen the Jews' sense of apartness. The sociologist Charles Silberman explains this exclusivist excess by noting the intensity with which the trauma continues to be felt by the Jews. This intensity would inevitably abate over the years were it not for the presence of a mighty

251

machinery designed to prevent any such ebbing of emotion. The historian Ismar Schorsh of the Jewish Theological Seminary pronounces a harsher judgment. He sees in the Jewish desire to monopolize the Holocaust memory a "distasteful" secular version of chosenness, an effort to establish the moral superiority of the Jews on the grounds that they have suffered more than any other people for no other reason than their Jewishness. (The Gypsies, of course, were also destined for annihilation for no other reason than that they were Gypsies.)

It is a matter of historic record that no country was eager to open its gates to Jewish refugees when the Nazi persecution of Jews began to assume dangerous dimensions. David Wyman, in his seminal work *The Abandonment of the Jews,* documented that the United States and Britain refused to rescue even a few thousand Jews from Europe, for fear that Germany would unload greater numbers of "undesirable" Jews on the West. Indeed, that is precisely what Hitler's Germany was interested in doing—until such reactions brought it to the conclusion that emigration was not a realistic way to get rid of large numbers of Jews.

Governments simply did not consider the fate of foreign Jews, or any foreigners for that matter, to be in any way their responsibility. It is difficult to believe that they would have changed their view had they known sooner what ultimate fate Hitler had in store for the Jews. Governments are moved by what they consider to be their self-interest. (Israel is no exception.) Humanitarian considerations come into play only afterward, and then only if they do not contradict the perceived self-interest. By the time the news about the Final Solution could no longer be ignored, the Allies were deep into fighting a world war. The rescue of Jews was not an Allied war aim. If it was on the agenda at all, it was as a low-priority item that would not be allowed to interfere with the war effort.

As a matter of fact, the rescue of European Jewry was not even a priority for the Jewish Agency—until, that is, it was too late to do anything but hatch quixotic plans. The Zionist leadership was interested in bringing Jews to Palestine only to the extent that their presence might further the aim of the creation of a Jewish state. (Similarly, the Israeli government today is not interested in freedom of emigration for Soviet Jewry, but only in their freedom to go to Israel.)

In 1938, Ben-Gurion actually opposed the Evian Conference at which the representatives of Western democracies met to discuss the German refugee problem. He feared that any positive result would weaken the Zionist thesis that only a Jewish state could serve as a haven for persecuted Jewry. As it turned out, he had nothing to fear: the Evian Conference did not open any avenues for Jewish emigration. In the same year, he told the meeting of his party's Central Committee that he would prefer to see emigration to Palestine of only half of Germany's Jewish children, rather than have all of them brought to safety in England. (England did accept a small number of Jewish refugee youngsters.)

To reproach countries like the United States for not having done more to rescue Jews from the Holocaust is like castigating the authors of the American Constitution for not having abolished slavery in 1789. In both cases, the criticism, although morally justified, retrojects into the past the spirit of later times.

Such an attitude has its attractions. By accusing the Western democracies of anti-Semitism, the Jews put them on the defensive. As long as guilt feelings can be profitably mined, advantages can be gained. But the lode is not likely to last forever. More important, guilt feelings are not a solid foundation on which to build any group's position, nationally or internationally.

Nonetheless, the belief in the permanence of gentile hostility seems to have become part of Israeli political culture. According to Charles Liebman, a professor of political studies at the religiously oriented Bar Ilan University, the core values of modern Israeli political culture include "elements of the religious tradition and in particular conceptions of Jewish moral-cultural uniqueness and superiority, the permanent hostility of the Gentiles, and the mandate to preserve this culture."

Religious tradition, moral-cultural uniqueness, superiority, the permanent hostility of the gentiles—these were not the spiritual building blocks used to create the Jewish state. And they are not the ones that can preserve it as a secular democracy, which the majority of Israelis seem to prefer. Yet somehow they have become the core values of Israel's political culture.

The phenomenon cannot be explained merely by the existence of a political system that obliges power-hungry politicians to truckle to the fundamentalist defenders of the true faith. It would not have come about had not a profound change transformed Israeli society, a transformation that made Israel forget its Zionist ideals and become receptive to the old-new call for redemption.

There is nothing abnormal about the decline of Zionist idealism. All revolutions—the French, the Russian, the nationalist revolutions in Europe and, later, in its dependencies—ran out of idealistic steam once their leaders attained power. Ideologies, of course, are harder to kill. They can be kept alive, like a comatose patient, on the life-support machinery of symbolic, sentimental, and rhetorical attachment to the values they had once created.

In Mandatory Palestine, the struggle for the establishment of a Jewish homeland was spearheaded by the Zionist pioneers. But although they were emblematic of the effort, they were actually a minority in the Yishuv. The fact was, the people who tilled the land, tended the citrus groves, and constructed the roads and houses were not the only ones responsible for erecting the edifice of the future state; it was not they alone who pushed the *medina bederekh*—"the state on the way"—toward the ultimate goal of independence.

The small shopkeeper, the fledgling manufacturer hammering away in a garage workshop, the tailor, the tinsmith and the tilemaker, even the real estate speculator—all were convinced that they, too, were contributing to the common effort. And they were—through their conviction alone, irrespective of the quality of their product or effort. So what if foreign toothpaste was tastier? Where else in the world was there a factory that produced toothpaste with Hebrew labels? In fact, speaking Hebrew was in itself a way of promoting the cause, which is why the polyglot population was constantly exhorted to use the ancient language.

Teachers were held in particular esteem, for they taught not only a regular curriculum in Hebrew but also Zionist values. The Bible was thus taught as history, and the Oral Tradition was regarded as nothing more than a Jewish curiosity, a part of the heritage that had little if any relevance to the present. Students were taught to emulate the best: the selfless pioneers.

The struggle demanded a constant readiness for personal sacrifice—the everyday pedestrian kind of sacrifice as well as the heroic kind: heroic not in the old passive way of the persecuted, martyred Jew, but in a new, un-Jewish meaning of the word. "Our" heroes were now like "their" heroes: they died with their boots on. Life was very hard, but it made sense.

All that changed with statehood. Now that defense was the army's responsibility, the Israel Defense Forces could no longer be a voluntary, comradely "underground" army like the Haganah or Etzel. It had to become a conscript army, forged through rigorous training into a formidable fighting force led by a professional officer corps. And while the old Yishuv virtually policed itself—old-timers will tell you that locking one's apartment was unheard of in the early days—after independence, a police force became a growing necessity. In fact, the need grew much faster than the force.

In the first years after independence, the agricultural conquest of the land was still a national goal. But there was no longer any need to occupy the land by sending a handful of courageous pioneers in the thick of the night to set up a "Tower and Stockade" settlement. The "Crown Lands" that the British administration of Palestine had closed to Jewish settlement now belonged to the State of Israel. Arab landlords did not have

255

to be cajoled to sell their land, as had been the case in the past. The state now could claim the right of eminent domain and confiscate land, compensating the owner in some way or another. More commonly, the office of the custodian of Absentee Property simply appropriated land abandoned by Arabs on the assumption that the original owners would not return; the assumption was based on the logical grounds that they would not be allowed to return. (With the unification of Jerusalem some "absentee owners" have found themselves back within Israel's borders—a privilege that does not include the right to recover their "absentee" property.)

The Sephardi immigrants from Arab countries who streamed to Israel in great numbers after independence also changed the character of the Yishuv. However much the state needed people, it was clear that these newcomers were not the sort of people that the social engineers of Zionism could use for the construction of the kind of society they originally had in mind for the Jewish state.

As a result, after a period of great difficulties and stringent austerity, the Israelis wound up creating a state not based on high-flown Zionist ideals or Judaic ethics but one modeled on Western consumer society—at least to the degree that circumstances (including the presence in its midst of a sizable Third World population) permitted it. Israel has since managed in a remarkable measure to assure its population a relatively high standard of living, albeit at the cost of a huge external debt and a constant reliance on massive financial support from the United States.

But was the Jewish state created for no other purpose than for the more or less satisfactory fulfillment of ordinary desires of ordinary people? Had not Ahad Haam way back in 1897 warned that Zionism would be a failure if it resulted in no more than the creation of yet another small state on the map of the world?

As long as the state was not yet in existence, that question, though hotly debated, went necessarily unanswered. And for the first twenty years after independence, it continued to generate little soul-searching. There were too many burning practical problems to be addressed. But then came the 1967 victory, which gave Israel a much trumpeted sense of having arrived, of having established itself as a permanent feature in the Middle East, and one that had to be reckoned with. But instead of being reassured, Israelis found themselves confronted with the challenge presented by the return not of the diaspora "Exiles," who stubbornly stayed where they were, but of the occupied territories whose addition would make the Land of Israel whole.

Zionism could not answer that challenge. Though rivers of Zionist rhetoric flowed as never before, the Zionist emperor who now ruled the whole of the Land of Israel had no clothes, his old ones having been torn to tatters on the thorns of Israeli realities. The Israeli was thus left not only without idealism but without an ideology. Consumerism, bad manners, and the groping for a compromise between Western culture and that brought along by immigrants from Moslem countries were obviously no substitute for ideological motivation.

Then came the 1973 Yom Kippur War. It shocked the Israeli public primarily because it shook, temporarily at least, the country's belief in the solidity of its military machine. It seemed that the Labor Party, which had been the principal political player since before independence, had not delivered whatever it was supposed to deliver in an era of fluctuating expectations. What was worse, labor no longer seemed able to send a clear message about its national goals. Unlike the old generation of Labor leaders such as Ben-Gurion, Golda Meir, and Levi Eshkol, the new generation was not ideological but managerial. Too many among them looked after their personal interests and fortunes, a thing previously unknown in Israel. They had lost credibility.

The stage was thus set for a drama with a new message, new in the political context. That message carried openly messianic overtones, and it was eagerly adopted by the political right. It drew crucial strength from the coming of age of the Sephardi electorate, that mass of voters made up of the inhabitants of development towns and the poorer quarters of Israeli cities, of working-class people and members of a lumpenproletariat, of lower-echelon civil servants and office workers, of an admixture of people who had made a lot of money yet had gained no respect or recognition, a mass that had been hitherto enfiefed to Labor. They had had enough of Labor's patronizing if well-meaning attitude to those of its "underdeveloped" brethren who refused to adapt to Labor's peculiar Ashkenazi and pseudo-socialist ethos.

What helped the Sephardim to assert themselves was not only the leadership's disarray during the 1973 war but the recognition that they no longer stood at the bottom of the social ladder: the Arabs from the occupied territories had taken their place as hewers of wood and drawers of water. No wonder the Sephardim wanted to keep what Israel had won.

Before the *intifada*, public-opinion polls consistently showed that two-thirds of the Israeli population favored the retention of the West Bank. (Since the uprising, opinion polls indicate a confusing shift: though a majority favors negotiations with the PLO "provided it keeps its promises," an even larger majority does not believe the PLO will do so.) In any case, since only some 15 percent of the population is religious, one must assume that the majority of both the conditional and unconditional "hawks" want to keep the territories for reasons other than the religious belief that the "wholeness" of the Land of Israel is a precondition for the beginning of redemption. Most likely, they consider Judea and Samaria to be part of the Jewish patrimony, and as such areas in which an Israeli presence must be maintained in one form or another. (Prime Minister Shamir's Likud has lately muted its redemptory rhetoric.)

But if there really is a higher justification for keeping the Land of Israel whole, all the more reason to keep the territories. At least this gives the Jewish people—with the Israelis in the forefront where they belong—a mission: to pave the way for the coming of the Messiah. Rabbi Kook had always held that that was precisely what the Godless socialist pioneers had been doing: they were fulfilling God's will by breaking His commandments.

For the pioneers, redemption meant something very concrete. It had no religious meaning. It meant tilling a piece of land, planting an orchard, building a road, bringing in illegal immigrants under cover of night, joining an underground fighting unit, creating the reality that would move the dream closer to reality. The work was the medium of personal redemption—redemption from the indignities of the Exile, redemption from enslavement to egotism. (Judaism knows only collective, not individual redemption.)

But that was in the past. No longer could redemption be furthered through a breach of commandments: now the commandments would have to be scrupulously observed. Only thus, the religious argument went, would the Jewish people become a Holy People and the Kingdom of God on earth be established. In principle, this notion applied to Jews everywhere. But the Jews of Israel carried a special responsibility, since certain commandments could only be fulfilled in the Holy Land.

And since the Holy Land is now the State of Israel, the argument continued, the state must assume a religious meaning never contemplated by any of the founding fathers of Zionism, including the few Orthodox Zionists who embraced the idea of a return to the land of the forefathers before the advent of the Messiah.

This is the doctrine the "redemptionists" propagate. This is the doctrine that has turned classical Zionism into a historical artifact. Of course, to convert Israel into a truly Jewish state, the supreme law of the land would have to be the *halakha*. The only remaining question would then be how to apply it to public life. *Halakha* is not subject to the decisions of the electorate.

The behavior of the religious parties in Israel provides a foretaste of the kind of government they envisage—until, that is, the coming of the Messiah puts an end to the state as an institution. (Karl Marx also predicted the "withering away of the state," but he was merely a political messianist, not a messianic politician.) There could still be a parliament (indeed, Iran has one), but any decision of importance would be made by unelected Torah sages. There would be no independent judiciary, only religious courts. There would be no other culture than religious culture.

The thesis that the State of Israel has theological significance, a view rejected by both the political and the cultural Zionists, has also made a great deal of headway in the diaspora —and not only among the Orthodox. For example, American Conservative Judaism, whose rabbis are anathema to Israel's religious establishment, added to the traditional version of the blessing after meals a prayer asking the "Merciful to bless the State of Israel, the dawn of our redemption."

There is nothing wrong with a revival of religiosity. It is a worldwide phenomenon. In Israel, it is strengthened by the evocation of Exilic experience—specifically, the notion that what allowed the Jewish people to maintain their identity through all those centuries of wandering was their adherence to their religion. But present circumstances are radically different. In Israel, a Jew does not need a religious identity to remain a Jew—he has a national identity. Indeed, the State of Israel was founded in order to enable Jews to do there what they could not, and cannot, do anywhere else. For the Israeli, Jewishness is unmediated, a matter that goes without saying. The diaspora Jew, on the other hand, has to say it all the time.

If an Israeli believes, and obviously quite a few do, that it is not enough to be a Jew defined by nationality, there is nothing to prevent him from obeying all the commandments. On the contrary, the state has been generous—all too generous, the majority of Israelis believe—in furthering religious education and being sensitive to the concerns of the Orthodox (among other things, by exempting religious women and many thousands of yeshiva students from military service).

But personal preferences is not what the *Kulturkampf* raging in Israel today is all about. It is about the declared desire of the religious sector to make *halakha* the law of the land, the only constitution the country will ever need. (It has none at present because of religious objections to a secular constitution.) In the tenth century, the great rabbinical scholar, exegete, philosopher, and poet Saadia ben Joseph declared that "our nation is a nation because of its possession of the Torah." But he lived in Exile— in Babylonian Exile, to be precise. The Jews of Israel do not live in Exile. And the "possession of the Torah" is not what makes Israel a nation-state. Besides, the world is moving into the twenty-first century.

Not that the Orthodox oppose technological progress. On the contrary, they welcome it. Computers are used to check Torah scrolls for copying errors. Programmable devices allow them to circumvent prohibitions against work on the Sabbath and holy days, such as pushing elevator buttons or switching on lights and appliances. The rabbis may one day even permit the use of fully automated public transport on the Sabbath. Even space travel does not seem to present major problems. A former Chief Rabbi of Israel, Shlomo Goren, has already worked out a prayer schedule for future Orthodox astronauts in orbit. (Typical for the Orthodox establishment, Rabbi Goren is primarily interested in the ritual.)

Orthodox rabbis insist that questions arising from new technologies can be answered by a sharpening of distinctions found in the sources and interpretative works. But important as this sort of thing may be in practical terms, such issues are peripheral. The central question is what political and social structure the Jewish state—Israel—should have. To this, Orthodoxy has one answer: in essence, the same structure Jewry knew before the walls of the European ghettos fell to the onslaught of the Enlightenment.

Far-reaching changes would have to occur before the wall of *halakha* could be erected around Israel, before Israel could be cut off spiritually and culturally from the rest of the world as were the Jews in their medieval ghettos. Above all, the secular majority would have to be convinced or coerced into giving up not only its materialistic way of life but its clear desire to be open to the rest of the world. It is a desire perhaps most evident in the wanderlust of the Israelis, in their (sinful?) interest in the fads, films, and follies of the Western world, to say nothing of the fertile intellectual curiosity of Israel's scientists, writers, artists, and thinkers.

It is highly questionable whether the state could survive a re-ghettoization. The *haredim*, the ultra-Orthodox who oppose the state, are right in claiming that in order for Jews to fulfill the mission they took upon themselves at God's command, no Jewish state is needed. If anything, the existence of a Jewish state that has no choice but to behave like any other non-Jewish state makes achieving that mission even more difficult than it needs to be. Their attitude is like that of the character in Shai Agnon's novel *Shirah* who says that "the Jews do not seek a state and a political Jewish life but simply to worship God and make a decent living."

There is, of course, a national Orthodoxy that wants to worship God and fulfill His commandments, and also wants the Jewish state to be a vehicle of redemption. Otherwise, the religious nationalists believe, Israel cannot be a truly Jewish state. According to George Santayana's famous dictum, "Those who cannot remember the past are condemned to repeat it." The Jews certainly remember the past, but the Orthodox, it seems, remember it *in order* to repeat it, albeit in different geographical and political circumstances. They are aware of these differences, but they firmly believe that they can bend them to their purpose—a purpose that is incompatible with that of a modern nation-state.

The Orthodox of all brands—national, non-national, anti-national, and chauvinist—have wrought perceptible changes in the Israeli sociopolitical landscape, particularly in that of Jerusalem. But they have a long way to go before the state will become a theocracy.

Because the Jews first became a nation through an act of religion, a strict separation of state and synagogue in Israel would be anti-historical. In any case, such a separation is not necessary to preserve the democratic character of the country. Other countries, such as Britain and the Scandinavian countries, are both democracies and have an official church. What is needed is a divorce of religion from politics, a divorce from which true religiosity and piety could only profit. Such a divorce would finally allow the politicians to observe the boundaries between the sacred and the profane.

Orthodoxy is trying to move Jewish history in a circular route back to the self-centered security of faith that is possible only in a ghetto. Such may be a valid route for an individual, but it is not a road on which the vehicle of the nation-state can travel. For if Israel were to dwell alone, the danger is that it won't ere long dwell at all. As the American poet Robert Frost reminds us: "Before I'd build a wall I'd ask to know/ What I was walling in or walling out."

XIII

At *the* Crossroads

In 1988—5748, according to the Hebrew calendar—Israel celebrated forty years of existence as an independent state. Like other
nations for whom independence is still a novelty, Israel likes to
give particular prominence to its birthday, especially when the
anniversary is one of "round" numbers. It is as if the state were
saying to the world and its own people: "Look, we have made it so
far and that is a reassuring portent of permanence."

Israel also had more pragmatic reasons for marking the year.
The fortieth-anniversary celebration would provide it with an
opportunity to place before the world, in word and image, its
achievements, its uncontroversial sides, a face with no disfiguring warts. The celebration would not simply attract attention,
but the right kind of attention.

It was to be an auspicious year. The number 5748 is represented by the Hebrew letters *taw, shin, mem, heth*, a sequence
that can be read as *tismach*, which means "You shall rejoice."
But though Israel planned to make the celebration a joyous one,
the unplanned and unforeseen upheaval in the occupied terri-

tories left Israelis with little reason for rejoicing.

Suddenly, after twenty years, the Palestinians under Israeli occupation had risen spontaneously in revolt against Israeli rule. Their frustration had reached the critical mass where violence offers the only relief.

The uprising itself was unlikely to lead to the speedy disappearance of Israeli troops and Israeli administration from the West Bank and the Gaza Strip, much less the destruction of Israel, which was the proclaimed aim stipulated in the charter of the Palestine Liberation Organization. (After a May 1989 audience with French President François Mitterrand in Paris, Yassir Arafat proclaimed the relevant paragraph of the charter "null and void.") Nonetheless, it did make some important political points. It showed that Israel can be bruised by youngsters throwing stones and bottle bombs, by merchants closing their shops, by workers failing to appear at their customary workplace in Israel proper, by screaming women waving their taunting fists into the faces of Israeli soldiers, by makeshift PLO flags fluttering from utility poles and telephone lines. Perhaps worst of all, the flames of the uprising jumped over the Green Line, which legally separates Israel from the occupied territories, to burn down proudly tended Jewish forests, groves, and fields.

The uprising certainly caused more damage to Israel and its image in a few months than Yasir Arafat's self-promoting diplomatic salesmanship and reams of United Nations resolutions were able to cause in two decades. The throwers of stones and bottle bombs proved to be more of a threat than the official Palestinian forces kept and armed at considerable cost. The rioting Palestinians were able to pin down larger Israeli forces than the PLO regulars could ever hope to engage. They also scored an important psychological point: their actions showed that they no longer feared the Israelis. (In a sense, this did for Palestinian self-esteem what the 1973 crossing of the Suez Canal and the storming of the "impenetrable" Bar-Lev Line did for Egyptian pride.)

In addition to all this, the uprising caused Israel substantial economic losses, something Arab boycotts have never been able to do. Occupancy rates in Israel's hotels plunged as tourists canceled their reservations. Israel's national airline suffered losses for the same reason. There was a tidal wave of cancellations by groups of American Jews. In times of tension, it seems, American Jews are ready to stand by Israel but reluctant to travel there.

In some branches of industry, the absence of Arab labor from the territories made itself painfully felt. The building industry, not given to speedy work in the best of times, slowed down to a snail's pace. The army required additional funds for the discharge of riot-control duty for which it was neither trained nor equipped, and for which most Israeli soldiers had little taste. (A handful of reservists preferred to go to jail rather than serve in the occupied territories.)

Even more severe was the damage to Israel's image abroad, the result of which was a series of diplomatic setbacks. New Zealand, Portugal, and Ireland suspended the appointment of nonresident ambassadors, while Greece reneged on its promise to raise the status of its diplomatic representation to the rank of an embassy, which would have implied de jure, not mere de facto recognition. (In the meantime, Greece recognized the Palestinian state.) Similarly, a number of African countries that had been on the verge of resuming diplomatic relations with Israel decided to remain poised on the verge. (Kenya did resume diplomatic relations with Israel in December 1988.) In some countries, such as Denmark, which was long known as a friend of Israel, unofficial boycotts pressured supermarket chains into refusing to carry Israeli produce.

American Jewry was particularly disturbed by the way in which television news cameras, with what seemed to be undisguised schadenfreude, kept their lenses trained on Israeli soldiers beating rioters, firing live ammunition and tear gas in order to disperse hostile crowds of "teenagers" (no one mentioned that the Israeli soldiers were mostly teenagers, too)—in short, behaving much like any other nation's soldiers would in similar circumstances.

As was the case during the 1982 invasion of Lebanon, the news media were accused of displaying an anti-Israel and anti-Jewish bias in their coverage of the 1988 uprising. In the relatively rare cases in which newsmen compared Israel's behavior to that of the Nazis, the accusation of bias was more than justified. The detention camps in which suspected Palestinian agitators were held did not bear the remotest resemblance to Nazi concentration camps, to say nothing of death camps. Nor was Israel guilty of using massive lethal power against civilians, a practice that Nazi Germany (and the Pol Pot regime in Cambodia) had employed with satanic abandon. If any parallel could be drawn at all, it might be with the French during the last years of their rule in Algeria. But even compared to the French, the Israelis behaved like human-rights activists.

The Western news media's anti-Israel bias expressed itself mainly in their tendency to judge Israel by a higher moral standard than they applied to any other nation. (Governments seem to do the same thing. Israelis quite naturally find it irritating that the world gets up in arms when a relatively small number of rioting Palestinians are killed or beaten, yet shrugs off Iraq's despicable use of poison gas in its war with Iran.) The Western press, of course, thrives on moral indignation. But why does it appear particularly eager not to spare the rod in the case of Israel? Perhaps it is because Israel, in the best tradition of the Zionist movement, has always tried to occupy the high moral ground. How self-righteously satisfying it must be to topple Israel (and the Jews) from that lofty perch by showing that Israel, in dealing with the Palestinian population, has adopted repressive policies.

In fact, Israel has been acting with restraint, much as the British were forced to do in Palestine. (It is an irony of history that the legal framework for Israel's security policy in the occupied territories has its basis in the emergency regulations inherited from the British Mandatory administration.) Of course, Britain's restraint was due primarily to internal policy considerations, while Israel's is dictated almost exclusively by foreign policy imperatives—first and foremost, the need to maintain the special relationship with the United States.

For the same reason, the Israeli government made only half-hearted efforts to restrict media access to localities where the uprising had turned violent. In fact, the authorities would have liked nothing better than to ban the media from the occupied territories entirely; barring the TV cameras, it was felt, would do much to dampen the Palestinians' enthusiasm for going out into the streets and attacking Israeli military patrols and civilian vehicles. But while South Africa was able to win its war with the media through the use of such tactics, Israel could not afford the Western outrage that such a move would inevitably provoke.

At home, by contrast, the Israeli government could count on wide popular support. Indeed, a large sector of the population—perhaps a majority—favored using harsher methods to suppress the uprising. The shift to the right in the 1988 elections and the steady popularity of Defense Minister Yitzhak Rabin reflected the popular mood in this matter—a mood that itself reflected a profound change in the attitude of Israelis toward the Arabs of Eretz Israel, as the Palestinians are called by those who would like to see Israel solve the problem without relinquishing control of the occupied territories. (The term appears in the Hebrew version of the Camp David Agreement.)

For a long time, the feeling on the Jewish side of the fault line was by and large free of hatred of the Arabs. To be sure, Israelis had little respect for the Arabs and no sympathy for the plight of the Palestinian refugees. As far as most Israelis were concerned, the refugees were the responsibility of Arab countries—which, it was felt, could have absorbed them much more easily than Israel had absorbed Jewish refugees from Arab countries. (The Arabs did not wish to do so precisely because they understood that the refugee problem was a time bomb that would one day blow up.)

For most of the last two decades, the Arabs of the territories had been docile. Though they worked in Israel for low wages, they were better off than they had been under Jordanian rule. (Over the last twenty years, the gross domestic product of the occupied territories has more than tripled.) The conventional wisdom was that while the Arabs did not like the Israelis, they liked the material advantages they had come to enjoy well enough to keep quiet, especially as there was no real alternative in the offing.

Few Israelis were perturbed when individuals thought to be agitators were expelled from the territories, or when homes that had sheltered someone connected with a terrorist act were blown up—a policy that reversed the Biblical injunction and punished the fathers for the sins of their sons. Nor did most Israelis find it unreasonable or unethical that the Palestinian workers from the territories were forced by administrative fiat to return to their homes every evening after working for their Jewish bosses in Israel proper. After all, that's where they lived. Surely, no one would want them hanging out idly at night in Jewish cities.

To most Israelis, the occupation simply did not present a moral dilemma. The territories were the spoils of war. No one saw any reason to look upon the Arabs of Eretz Israel as "strangers within thy gates," who, according to the Bible, were entitled to an equitable and just treatment. Least of all the Orthodox establishment, which had wholeheartedly embraced the postulate of territorial "wholeness" and was thus more inclined to see the Arabs as Amalek, the hereditary enemy.

Nor did the occupation as such raise any *halakhic* problems. The administration of the territories simply did not concern the rabbinical establishment. The rabbis felt no need to pass judgment on the measures taken by the military administration either before or during the uprising—just as they felt no need to take a stand, say, on the question of nuclear weapons.

Underneath this moral complacency, however, hatred of the Arabs was lying dormant, like an inactive virus, in many an Israeli breast, especially among those whose diaspora experience left them ill-disposed to look upon Arabs with forgiving kindness. The uprising was bound to activate the virus, the more so as it was accompanied by renewed calls for the destruction of Israel. The uprising thus appeared in Israeli eyes not merely to be directed against the Israeli presence in the West Bank and Gaza, but as a first step in an escalating furor that would eventually lead to the annihilation of the Jewish state.

The uprising also threw into sharp relief the apparent intractability of the Palestinian problem—a problem whose existence the Israelis for a long time tried to deny. Now everyone could see that the conflict was not primarily between Israel and the Arab states, but amounted to a resurgence of the struggle between Jews and Palestinian Arabs over the same land, a struggle that first began in earnest at the end of World War I.

In practical terms, the uprising did not mark a return to square one. The Jews are no longer a weak minority in Palestine. On the contrary, they possess a powerful military machine. Still, on an emotional level, the sense of déjà vu is overwhelming. It is so easy to view the conflict as one that simply pits the Israelis' desire to get rid of the Arabs against the Palestinians' long-cherished yearning to throw the Jews into the sea—illusory as both dreams may be.

In fact, most Israelis and diaspora Jews are convinced that the Arabs would slaughter the entire Jewish population of Israel if they had the power to do so. (They would probably get away with it, too, as international opinion would forgive them as it forgave Iraq the use of poison gas in 1988.) After all, Arab countries have been reluctant to offer unambiguous assurances to the contrary. And savage fantasies of revenge are kept burning among Palestinian refugees who have little else to dream about.

Nothing new there. What *is* new is the emergence among Jews of a mirror-image of the Arab phantasm. Since it is now clear that there is no way the Palestinians can be persuaded (or bribed) to abandon their homes peacefully, the thoughts of some Israelis have turned to cataclysmic scenarios in which, during a war bloodier than any Israel has had to fight until now, the mass exodus of some one and a half million Arabs could be conceivably engineered. There are people in Israel who find such a course unfortunate but not abhorrent.

In the midst of all this, the Israeli government seems curiously paralyzed. It is one of the peculiarities of the Israeli style of governance that while every care is taken to prepare for military contingencies, political planning is sorely neglected. As noted earlier, Israel has always preferred the status quo to the uncertainty of a new political situation; new situations, after all, inevitably entail concessions. Thus, instead of planning for them in advance, Israel prefers to deal with political situations as they arise and to adapt its policies in reaction to them. This antipathy toward political planning is reflected in Israel's official attitude toward the occupied territories: Israel is as reluctant to vacate them as it is to annex them.

There are good reasons for this ambivalence. Withdrawal seems unacceptable, not because of the security questions it would raise (a solution to these could be negotiated with the PLO, whose leader, Yasir Arafat, has at last explicitly accepted the U.N. resolution endorsing Israel's right to live "within secure and recognized borders"), but because it would mean the betrayal of the "wholeness" concept, for which there is no negotiable substitute. Annexation, on the other hand, would create a binational state in which the majority status that the Jews currently enjoy in Israel (and nowhere else) would be quickly eroded. (Though they claim to be victims of genocide, the fact is that the Palestinians have one of the highest birthrates in the world.) In any case, the dilemma seems clear: How can the Land of Israel remain whole and at the same time avoid having to grant Israeli citizenship to its Arab residents? Accommodating these apparently antithetical objectives would probably entail a policy involving Israeli control of the territories combined with some sort of autonomy for the local population—in short, something very much like the status quo. (That is the solution desired by Prime Minister Shamir.)

The status quo worked for twenty years even without local autonomy. Certainly, the majority of Israelis were able to live with the situation, even be quite happy about it. They paid little heed to the growing chorus of voices that warned that the status quo could not be preserved indefinitely, that a real solution was urgently needed. For the most part, Israel and its leadership preferred not to cross that bridge until they came to it.

Whatever else one can say about it, the 1988 Palestinian uprising brought the country a giant step closer to the bridge.

To be sure, Israel is not there yet. As dire as the situation may be, the country has still not passed the point of no return. But while catastrophe is not inevitable, both Israel and the Palestinians will have to go through some fundamental changes if they are to avoid the abyss.

To begin with, before any real steps can be taken to resolve the bitter conflict through negotiations—and negotiations are essential, for no military solution exists—both parties will have to clear away the psychological barriers each has been busily building up over the years. The simple fact is that no move toward mutual understanding will be possible without a change in basic conceptions and language on both sides.

For their part, the Palestinians would have to cease regarding Zionism and the state it sired as a colonial phenomenon that is inevitably doomed to destruction by the forces of history. They would also have to acknowledge that the territories Israel would vacate in any peace arrangement or treaty would only be those occupied as a result of the 1967 conquest, and not all of the former Mandatory Palestine.

For its part, Israel would have to cease reacting to the PLO as Pavlov's dog to the dinner bell and accept that the PLO is not synonymous with "terrorism." It would thus have to acknowledge that the Palestinians have legitimate national aspirations that can only be satisfied by territorial and political concessions and that the breadth and width of these concessions cannot be negotiated with third parties. In other words, the conflict cannot be solved without recognizing the partner directly concerned and without a division of the land between the two peoples that have a just claim to it.

Both sides will have to give up all pretensions that they are waging a holy war. The injection by either side of religion into the

272

conflict can only make the prospects of a solution even dimmer than they already appear to be. A holy war does not permit any compromise. Its nature dictates that it can only end with the physical (or at least the moral) destruction of the enemy.

True, as distinct from Islam, the very notion of a holy war is alien to Judaism. But the desire to preserve the "wholeness" of Eretz Israel at any price, on the grounds that it is essential to the fulfillment of the Jewish people's destiny, comes very close to being a holy war. Though no one may be calling for the wholesale slaughter of the enemy, the desire for Jewish control of the whole Land of Israel often finds virulent and at times violent expression in a sector of Israeli society.

This is the view of a minority, to be sure, but it is a minority that draws disproportionate strength from the claim that it alone is obeying God's command. And its thinking fits in with that of those who want to retain the territories for less eschatological reasons. After all, no one among the Zionist leadership, not even so perseverant a pragmatist as David Ben-Gurion, ever renounced the claim of the Jews to all of their historic homeland.

In essence, the only hope for a solution to the conflict that would allow the two nationalisms to live side by side in peace rests on the willingness of both to trade off the "wholeness" of Eretz Israel against the Arab dream of no Israel at all. Sanity would seem to recommend such a course. Unfortunately, sanity is rarely the stuff of which the harrowing and heroic pages of history are made.

Still, though the *intifada* only marginally affects the daily life of the Israeli population (except for those who live in the settlements directly threatened by hostile Arabs), and though the belief is widespread that it must be suppressed (by an iron hand, if need be) before any dialogue about the future of the territories can get under way, the fact remains that the uprising has driven home a few unpleasant truths. These truths are particularly unpleasant for those who believe that Israeli control of the territories can somehow be maintained.

Despite all the official rhetoric about the material advantages it brought the population of the West Bank, no one ever really believed that the Palestinians there welcomed the Israeli administration. Nonetheless, the idea gained wide currency that West Bank Arabs would eventually acquiesce to Israeli control —in part, because of the deterrent a heavier Jewish settlement of the area would supposedly present; in part, as a result of the security services' ability to hold in check Palestinian agitators, terrorists, and their allies. This idea still guides the present government, although a recognition that the status quo is untenable is slowly seeping into the consciousness of the hawks.

In fact, the uprising has ground down the idea of continued control into a thin irrational sliver of hope. It has also thrown into dramatic and bloody relief the demographic time bomb represented by the rapid growth of the Palestinian population under the age of twenty. After all, the *intifada* is almost exclusively the work of the *shebab*, the undereducated, unemployed, and ungovernable juveniles who graduated from idly roaming the streets of the West Bank to the nationalist thrill and glory of confronting the Israeli army.

It wasn't until the *intifada* had become an obvious success that local Arab intellectuals were prodded to assume leadership of the resistance movement—which by its second year had come to be embraced by a Palestinian population that was ready as never before to make material sacrifices and obey its orders. Yasir Arafat then took advantage of the situation, seizing upon the uprising as the lever with which to implant the idea of a Palestinian state on the West Bank and in the Gaza Strip both among Palestinian political exiles and in the minds of almost everybody else.

By accepting Arafat's leadership, the militants of the *intifada* embraced (at least ostensibly) what for all practical purposes became official Palestinian policy, even if it was rejected by the more radical exile groups. To be sure, the Palestinian population had always by and large supported the PLO, even though the PLO had never been able to affect Israeli policies in the occupied territories—and consequently the conditions of Pales-

274

tinian existence there. But now the militants on the West Bank were ready to take on the task of generating the "military" pressure that would eventually force Israel to yield. If nothing else, this seemed likely to make it increasingly difficult for Israel to continue to insist that the Palestinian population and the PLO were not in fact two arms of the same body politic.

The chain reaction ignited by the *shebab* has not actually brought the Palestinians any closer to their oft-stated aim of destroying the Jewish state. But it has placed Israel in the most difficult political situation it has ever encountered. Faced with Washington's acceptance of Arafat as a legitimate negotiating partner, the Jerusalem government is going to find it extremely difficult to maintain its opposition to holding any sort of a dialogue with him. And while Washington may still agree with Jerusalem that the establishment of a separate Palestinian state between Jordan and Israel is not a good idea, any kind of American dialogue with Arafat is bound to erode that position. After all, what is there to negotiate with Arafat if not the boundaries of his proclaimed Palestinian state and the modalities of its relationship with Israel? And if such negotiations were to get under way, perhaps under some international umbrella, what will be said about the thorny question of Jerusalem? Given the fact that the United States never recognized Israel's July 1980 unilateral unification of Jerusalem, Israel could find itself completely isolated here.

Israel, in an act that has historic precedent—and thus would not be out of character for it—could then decide to go it alone and damn the consequences. Whatever those consequences might prove to be, they are unlikely to resemble peace. The fact is, if a peaceful solution is at all possible, it can only be achieved in concord with the United States. And it can become reality only if the right wing Likud accepts it.

Not all of Israel will rejoice if and when peace breaks out as a result of a compromise between the two nations, the Israelis and the Palestinians. On the contrary, the event may well be felt as an earthquake stronger than the one the country experienced after

275

the Yom Kippur War of 1973. If any credence can be given to the vows of the hard-line religious nationalists, they would oppose any and all territorial concessions that affect the settlements in which they live. Clashes between settlers and security forces have already occurred, much to the glee of the Palestinians. In case of any Israeli withdrawal from the territories, the intensity of the intra-Israel confrontation could assume the character of a civil war. If that were to happen, the religious nationalists would be waging a "holy war"—against their fellow Jews.

The shrinking of Israel would be a hard blow to the virile self-image of the numerous partisans of a Greater Israel. It would mean that the messianic dream of a "whole" Eretz Israel was nothing more (or less) than a dream that cannot be translated into reality by mundane means. And it would serve as a distressing reminder that religion and realpolitik do not make good bedfellows.

The inevitable withdrawal pains would be all the greater as Israel would undoubtedly be required not only to vacate the near totality of the West Bank and all of Gaza (though a formula might be found to allow Jewish settlements to remain in place), but also to agree to some limitations of its sovereignty in Jerusalem. That issue is so explosive that the Israeli advocates of a compromise refrain from mentioning it at all.

Could the earthquake be of sufficient force to threaten the very survival of Israel? That's a possibility—but only if Israel lets it happen. For the past twenty years, Israel has been painting sweeping vistas, both secular and religious, into its national psyche. If the nation is not prepared for it, the sudden realization that those vistas were only a mirage could destroy Israel's moral texture.

Nothing would be easier than to blame the loss on the eternal hostility of the gentile world—to claim that it was the result of anti-Semitism that Israel was denied the right to its historic homeland, that alone among the nations Israel was not allowed to keep the fruits of its hard-won victories. In such a context, it would also be easy to argue that there would be no assurance that the goyim would permit "little" Israel to live at all. International guarantees? Recent history is littered with worthless proclamations and promises of that sort.

Such a train of thought might well lead to despair, to a questioning of whether the Jews were destined to have a state of their own for any length of time. (Ben-Gurion was known to have privately harbored nagging doubts about the state's viability, doubts of which not even the slightest whiff escaped into his public posture.) Certainly, if past history can provide any guidance, the answer to that question is not reassuring. After all, the Jews have spent far longer in exile than living in a sovereign country of their own. Could it be that the diaspora is the natural habitat of the Jewish people?

The *haredim* are not the only ones who maintain that the Jews are destined to remain in dispersion. At the other end of the scale are those secularists who see the historic role of the Jews as being the leavening agent of European (and, by extension, American) cultural and intellectual life. Since emancipation, Jews have often been the pike in the carp pool of intellectual complacency and moral hypocrisy. Evidently, only in the diaspora can Jews take on this "historic" role.

If that is indeed the true calling of the Jews, one would do well to recall the question of Jewish co-responsibility for the Holocaust. George Steiner, for example, once asked, in a rhetorical question to which the answer is affirmative, whether "the critical, deconstructive power of Central European Jewish thought, music, literature [was] wholly without responsibility for that which it [partly] foresaw?" In Steiner's view, and he is by no means alone, European Jews played a critical role in the "dissolution of European values, the erosion of the social and private centers of gravity before and during the crises of world war and economic chaos."

Were the Jews only endowed with an uncanny, tragic foresight, or were their premonitions self-fulfilling prophecies? Was the Jewish intellectual simply better equipped to see through the hollow conventions of society because he was doubly alienated: from traditional Judaism because of his plunge into modernity, and from gentile society because of its (and his own Jewish) reluctance to allow him to fuse with it seamlessly, as the American sociologist Thorstein Veblen proposed? (Freud readily acknowledged that his Jewish marginality provided much of the motivation for his research.) Or was the "erosion of the social and private centers of moral gravity" critically aggravated by the relentless probing of Jewish intellectuals, as Cuddihy implies when he speaks of their "punitive objectivity" and "vindictive objectivity," which he firmly believes "continue unabated into our own time"? In other words, Jewish thinkers, musicians, writers, and artists of the diaspora are still playing with the flames of a dangerous deconstructive power, ultimately dangerous to the Jewish people.

The existence of the State of Israel seemed to have laid many of these doubts to rest. But they could re-emerge in the wake of the kind of traumatic experience a withdrawal from most of the territories would be likely to produce, a trauma that could be aggravated by the familiar Jewish capacity for self-destructiveness.

On the other hand, the trauma might well strengthen the hand of Orthodoxy. The failure to advance on the path to redemption, of which the "wholeness" of Eretz Israel had become an important element, could be imputed to the unworthiness of the present Jewish state to serve as a vehicle of redemption. Following the inner logic of this proposition, the remedy can only lie in a collective withdrawal into the Jewish religious self, a retreat into the womb of the certainty of faith, a reversion to the ahistoric existence from which the Enlightenment and emancipation had lured the Jews, the former by the might of its idea, the latter by the mirage of its promises.

Fundamentally, this concept obviates the need for a nation-state. In any case, it makes the nation-state ultimately redundant. Of course, until the state withers away, there remains a case to be made for its usefulness as a protection against the hostile outside world, a technically advanced and more effective kind of ghetto wall. In this scheme of things, the state can fulfill its role—nay, survive—only if its people live in the closed universe of Orthodox tradition and religious authority, in which *halakha* holds absolute and total sway.

For Orthodoxy, the state makes sense only as a stage, a milestone, a phase, an instrument toward a higher goal. Seen from the outside, the Orthodox view of history is deterministic, its ideology totalitarian. In its own mind, Orthodoxy recognizes neither history nor ideology, only God's commandments.

Such a view of the state was never part of the vision of the founding fathers of the Zionist movement and of the Jewish state. Even the movement's religious faction didn't subscribe to it (though it does so now). The Zionist vision of a renewed Jewish commonwealth was secular. It wanted the Jewish state to embody the ideals of a democratic and humanistic worldview into which it wove the philosophy and moral message of Prophetic Judaism. The Declaration of Independence of Israel symbolically reflects this aspiration. This is clearly spelled out in the paragraph in which the declaration gives the assurance that Israel "will be based on freedom, justice, and peace as envisaged by the Prophets of Israel; it will ensure complete equality of social and political rights to all its inhabitants irrespective of religion, race, or sex, it will guarantee freedom of religion, conscience, language, and education..."

The secular Jewish state never intended to reject its Jewish heritage. But it never considered that heritage to be narrowly circumscribed by the Torah and its exegesis, past and present. After all, the work of the *Maskilim* is part of the Jewish heritage, to say nothing of Zionism. And so is the work of (the apostate) Heinrich Heine, of Karl Marx and Sigmund Freud and Marc Chagall and of thousands of other Jews whose contributions to Western civilization the Jews never cease to extol. It would be preposterous to look for the Jewish root, the Jewish spark, the Jewish radiance in every work by any Jew, as Jews tend to do, sometimes obsessively—yet at the same time claim that it is not part of the Jewish heritage because it lies outside the religious sphere.

The founding fathers of the Jewish state wanted its citizens to live in free intellectual, moral, and aesthetic communion not only with its religious and secular past but also as creative equals with (as opposed to subservient imitators of) the non-Jewish world. Modern Hebrew literature and drama certainly attest to this desire. So does contemporary Israeli art.

It was the essence of the Zionist revolution to make the Jewish people participate in history, with all the toil and trouble, the tribulations, travails, and (rare) triumphs that are the lot of every nation that wishes to direct its fate as best it can in the here and now. (Indeed, this was the most revolutionary aspect of Zionism.) This is a difficult task, one that requires enormous effort, courage, and determination. No state, least of all a small one like Israel, could perform such a task if it had also to carry the additional burden of being an instrument in the fulfillment of messianic ambitions.

Moreover, a nation-state is by its nature incapable of taking on religious significance and functions (unless it lives in total isolation, as Tibet once did). For Israel to attempt to do so can only result in the perversion of both religion and the state. After all, the survival of the State of Israel depends on different elements than the survival of Judaism; indeed, some of the state's needs, by dint of the cruel demands of politics, stand in glaring contradiction to Judaic precepts. For Judaism to survive, it must cut itself loose from involvement in worldly politics and rely on the strength of its spiritual message alone. Judaism can only flourish in a different sphere and function on a separate plane from the worldly structure within which it exists. If Judaism has to resort to the coercive powers of the worldly state to get its message across, it casts doubts on its spiritual strength.

But what should Israel's relationship to Judaism be if the Jewish state cannot be an instrument of eschatological aims? For the State of Israel, it is not so much a matter of a strict separation of church and state (Judaism, after all, is not a church) as it is one of the need to refrain from blurring the borders between the sacred and the profane. While the Jewish state need not seek a divorce from Judaism, it must separate itself from a subservience to the claim that Orthodoxy is ultimately the sole arbiter of what is Jewish and what is not. It must reject the Orthodox thesis that the absolute primacy of *halakha* is the sole guarantee for the preservation of the Jewish character of the state and the unity of the Jewish people.

Indeed, in order to survive, the Jewish state must reverse the trend toward any kind of re-ghettoization, and put its efforts into normalization—normalization of the relationships within its polis as well as those with the outside world. In a sense, this represents a return to a principal paragraph of the old Zionist agenda.

It would in no way detract from the unique historic experience of the Jewish people if Israel were to be content to be a nation among nations trying to live up to reasonable moral standards—reasonable, that is, in terms of the peculiar morality of politics. There is no reason for Israel to aspire anymore to be a "beacon unto the nations"—a task, in any case, at which the Jewish people have been singularly unsuccessful. The world is not likely to blame Israel for not having done everything that Jewish (and some Christian) fundamentalists believe necessary to advance the coming of a messiah in whom the majority of mankind does not believe.

There was never any chance that the State of Israel could ever become the "Old New" land of Herzl's utopian dreams. But it can strive to become a normal nation that will be counted among the nations. To do so, the state must discard messianic politics and territorial aspirations under whatever guise, secular or religious. Israel will simply not be permitted to indulge in such policies—not because it is a Jewish state, but because it came into being at a time when map-changing power games were no longer acceptable.

Internally, the future of the Jewish state will be determined by the tug of war between the spiritual and intellectual forces that are present there. The *Kulturkampf* has been raging for quite some time now. On both sides of the barricade, the secular as well as the religious, Balaam's curse rekindles dangerous atavistic reflexes—reflexes that could affect external as well as internal relations. The desire to bend into a circle the phase of Jewish history that began with the exodus from the ghetto could very well engender a parallel change in the attitudes of the non-Jewish world.

The longing for the spirit, if not the physical conditions, of the ghetto is powered by the yearning for the certainty of faith that modernity has undermined. It is a ubiquitous yearning, but it seems to have gripped the Jews with greater intensity than other Westerners. It finds expression in the almost obsessive and often exclusionist preoccupation with Jewishness, Jewish rituals and customs, Jewish studies and Jewish books, Jewish sentimentality and superstitions, all of it dressed up as Jewish values, suffusing in a Jewish ethical aura matters that are value-neutral. As a result, Jewishness as such is being elevated to the rank of a moral precept irrespective of the individual Jew's moral worth.

Whatever the outcome of the *Kulturkampf*, the result will be the Jews' own doing. By embracing the idea of the nation-state, they have contracted to take their fate into their own hands. It is an awesome responsibility before history, not before God. It cannot be avoided, unless the Jewish people want to opt out of history again. In that case, there would be no need for a Jewish state.

But the Jewish people, except for an ultra-Orthodox minority, do want to have a state they can call their own—even the diaspora majority that has no intention of living there. More than that, most Jews strongly believe that the State of Israel is essential for the survival of the Jewish people. (In fact, this is pure conjecture not supported by past history.) A great number of Jews even believe that Israel is central to Judaism. (This is false: God is central to Judaism.) But whatever its real significance, the Jewish nation-state cannot take upon itself the metahistoric mission of Judaism. The nature of the nation-state precludes it. That, of course, does not mean that the Jewish people are not free to pursue that vision as a people. Indeed, they can have the best (or worst) of both worlds: they can be a nation like other nations in Israel and they can pursue their metahistoric destiny as a matter of faith.

Glossary

(Note: The transliteration of Hebrew terms follows the customs of general publications, not the rules applied in academic works such as the *Encyclopaedia Judaica*.)

Aliyah (also **aliya**). The immigration of Jews to Eretz Israel. Literally "ascension," the term implies a spiritual elevation.

Amalek. The first enemy the Israelites encountered after crossing the Sea of Reeds. During a battle in the northern part of the Sinai Peninsula, Moses proclaimed: "The Lord will be at war against Amalek throughout the ages." Since it is Israel which fights the Lord's battles "throughout the ages," Amalek has become a synonym for hereditary enemy.

Ashkenazi. A Jew living in Ashkenaz (from the twelfth century on, the Hebrew name for Germany). Ashkenazim are people of a cultural legacy emanating from centers in France and Germany which later spread to Eastern Europe. In Slavonic countries, the use of Yiddish was part of this legacy.

Dybbuk (also **Dibbuk**). According to Hasidic legend, an evil spirit or the spirit of a dead person inhabiting a human being. The spirit can be exorcized.

Edom. A region in the southeast of today's Kingdom of Jordan inhabited in Biblical times by a population of mixed ethnic origin related to Israel through Esau. Conquered by King David. In religious literature, Edom was used as a synonym for Christian Rome and hence for Christianity as the enemy of the Jews.

Eretz Israel (also **Eretz Yisrael**). The Hebrew name for the Land of Israel. Offi-

284

cial Hebrew designation of British Mandatory Palestine.

Etzel. Hebrew acronym for Irgun Tzvai Leumi ("National Military Organization"), an armed underground force founded by dissident Haganah officers in 1931. Etzel merged with Betar (acronym for Brith Trumpeldor) of the Revisionist Zionist movement. From 1943 until its disbandment, it was commanded by Menachem Begin.

Galut (also **Gola**). Hebrew for Exile. Modern historians generally consider the period from the destruction of the Second Temple in 70 B.C. until the creation of the State of Israel as that of Exile. Some Zionists call the present diaspora Jewry "exiles."

Golem. From the Hebrew *gelem* ("unformed"), a robotlike being created with the help of sacred magic. The best-known golem was the one fashioned according to legend by Rabbi Juda Liwa ben Bezalel, a.k.a. the High Rabbi Loew of Prag. The subject of many works of Western literature, drama, and film, the golem served as the model for the monster in Mary Wollstonecraft Shelley's novel *Frankenstein.*

Goy (plural **goyim**). Hebrew for "people," any people. In our time, it is a slightly pejorative designation for a non-Jew.

Hagada (also **Haggadah**). From the Hebrew root "to tell." The Hagada is a collection of prayers, psalms, stories, comments, and songs read at the traditional Passover meal, the Seder ("order"). Its composition varies in different communities. The three basic types are Ashkenazi, Sephardi, and Italian. The oldest known Hagada is from Guadalajara, Spain, dating from around 1482.

Haganah. Hebrew for "defense." The Haganah was the clandestine military organization of the mainstream Yishuv. Founded in 1920 as an outgrowth of the Jewish watchman's organization Hashomer, its purpose was to place the defense of the Yishuv into Jewish hands and not rely only on British forces.

Halakha. From the Hebrew root "to go." The halakha comprises the entire legal system of Judaism, encompassing detailed prescriptions for observances, interdictions, and customs, elaborated by rabbinical exegesis. In short, it shows the Orthodox Jew the way "to go"—i.e., to live.

Hared (plural **haredim**). Hebrew for "fearing," i.e., God-fearing. Generic name for the ultra-Orthodox community living in Israel that does not recognize the Jewish state.

Hashomer. Hebrew for "watchman." The first Jewish defense organization in Palestine, established in 1909 to protect settlements against Arab marauders.

Hasid (plural **Hasidim**). Hebrew for "pietist," an adherent of Hasidism, the mystic, charismatic, ecstatic, and sometimes ascetic branch of Orthodox Judaism. Its beginnings go back to the middle of the eighteenth century. At first localized in the corner formed by Poland and Lithuania, it eventually spread to Ashkenazi communities all over the world. Israel ben Eliezer (1699–1760), better known as Baal Shem Tov ("Master of the Good Name") or the Besht, is considered the founder of the movement.

Haskala. Hebrew for "enlightenment." The Haskala movement began in the third decade of the eighteenth century in opposition to Rabbinical Judaism. It emphasized rationalism, secular education, and the use of Hebrew as literary language. Moses Mendelssohn is considered the father of the movement.

Heder. Hebrew for "room," it refers to private elementary schools owned and run by individual teachers for children age three to thirteen. Depending on their age, *heder* students were taught the prayer book, the Pentateuch, and the Talmud with commentary by Rashi.

Hibat Zion (also **Hibbat Zion**). Hebrew for "love of Zion." A forerunner of political Zionism, Hibat Zion engaged in philanthropic assistance to settlers in Palestine. Founded in Russia in the nineteenth century.

Hovev Zion (plural **Hovevei Zion**). An adherent of Hibat Zion.

Kashrut. Observance of the dietary laws.

Maccabee. Agnomen of Judah, son of Mattathias, the military leader of the revolt against the Seleucid rule in the second century B.C., and his entire clan. As a dynasty, the Maccabbees were known as Hasmoneans.

Marrano (plural **Marranos**). A derogatory term for Spanish and Portuguese Jews who converted to Catholicism in the fifteenth and sixteenth centuries, as well as for crypto-Jews of the same origin. Most probably derived from the Spanish word for "pig."

Maskil (plural **Maskilim**). Proponent(s) of Haskala.

Mil. The smallest coin of British Palestine, equal to one-thousandth of a Palestine pound. The pound was equal in value to the British pound sterling.

Mishna (also **Mishnah**). From the Hebrew root *shanah*, "to repeat." The Mishna is an important part of the Jewish oral tradition that was put into writing in the second century. It comprises sixty-three tractates in six volumes (cf. Talmud).

Misnagdim. Ashkenazi pronunciation of *mitnagdim*, Hebrew for "opponents." A movement initiated by Solomon Zalman, the Gaon of Vilna (1720–1797) in bitter, often ruthless opposition to Hasidism. Adherents were known for their sharp, cerebral approach to the Talmud.

Moshav. An Israeli cooperative smallholders' village on national land.

Oleh. A person "making" aliyah.

Seder. See Hagada.

Sephardim. Descendants of Jews and crypto-Jews who left Spain and Portugal because of persecution by Catholic Church. They maintained a particular culture and Jewish-Spanish language called "Ladino." Nowadays "Sephardim" refers to all non-Ashkenazi Jews.

Shiksa. From the Hebrew root for "abomination." A non-Jewish woman. The term is no longer considered derogatory.

Shoah. Hebrew for "catastrophe" and, hence, the Holocaust.

Shtetl. Yiddish for "small town." The first shtetl arose in Poland in the sixteenth century under the favorable conditions granted to Jews by the country's rulers and its nobility. Characterized by a special communal culture, shtetls could be found all over Eastern Europe before World War II.

Shul. From the German for "school." Yiddish for a Jewish Orthodox place of worship. Colloquially applied to all Jewish houses of worship.

Talmud. From the Hebrew root for "learning." The Talmud is a vast compilation of rabbinical exegesis, comments, homiletics, observations, and stories. The Mishna is one part of it. The rest is called "Gemara." All of it is the Oral Tradition.

Thirty-Six Righteous *(Lamed Vav Tsadikim).* According to an Ashkenazi legend, thirty-six righteous men can be found in every generation, hidden saints whose existence saves the world.

Torah. Hebrew for "doctrine." The Five Books of Moses (Pentateuch).

Yad Vashem. The Martyrs' and Heroes' Remembrance Authority of Jerusalem, an Israeli institute for the perpetuation of the Holocaust memory through research, publications, exhibitions, and conferences. It includes a planted alley of trees, each honoring a "Righteous Gentile" who risked his or her life in saving Jews.

Yeshiva. Hebrew for "sitting." An institute of Talmudic studies of various scholarly levels.

Yishuv. The Jewish population that settled in Eretz Israel for Zionist reasons.

Selected Bibliography

Abramov, Zalman S. *Perpetual Dilemma: Jewish Religion and Jewish State.* Rutherford: Fairleigh Dickinson University Press, 1976.

Adler, Joseph. *The Herzl Paradox: Political, Social and Economic Theories of a Realist.* New York: Hadrian Press, 1962.

Ahad Haam. *Nationalism and the Jewish Ethic.* New York: Schocken Books, 1962.

——. *The Supremacy of Reason.* New York: Maimonides Octocentennial Committee, 1935.

——. *Ten Essays on Zionism and Judaism.* London: George Rutledge, 1922.

Arendt, Hannah. *The Jew As Pariah.* New York: Grove Press, 1978.

——. *Rahel Varnhagen.* London: East and West Library, 1951.

——. "Reflections on Eichmann in Jerusalem." *Midstream,* Sept. 1963.

——. "Zionism Reconsidered." *The Menorah Journal,* Oct.–Dec. 1945.

Avi-hai, Avraham. *Ben-Gurion, State Builder: Principles and Pragmatism.* New York: Wiley, 1974.

Avineri, Shlomo. *The Making of Modern Zionism.* New York: Basic Books, 1981.

Avishai, Bernard. *The Tragedy of Zionism.* New York: Farrar, Straus & Giroux, 1985.

Baer, Jean. *The Self Chosen.* New York: Arbor House, 1982.

Bar-Zohar, Michael. *Ben-Gurion: A Biography.* New York: Delacorte, 1979.

Bauer, Bruno. *The Jewish Problem.* Cincinnati: Hebrew Union College, 1958.

Bell, Daniel. "Reflections on Jewish Identity." *Commentary,* June 1961.

Belloc, Hilaire. *The Jews.* Boston and New York: Houghton Mifflin, 1922.

Ben-Gurion, David. *Memoirs.* (Hebrew) Tel Aviv: Am Oved, 1971.

————. *Rebirth and Destiny of Israel.* New York: Philosophical Library, 1954.

Ben-Horin, Meir. *Max Nordau.* New York: Conference of Jewish Social Studies, 1956.

Bentwich, Norman. *Ahad Ha'am and His Philosophy.* Jerusalem: Keren Hayesod and Keren Kayemet, 1927.

Ben-Yeruham, Hayyim. *The Betar Book.* (Hebrew) Tel Aviv: Betar, 1969.

Berger, Elmer. *Judaism or Jewish Nationalism: The Alternative to Zionism.* New York: Bookman Assoc., 1957.

Bergmann, Hugo. *Yavne and Jerusalem.* (German) Berlin: Jüdischer Verlag, 1919.

Berlin, Isaiah. *Chaim Weizmann.* London: Weidenfeld & Nicolson, 1958.

————. *Jewish Slavery and Emancipation.* In Pamphlet No. 13. New York: Herzl Press, 1961.

————. *Karl Marx.* London: Thornton Butterworth, 1939.

Birmingham, Stephen. *Our Crowd.* New York: Harper & Row, 1967.

————. *The Rest of Us: The Rise of America's Eastern European Jews.* Boston: Little, Brown, 1984.

Boehm, Adolf. *The Zionist Movement.* (German) Berlin: Jüdischer Verlag, 1937.

Brandeis, Louis D. *Zionism and Patriotism.* New York: Federation of American Zionists, 1915.

Brandes, Georg. "My Attitude to National Judaism." (German) *Der Jude,* Vol. 2, 1917–1918.

Breuer, Isaac. "The Challenge to Israel." In *Judaism in a Changing World,* ed. by Leo Jung. New York: Oxford University Press, 1939.

————. *The Jewish National Home.* (German) Frankfurt: J. Kauffmann, 1925.

————. *Jewish Problems.* Frankfurt: J. Kauffmann, 1922.

Buber, Martin. *Israel and Palestine: The History of an Idea.* London: East and West Library, 1952.

————. *About the Spirit of Judaism.* (German) Leipzig: Wolff, 1916.

Cattani, Georges. "Marcel Proust and the Jews." *Jewish Review* 3, Dec. 1932–March 1933.

Cohen, Hermann. *Germanness and Judaism.* (German) Giessen: A. Töpelmann, 1915.

Cohen, Michael J. *Churchill and the Jews.* London and New York: Frank Cass & Co., 1985.

Cox, Harvey. *Religion in the Secular City.* New York: Simon & Schuster, 1983.

————. *Toward a Postmodern Theology.* New York: Simon & Schuster, 1984.

Cuddihy, John Murray. *The Ordeal of Civility.* New York: Basic Books, 1974.

Davis, Moshe, ed. *Zionism in Transition.* New York: Arno Press, 1980.

Dayan, Moshe. *Living with the Bible.* New York: William Morrow, 1978.

————. *Story of My Life.* London: Weidenfeld & Nicolson, 1966.

Dimont, Max I. *The Indestructible Jews.* New York: World Publication, 1971.

Dinur, B., and Y. Klausner. *In Memory of Ahad Haam.* (Hebrew) Jerusalem: Hebrew University, 1955.

Dubnow, Simon, and K. S. Pinson, eds. *Nationalism and History: Essays on Old and New Judaism.* Philadelphia: Jewish Publication Society, 1958.

Eban, Abba. *Abba Eban: An Autobiography.* London: Weidenfeld & Nicolson, 1978.

―――. *Heritage: Civilization and the Jews.* New York: Summit Books, 1984.

―――. *The Toynbee Heresy.* New York: Yeshiva University, 1955.

Eldad, Israel. *The Jewish Revolution: Jewish Statehood.* New York: Shengold, 1971.

Elon, Amos. *Herzl.* New York: Holt, Rinehart & Winston, 1975.

―――. *The Israelis: Founders and Sons.* New York: Penguin, 1983.

Fackenheim, Emil L. *The Jewish Return into History: Reflections in the Age of Auschwitz and a New Jerusalem.* New York: Schocken Books, 1978.

Fischman (Maimon), Harav Yehuda Leib Hacohen. *Religious Zionism and Its Development.* (Hebrew) Jerusalem: Hanhalat Hahistadrut Hazionit Haolamit, 1936.

Friedman, Maurice S. *Martin Buber's Life and Work: The Early Years.* London and Tunbridge Wells: Search Press, 1982.

Friedmann, Georges. *The End of the Jewish People.* (French) Paris: Gallimard, 1965.

Friesel, Evyatar. *Zionist Policy after the Balfour Declaration. 1917–1922.* (Hebrew) Tel Aviv: Tel Aviv University, 1980.

Gavron, Daniel. *Israel after Begin.* Boston: Houghton Mifflin, 1984.

Gilbert, Martin. *The Holocaust: A History of the Jews of Europe during the Second World War.* New York: Holt, Rinehart & Winston, 1986.

Glazer, Nathan. "The Exposed American Jew." *Commentary* 59, June 1975.

Goitein, Solomon D. *A Mediterranean Society: The Jewish Community of the Arab World.* Berkeley: University of California Press, 1967.

Goldmann, Nahum. *About the Significance and Task of Judaism in World Culture.* (German) Munich: F. Bruckmann, 1916.

―――. *The Jewish Paradox.* New York: Fred Jordan Books/Grosset & Dunlap, 1978.

Grose, Peter. *Israel in the Mind of America.* New York: Alfred A. Knopf, 1983.

Grossman, David. *The Yellow Wind.* New York: Farrar, Straus & Giroux, 1988.

Haag, Ernest van den. *The Jewish Mystique.* New York: Stein & Day, 1969.

Halkin, Hillel. *Letters to an American Jewish Friend: A Zionist Polemic.* Philadelphia: The Jewish Publication Society of America, 1977.

Halpern, Ben. *The American Jew: A Zionist Analysis.* New York: Schocken Books, 1983.

Heller, Joseph. *The Zionist Idea.* London: Joint Zionist Publication Committee, 1947.

Heller, Otto. *The Fall of Judaism: The Jewish Problem, Its Critique and Its Solution through Socialism.* (German) Vienna: Verlag für Literatur und Politik, 1931.

Herman, Simon. *Israelis and Jews.* New York: Random House, 1970.

Hertzberg, Arthur. *The Zionist Idea.* New York: Harper Torchbooks, 1966.

Herzl, Theodor. *The Jewish State.* (German) Berlin: Jüdischer Verlag, 1918.

———. *Old-New Land.* Haifa: Haifa Publishing Company, 1960.

Himmelfarb, Milton. *The Jews of Modernity.* New York: Basic Books, 1973.

Horowitz, Irving Louis. *Israeli Ecstasies, Jewish Agonies.* New York: Oxford University Press, 1974.

Howe, Irving. "Sholom Aleichem: Voice of Our Past." In *A World More Attractive: A View of Modern Literature and Politics.* New York: Horizon Press, 1963.

Jabotinsky, Vladimir. "The Betar View on State and Social Problems." *Hadar* 5–8, Nov. 1940.

———. *The Story of the Jewish Legion.* New York: B. Ackerman, 1945.

Jung, Leo, ed. *Judaism in a Changing World.* New York: Oxford University Press, 1939.

Kaplan, Mordecai M. *Judaism As a Civilization.* New York: Macmillan, 1934.

———. *A New Zionism.* New York: Theodor Herzl Foundation, 1955.

Keren, Michael. *Ben-Gurion and the Intellectuals: Power, Knowledge, and Charisma.* DeKalb: Northern Illinois University Press, 1984.

Koestler, Arthur. *Promise and Fulfillment.* New York: Macmillan, 1949.

Kook, Abraham Isaac. *The Lights of Penitence, the Moral Principles, Lights of Holiness, Essays, Letters, and Poems.* New York: Paulist Press, 1978.

Kornberg, Jacques, ed. *At the Crossroads: Essays on Ahad Ha'am.* Albany: State University of New York Press, 1983.

Kraus, Karl. *One Crown for Zion.* (German) Vienna: Verlag von Moritz Frisch, 1899.

Kurzman, Dan. *Ben-Gurion: Prophet of Fire.* New York: Simon & Schuster, 1983.

Kurzweil, Baruch. *Our New Literature—Continuation or Revolution.* (Hebrew) Tel Aviv: Schocken, 1959.

———. "Pluralism of Anomaly as a Basis for Jewish Existence." (Hebrew) *Haaretz,* June 30, 1967.

———. *The Struggle over the Values of Judaism.* (Hebrew) Tel Aviv: Schocken, 1976.

Landes, David. *Revolution in Time: Clocks and the Making of the Modern World.* Cambridge: Harvard University Press, 1984.

Laqueur, Walter. *A History of Zionism.* London: Weidenfeld & Nicolson, 1972.

Lazare, Bernard. *Job's Dungheap.* New York: Schocken Books, 1978.

Leschnitzer, Adolf. *The Magic Background of Modern Anti-Semitism: An Analysis of the German-Jewish Relationship.* New York: International University Press, 1956.

Levi, Primo. *The Drowned and the Saved.* New York: Summit Books, 1987.

Liebman, Charles S. *The Ambivalent American Jew.* Philadelphia: The Jewish Publication Society of America, 1973.

Liebman, C., and E. Don-Yehia. *Civil Religion in Israel: Traditional Religion and Political Culture in the Jewish State.* Berkeley: University of California Press, 1983.

Litvinoff, Barnett, ed. *The Essential Chaim Weizmann: The Man, the States-man, the Scientist.* London: Weidenfeld & Nicolson, 1982.

Lowenberg, Peter. "Theodor Herzl." In B. Wolman, ed. *The Psychoanalytic Interpretation of History.* New York and London: Basic Books, 1971.

Lowenthal, Marvin, ed. *The Diaries of Theodor Herzl.* New York: Dial Press, 1956.

Maron, Stanley. *Zionism between Assimilation and Revival.* (Hebrew) Tel Aviv: Am Oved, 1983.

Melzer, Michael, ed. *Zionism Reconsidered: The Problems of Jewish Nation-alism and Normalcy—Dissenting Views.* New York: Macmillan, 1970.

Mendes-Flohr, Paul, and Yehuda Reinharz, eds. *The Jew in the Modern World.* New York: Oxford University Press, 1980.

Morse, Arthur. *While Six Million Died.* New York: Random House, 1967.

Mumford, Lewis. "Herzl's Utopia." *Menorah Journal* 3, August 1923.

Naiditch, Isaac. *Edmond de Rothschild.* Washington: Zionist Organization of America, 1945.

Nedava, Joseph, ed. *Ze'ev Jabotinsky: The Man and His Teachings.* (Hebrew) Tel Aviv: Misrad Habitachon, 1980.

Neusner, Jacob. *Israel in America: A Too-Comfortable Exile?* Boston: Beacon Press, 1985.

———. *Stranger at Home: "The Holocaust," Zionism, and American Ju-daism.* Chicago: University of Chicago Press, 1981.

Newman, Louis I. *The Hasidic Anthology.* Northwale, N.J. and London: Jason Aronson, 1987.

Nordau, Anna and Maxa. *A Biography.* New York: The Nordau Committee, 1943.

Nordau, Max. "Ahad Haam on 'Old-New Land.' " (German) *Die Welt*, March 13, 1903.

———. *Memoirs.* (German) Leipzig and Vienna: Renaissance Verlag, 1928.

Nussenblatt, Tulo. *A People on the Way to Peace.* (German) Vienna and Leip-zig: Reinhold Verlag, 1933.

———. *Theodor Herzl Yearbook.* Vienna: Dr. Heinrich Glanz Verlag, 1937.

O'Brien, Conor Cruise. *The Siege: The Saga of Israel and Zionism.* New York: Simon & Schuster, 1985.

Oppenheimer, Franz. *The State.* New York: Vanguard Press, 1926.

Oz, Amos. *In the Land of Israel.* New York: Harcourt Brace Jovanovich, 1983.

Painter, George D. *Proust: The Early Years.* Boston and Toronto: Little, Brown, 1959.

Peres, Yohanan. *The Fusion of the Exiles.* (Hebrew) Jerusalem: Hebrew Uni-versity, 1969.

Perlmutter, Amos. *Israel—the Partitioned State.* New York: Scribner's, 1985.

Perlmutter, Nathan, and Ruth Ann Perlmutter. *The Real Anti-Semitism in America.* New York: Arbor House, 1982.

Podhoretz, Norman. "Hannah Arendt on Eichmann: A Study in the Perversity of Brilliance." *Commentary* 3, 1963.

———. *Making It.* New York: Random House, 1967.

———. "Now Instant Zionism." *New York Times Magazine,* Feb. 3, 1974.

Poliakov, Leon. *The History of Anti-Semitism.* New York: Vanguard Press, 1965.

Prinz, Joachim. *Life in the Ghetto.* (German) Berlin: Ernst Loewe, 1937.

Proust, Marcel. *Remembrance of Things Past.* New York: Random House, 1927, 1929, 1930, 1932.

Rabinowicz, Oskar K. *Fifty Years of Zionism: A Historical Analysis of Dr. Weizmann's "Trial and Error."* London: R. Anscombe, 1952.

———. *Vladimir Jabotinski's Conception of a Nation.* New York: Beechhurst Press, 1946.

Rotenstreich, Nathan. *Jews and German Philosophy: The Polemics of Emancipation.* New York: Schocken Books, 1984.

Rozenblit, Marsha L. *Jews of Vienna, 1867–1914: Assimilation and Identity.* Albany: State University of New York Press, 1983.

Rubinstein, Amnon. *The Zionist Dream Revisited.* New York: Schocken Books, 1984.

Sachar, Howard M. *The Course of Modern Jewish History.* New York: Dell, 1958.

———. *A History of Israel.* New York: Alfred A. Knopf, 1976.

Samuel, Maurice. *The Gentleman and the Jew.* New York: Alfred A. Knopf, 1950.

Sartre, Jean-Paul. *Anti-Semitism and Jew.* New York: Schocken Books, 1948.

Schama, Simon. *Two Rothschilds and the Land of Israel.* New York: Alfred A. Knopf, 1978.

Schechtman, Joseph B. *The Life and Times of Vladimir Jabotinsky: Rebel and Statesman.* New York: Thomas Yoseloff, 1956.

———. *The Life and Times of Vladimir Jabotinsky: Fighter and Prophet.* New York: Thomas Yoseloff, 1961.

Schiff, Ze'ev. *The October Earthquake.* (Hebrew) Tel Aviv: Zmora, Bitan, Modan, 1974.

Schmidt, Helmut D. "Anti-Western and Anti-Jewish Tradition in German Historical Thought." In *Leo Baeck Institute Yearbook of 1959.* London: East and West Library, 1959.

———. "The Terms of Emancipation, 1781–1812: The Public Debate in Germany and Its Effect on the Mentality and Ideas of German Jews." *Leo Baeck Institute Yearbook I,* Robert Weltsch, ed. London: East and West Library, 1956.

Segre-Avni, Dan. *Crisis of Identity: Israel and Zionism.* New York: Oxford University Press, 1980.

Shaked, Gershon. *Hebrew Literature.* (Hebrew) Tel Aviv: Ktav-Hakibbuts Hameuhad, 1981.

Shapira, Anita, and Raya Adler. *The Religious Trend in Zionism.* Tel Aviv: Am Oved, 1983.

Sherwin, Byron L. *Mystical Theology and Social Dissent: The Life and Works of Judah Loew of Prague.* London and Toronto: Associated University Press, 1982.

Sholem, Gershom G. *Major Trends in Jewish Mysticism.* New York: Schocken Books, 1961.

Silberman, Charles E. *A Certain People.* New York: Summit Books, 1985.

Silberner, Edmund. "Ferdinand Lassalle: From Maccabeism to Jewish Anti-Semitism." Cincinnati: Hebrew Union College Annual No. 24, 1952–1953.

Silver, Abba Hillel. *Where Judaism Differed: An Inquiry into the Distinctiveness of Judaism.* New York: Macmillan, 1956.

Smooha, Sammy. *Israel: Pluralism and Conflict.* Berkeley: University of California Press, 1978.

Steinsalz, Adin. *The Essential Talmud.* New York: Basic Books, 1976.

Strum, Philippa. *Louis D. Brandeis: Justice for the People.* Cambridge and London: Harvard University Press, 1984.

Talmon, Jacob Leib. *Political Messianism, the Romantic Phase.* New York: Praeger, 1960.

————. "Uniqueness and Universality of Jewish History: A Midcentury Revaluation." In *The Unique and the Universal: Some Historical Reflections.* New York: Braziller, 1965.

Teitelbaum, Michael S., and Jay M. Winter. *The Fear of Population Decline.* San Diego: Academic Press/Harcourt Brace Jovanovich, 1985.

Tevet, Shabtai. *Ben-Gurion and the Palestinian Arabs: From Peace to War.* New York: Oxford University Press, 1985.

————. *Ben-Gurion: The Burning Ground, 1886–1948.* Boston: Houghton Mifflin, 1987.

Tuchman, Barbara. *Bible and Sword: England and Palestine from the Bronze Age to Balfour.* New York: New York University Press, 1956.

Urofsky, Melvin I. *American Zionism from Herzl to the Holocaust.* New York: Doubleday Anchor, 1975.

Vital, David. *The Origins of Zionism.* London: Oxford University Press, 1975.

————. *Zionism: The Formative Years.* Oxford: Clarendon Press, 1982.

Weber, Max. "Judaism, Christianity and the Socio-Economic Order." In *The Sociology of Religion.* Boston: Beacon Press, 1963.

Weizmann, Chaim. *The Letters and Papers of Chaim Weizmann.* Series B, Papers Vol. 1., Aug. 1898–July 1931. Jerusalem: Israel Universities Press, 1983.

————. *Trial and Error.* New York: Harper, 1949.

Wyman, David S. *The Abandonment of the Jews: America and the Holocaust, 1941–1945.* New York: Pantheon Books, 1948.

Yehoshua, Abraham B. *Between Right and Right.* Garden City, N.Y.: Doubleday, 1981.

Zucker, Norman L. *The Coming Crisis in Israel: Private Faith and Public Policy.* Cambridge: MIT Press, 1973.

INDEX